# SMALL GROUP TEACHING:

# A TROUBLE-SHOOTING GUIDE

Richard G. Tiberius

Monograph Series/22
OISE Press/The Ontario Institute for Studies in Education

The Ontario Institute for Studies in Education has three prime functions: to conduct programs of graduate study in education, to undertake research in education, and to assist in the implementation of the findings of educational studies. The Institute is a college chartered by an Act of the Ontario Legislature in 1965. It is affiliated with the University of Toronto for graduate studies purposes.

The publications program of the Institute has been established to make available information and materials arising from studies in education, to foster the spirit of critical inquiry, and to provide a forum for the exchange of ideas about education. The opinions expressed should be viewed as those of the contributors.

**Canadian Cataloguing in Publication Data**
Tiberius, Richard G., 1941-
  Small group teaching

(Monograph series ; 22)
Includes bibliographical references.
ISBN 0-7744-0344-6

1. College teaching — Handbooks, manuals, etc.
2. High school teaching — Handbooks, manuals, etc.
3. Group work in education — Handbooks, manuals, etc.
4. Small groups — Handbooks, manuals, etc.
I. Title. II. Series: Monograph series (Ontario
Institute for Studies in Education) ; no. 22.

LB2331.T52   1989        378¹.1795       C89-090532-0


We gratefully acknowledge permission to reprint from Bergquist, W. H., & Phillips, S. R. (1975). A handbook for faculty development. Washington, DC: The Council for the Advancement of Small Colleges, p. 103; Rasmussen, R. V. (1984). Practical discussion techniques for educators. The Journal of the Alberta Association for Continuing Education. 12 (1), 38-47; Rudduck, J. (1978). Learning through small group discussion: A study of seminar work in higher education. Guildford, Surrey: Society for Research into Higher Education, pp. 120-121; and Schmidt, J. A., & Davidson, M. L. (1983). Helping students think. The Personnel and Guidance Journal. 61 (9), 563-569.


ISBN 0-7744-0344-6      Printed in Canada
1  2  3  4  5  WEBCOM  49  39  29  19  09

# Table of Contents

Acknowledgments      iv

Preface      v

Introduction      1

Part One:    Group Goals      5

     Troubleshooting Guide      5
     Chapter 1: Goals are Unclear      9
     Chapter 2: Goals are Unattainable      17
     Chapter 3: Goals are Unacceptable      36
     References for Part One      55

Part Two:    Group Interaction      59

     Troubleshooting Guide      59
     Chapter 4: Lack of Interaction      65
     Chapter 5: Teacher Dominates Interaction      99
     Chapter 6: Students Participate Unequally      119
     References for Part Two      136

Part Three: Group Motivation and Emotion      139

     Troubleshooting Guide      139
     Chapter 7: Students are Tuned Out      144
     Chapter 8: Teacher is Tuned Out      156
     Chapter 9: Students Don't Co-operate 171
     References for Part Three      193

Beyond Troubleshooting      195

     Chapter 10: Using Outside Help      196

Index of Names      213

# Acknowledgments

I am indebted first to the students and the teachers who provided the material — the problems, causes, and remedies — for the book. Drawing from this material, I was able to construct a rough outline of the problems and remedies of small group teaching which I used as a handout to accompany my workshops on small group teaching. The second group to whom I am indebted are the participants of these workshops who helped me refine the organization of the handout and who encouraged me to illustrate the material with anecdotes from my consultations. Around 1978 a Cerlux bound version of the materials was read by several of my colleagues who encouraged me to seek a publisher and who made valuable editorial comments: Martha Lonsdale, Jane Wilson, and Terry Miosi come to mind, but doubtless there were others.

In 1982 a revised Cerlux bound edition was presented to the biweekly interest group which we affectionately called the "Hunt Group" in honor of the convenor and group leader, David Hunt. I cannot remember everyone who was at that session — Pat Doyle, Terry Miosi, Michael Orme, Rosemary Peikes, Michael Skolnik — but I remember clearly how valuable their contributions were. They debated at length the assumptions underlying the book, such as the validity of attributing specific causes to teaching problems or attaching specific remedies to causes.

When I signed an agreement with OISE Press and began to work on the book in earnest, I discovered several ways in which the workshop materials could not stand alone. For one thing they often simply did not say what was intended. I had depended on the workshop discussion and on anecdotes to convey the message. My friend, colleague, and writing coach, Rene Gold, spent many hours pointing out the difference between what was said and what was intended and in helping me to say what I wanted to say. Second, examples were missing to illustrate some of the key ideas. For these I turned to members of my family with immediate university experience: my wife Joyce, my daughter Valerie, and my brother and sister-in-law Rob and Lynn. Finally, a professional editor from OISE Press, Frances Rooney, uncovered apparent contradictions, ellipses, and duplications which would have annoyed and frustrated the reader.

It would not have been possible to make the substantial time commitment required for this book if it were not for the indulgence of my wife, Joyce, who did more than her share of our household chores during the editing phase and for the generosity of the Acting Director of the Centre for Studies in Medical Education, Niall Byrne, who carried much of the burden that would have fallen to me during this period.

I am deeply indebted to all of these people and doubtless others whom I have omitted. Looking back on this whole project I am struck with a feeling of optimism that such close co-operation is possible between editors and educators. Without such co-operation, my experience would never benefit future teachers.

# Preface

This a trouble-shooting manual for teachers. Perhaps the best way to describe what it is about is to tell you how I came to write it.

I work as a teaching consultant in the medical school of a large university where my job is to help professors improve their teaching. When they ask me for help I usually begin by interviewing them, and often their students, in great detail in order to understand each problem in its context. I do this because my belief that each teacher-student relationship has its own unique problems and strengths has led me to conclude that the only way to improve teaching and learning is by individual consultation. At first I did not think it possible to devise a teaching improvement manual because the problems and remedies appeared to be unique to each situation. After ten years and hundreds of interviews I have come away with three overriding impressions: that even unique situations have common problems, that these problems arise from common causes, and that they share common solutions.

First, while there is a vast array of problems, a large majority of them belong to a few categories which come up again and again. For example, lack of interaction in small groups is a frequent problem. Second, while each of these common problems has a large number of *possible* causes, only a few of these causes are operative in most of the cases. The problem I have just mentioned, lack of interaction in small groups, is very frequently caused by the overwhelming authority of the teacher. And third, while there are, theoretically, a large number of remedies for each cause, only a few of them turn out to be of practical use. To be less overwhelming and encourage interaction, the teacher may need to do less talking and more listening.

I keep notes of my consultations, and digging through my old files confirmed these three impressions. As I read the notes I began to classify the problems, causes, and remedies they contained. I began to think that these notes, suitably organized, might be useful for teachers. I made a small, Cerlux-bound version of this manual which turned out to be more useful than I had expected, judging by the number of teachers and teaching consultants who have asked for copies of it. People began to suggest that I seek a publisher. Then, one day while I was repairing the hinges on my cupboards with the help of one of the Time/Life Fix-it-Yourself books, I was hit by the idea of organizing the manual like a do-it-yourself trouble-shooting manual. Embellished, with some refinements and additions, here it is.

Unless teachers are singularly fortunate or exceptionally oblivious, they become aware of problems in their teaching from time to time. For example, a class is bored, hostile, uncomprehending, or simply not learning. Teachers become aware of these problems in one of two ways. They either sense that something is wrong — "I don't know what's going on this year, but the class seems dead" — or their students tell them in conversations or in written year-end-assessments — "You should see what one of my students wrote on the evaluation. Ouch!" A list of problems, causes, and remedies appears at the start of each section. Of course, there are times when a teacher either is vaguely aware that something has gone wrong but cannot describe it clearly enough to know where to begin in a manual, or is so overwhelmed by a problem that action is difficult if not impossible. The final chapter, therefore, offers assistance for those times when you just can't do it by yourself. While the first nine chapters provide a kind of home repair manual, the last chapter discusses how to use a teaching consultant.

At a break between classes I once overheard three teachers sharing experiences of their first meeting with their students. One slumped down in his chair, poured a coffee and said, "They're dead. Completely dead!" The other replied: "I'm afraid I put my group to sleep." The third added: "Well, there are only 24 more meetings," and they all laughed. My purpose in this book is to help teachers stop blaming the students, blaming themselves, or becoming cynical. I would be pleased to hear that the book has influenced people to seek the causes behind their own and their students' behavior. Knowing why students are silent is a first step toward discovering some action which will create a more co-operative and satisfying teaching and learning relationship. I would like to hear the first teacher begin his conversation with: "They were silent today. I wonder why?" I would like to hear the second teacher say, "They appeared sleepy. I wonder if they were?" And I would like to hear the third teacher say, "It's a good thing this is only the first class. I have plenty of time to find out what's happening here and try a few things out."

This book is intended for several groups. While college and university teachers are its main target, most recommendations apply equally to high school teachers. I hope that those who, like me, are teaching consultants, will enjoy sharing my experiences, and that educational administrators may, by reading the book, reach a more sympathetic understanding of the problems of the people they administer. Further, I hope that students will read the manual and gain some insight into the problems their teachers encounter — often in silence, without students' awareness of them. Finally, I hope that this book will help teachers relax and enjoy their teaching.


## Philosophy

A do-it-yourself manual should not begin with a long-winded discourse on the assumptions underlying the book. My theory of teaching and learning and my values will be apparent from the text without my flogging them here. However, I also do not want to obscure my bias. Therefore, let me confess right at the start that the book is based on the assumption that teaching and learning should be a process of co-operative interaction for the purpose of helping the learner. The best way I can express this point of view is to tell you a story.

Some time ago, at a teaching and learning conference, I attended a special problem-solving session in which problems were posed by teachers for solution by a panel of faculty development people. One problem was the following: "I am faced with 160 students who sit in the back of the room. How do I get them to sit closer to the front?" The first person to answer provided a legalistic solution. He said: "As a teacher you have some rights too. Just tell them that you want them to sit down in front." The second provided a behavioristic response. She described arrangements which would reward the students for sitting in the front: "Speak very softly so that the students cannot hear you unless they sit up close." I spoke third, from what I call the interactionist point of view: "Find out why the students want to sit in the back and ask yourself why you want them to sit in the front, and only then try to reconcile the two needs."

I have in fact taken my own advice in a number of classes that suffered from this very problem and I found that the reasons students gave for choosing to sit at the back were often surprising. In one class students said that, because the room was slanted downward to the front, the middle of the classroom was actually at eye level with the teacher, who was standing on a raised platform. So students were choosing to be on eye level rather than look up at the teacher; a reasonable desire. The teacher said that he wanted them in front because he could make more eye contact with them when they sat closer to him. So they were all really saying the same thing. There was no conflict except in the teacher's interpretation of the students' motives. My experience has been that many problems in teaching arise out of misunderstanding and misinterpretation rather than lack of teaching techniques.

**A note to scholars in the field**
This book was written for teachers. I have not intended to write a distillation of the literature, but to present a list of suggestions that teachers might try when faced with certain common problems. I deliberately chose the word "suggestions" because these ideas have grown not out of controlled research but rather from my discussions with students and my consulting experience. The dilemma that this kind of book poses for me as a writer is that most if not all of these suggestions are no doubt already mentioned somewhere in the educational literature. Indeed, I don't think there is anything the students and I could come up with that some educator has not already written somewhere. If I were to search the literature carefully enough to find out who first made each of these suggestions, I would never finish the book. Wherever I have been aware of authors who have written about a similar idea I have referenced them. However, this book covers broad territory, and I obviously have not read everything. The strength here lies in the book's concrete style and readily accessible format. It should not be cluttered with hundreds of references for an idea which has become common knowledge in the field. However, if you discover that some of these ideas have been championed elsewhere, please write me and I will reference the authors in the next edition. References will not make the ideas more useful, but teachers might enjoy having alternative resources to read, and cross referencing is a way for us workers in this field to discover and perhaps to help one another.

**Confidentiality**
Since this book includes many examples drawn from my own consultancy, I have atempted to protect the confidentiality of teachers by changing the gender of the teacher, the discipline, or some other feature of the example that may reveal the identity of the teacher.

I want *Small Group Teaching* to be a living, working tool. While it looks at many common problems and makes numerous suggestions for dealing with them, it does not cover all the situations that arise in small groups, and as daily practitioners you will be certain to experience more situations and know of other solutions. If you will send me your teaching problem, cause, and solution, I will include it in the next edition. If you will permit me to,

I will attribute the contribution to you. Thank you; may we all enjoy our subjects, our students, and ourselves.

Richard G. Tiberius
CSME
Faculty of Medicine
University of Toronto
Toronto, Ontario M5S 1A8
Canada
Tel: (416) 978-2124
Fax: (416) 978-7186

# Introduction

## Small Groups and Large Ones

There is a belief, widespread among educators and deeply entrenched in the literature, that the teaching of small and large groups are distinct enterprises that must be considered separately. This book has followed that tradition. It deals exclusively with small group teaching and learning. A second volume will deal with large group teaching.

But although I will respect this tradition, I would like to take a moment to examine the differences between large and small group teaching. The most common questions are, first, How small does a group have to be before it is considered small for teaching purposes? Is there a magic number? And, second, What size of group is best? Is it always better to be taught in a small group or are there some kinds of teaching which are better suited to a large one?

It is obvious that the more students there are, the less time the teacher can spend with each of them. As the number of students becomes larger, a point is reached where the teacher must spend most of the time talking to them all at once, that is, lecturing. Clearly, large groups impose constraints on teaching not encountered in small ones.

But you could also lecture to a small group. It would be physically possible, though rather odd, to deliver a formal lecture to an audience of one. Whenever I talk to students from the Faculty of X (it shall remain nameless) one of them invariably tells me the story of the teacher who lectured to a class of only one student. The punch line is practically shouted: "He actually asked if there were any questions and the lone student raised his hand!" The emotional intensity with which the story is told does not seem to diminish over the years. Students view it as indisputable proof of the lack of interest in teaching their faculty. That this story strikes both teachers and students as absurd makes clear that the number in a class affects not only the physical possibilities of what can be done but also our expectations of what ought to be done.

These expectations are embedded in our culture. Our experience of small groups is based first on the family, later on groups of friends, and later still on clubs and the other small social groups. When such small groups come together, they display characteristic patterns of behavior. On the whole, people speak one at a time. There is an implicit assumption that everybody should get a turn to speak. Subgroups form and coalesce into a conversation, break up, and then join other subgroups. Whenever we are in a small group, whether it is a card game, a dinner party, or a class, we expect it to behave in this kind of way.

Similarly, our expectations of large groups are based on our experiences of cultural events where we submit ourselves to performances which we do not interrupt. Members of an audience are permitted ritual displays of emotion such as applause, laughter, and occasional weeping. But they are not expected to engage Hamlet in a discussion on the value of existence. These conventions mould the social expectations that greet the lecturer. In fact, a lecturer who actually wishes the audience to interrupt must give explicit permission to do so. (These large group conventions vary in different cultures.

In parts of Indonesia, the closest thing to formal large group teaching is Wayang theatre, a form of shadow puppet theatre, which proceeds for six or eight hours while members of the audience come and go, eat and talk. Apparently this custom of casual attention spills over into the lecture halls where students treat formal lectures like cafe theatre. Closer to home, one of my colleagues from a neighboring university told me about a large undergraduate course which was held in a sports arena. The students sat in the bleachers and they stood up and cheered when the professor took his place at the podium. When the seats were rearranged into the typical rows of a threatre, the cheering stopped.)

The teacher must take into account social expectations of this kind and could, of course, challenge them. But it is much more efficient to satisfy them. A lot of the problems discussed in this manual arise from a failure to do so.

From what I have written so far, it should be obvious that there is not a sharp distinction between small groups and large ones. In fact, there are circumstances which can give a large group the feel of a small one. A skilful teacher can sustain a discussion in a relatively large group, making intellectual and even physical sorties into the body of the lecture theatre and giving a sense of that intimate interaction with individual students more usually associated with a small group. So you could say that increased skill in the teacher decreases the subjective size of a group.

Other circumstances can also accomplish this. As the members of a group get to know one another, they become more informal and interact more. The length of time the group has been together influences its interaction and thus its subjective size. I have seen a very capable teacher interact with and stimulate interaction among a group of 50 third-year engineering students. Grade school teachers accomplish this frequently.

On the other hand, if you are an inexperienced teacher who faces a group you have never seen, and whose members do not know each other, 8 to 12 students might be the upper limit for a small group.

Assuming that one has a choice, the next question is, What size of group is best? When should a small group be used? As we have seen, teachers and students both can and expect to interact with one another more in a small group than in a large one. Is this always an advantage?

Actually doing something, like talking, instead of just looking and listening, increases people's involvement in learning. And there is evidence that active involvement motivates people to learn and allows them to do so more effectively. Talking provides an opportunity to practice skills and rehearse newly learned material. The advantage of this oral rehearsal is so obvious in some disciplines, such as languages, that it is thought essential. But virtually any subject is better understood through active participation. Problem solving — "thinking on your feet" in response to questions and applying abstract principles to concrete situations — also helps. Recently, some educators (Simpson & Galbo, 1987) have argued that interaction aids the thinking process itself by helping to connect the subject matter with thoughts that are most meaningful to the learner; so that even subjects that do not require verbal practice may benefit from the process of interaction fostered by small groups. Finally, student action, especially self-directed action, may help to strengthen the student's independence from the teacher.

Moreover, by talking to each other, students can also place their own views within the spectrum of their peers' opinions; they can make valuable inferences about their own strengths and weaknesses by observing other students struggle with the same material; they can observe how others respond to their ideas and actions; they can benefit from information other students have; and they can broaden their understanding of ideas by seeing them through the eyes of their fellow students. Finally, under the guidance of an exemplary small group leader, they can learn valuable interpersonal skills: how to interact with others sensitively, humanely, and with facility; how to tap the resources of the group; how to contribute in constructive ways, to build a co-operative group climate; and how to develop a sense of group identity, of teamwork, and of commitment to group goals.

The increased interaction permitted by the small group also helps teachers. It helps them to discover how well, and in what manner, each student has understood the subject matter, and to assess the extent to which the student can integrate and apply it. This enables the teacher both to deliver finely tuned corrective feedback to the students and to detect students' unconscious resistance to learning.

Finally, it appears that whether or not small groups improve teaching, both students and teachers generally prefer them. People are excited by participating in the group, by their ability to determine its direction, and by being able to use such educational devices as problem-based learning, in which the group generates a problem that serves as the basis for further study outside.

From what has been said it might be concluded that the right answer to the question, "When should you use small groups?" is, "Whenever possible." Some educators do hold this view. On the other hand, both the experimental evidence (see McKeachie & Kulik, 1975) and the collected experience from many universities (see, for example, Abercrombie, 1971; Rudduck, 1978) suggest that small groups are not more effective, and usually much less efficient than formal lecturing, in teaching facts. In the language of the Hale report: "Lectures have certain advantages over discussion periods in that continuous exposition, free from interruptions, can be better prepared and more profound than teaching in a discussion period, can cover more ground and can enable an inspiring teacher to influence more students" (cited in Abercrombie, 1971, p. 8).

In summary, the evidence seems to indicate that small groups are probably more efficient for higher orders of activity such as learning how to analyze, evaluate, synthesize, and apply ideas and perhaps less efficient for learning bare facts (McKeachie, 1986). Even here the small group may be superior to the large lecture but any advantage, if it exists, is probably too marginal to justify the cost in time for both teachers and students. The main disadvantage of the small group is that it is costly in time for all concerned.

The small group does have another rarely appreciated, but very real, disadvantage which arises from that very circumstance that makes the small group, in most respects, so superior. Because it gives the student such an intimate contact with the teacher's competence and style of exposition, any ignorance of the subject is detected quickly and with unerring precision by the students. There's no podium to hide behind. This book cannot remedy lack of knowledge, but it can assist to overcome some of the technical problems which arise in the very delicate task of managing small groups of students.

## The most common problems of small group teaching

The most common problems of small group teaching fall into three major categories: the first involves the goals of the group (Part One); the second concerns interaction within the group (Part Two); and the third encompasses the motivations and emotions of the group (Part Three).

Each of these three common problem areas contains several types of problems, which in turn are amenable to various remedies. Each problem type is organized as a chapter. At the beginning of each Part is a table summarizing all the problems, causes, and suggestions (remedies) discussed in that Part.

# Part One/ Group Goals

**Troubleshooting Guide**

**Chapter One: Goals are Unclear /9**

Possible cause 1: Failure to establish the goals of the group /9
    Suggestion 1: Set goals for the course /10
    Suggestion 2: Negotiate goals for the course /11
    Suggestion 3: Be prepared to negotiate difficulties that may
    come up /11
    Suggestion 4: Establish goals for each meeting /12
    Suggestion 5: Include criteria for success /13
    Suggestion 6: Modify goals if necessary /13

Possible cause 2: Digression from goals /13
    Suggestion 1: Precirculate questions or issues /14
    Suggestion 2: Get right into it /14
    Suggestion 3: Incorporate students' agendas into the class
    goals /14
    Suggestion 4: Restate the agenda or summarize /15

Suggestion 5: Paraphrase /15
Suggestion 6: Use a flip chart or chalk board /15
Suggestion 7: Identify irrelevant remarks /15
Suggestion 8: Evaluate the group product or process (but not the persons) /16
Suggestion 9: Give praise when it's due /16

## Chapter Two: Goals are Unattainable /17

Possible cause 1: Wrong group structure and process /17
Suggestion 1: Familiarize yourself with the many kinds of groups that provide information, stimulation, or provocation /18
Suggestion 2: Familiarize yourself with the types of groups that encourage participation /20
Suggestion 3: Familiarize yourself with the types of groups that help members understand the feelings or points of view of others /23
Suggesstion 4: Use more than one type of group if appropriate /26
Suggestion 5: Consider projects that take place outside the group and report back to it /26
Suggestion 6: Practise /27
Suggestion 7: Discuss the group structure in class /27

Possible cause 2: Students are not active enough /27
Suggestion 1: Use learning cells /28
Suggestion 2: Use helping trios /28
Suggestion 3: Arrange practice sessions /28

Possible cause 3: Distortion caused by evaluation of group performance /29
Suggestion 1: Evaluate the product of the group rather than its participation /29
Suggestion 2: Reduce anxiety about the exam /29

Possible cause 4: Poor time planning /29
Suggestion 1: Consider time in planning /29
Suggestion 2: Remind the group of the schedule /30
Suggestion 3: Assign preparation tasks /30

Possible cause 5: Superficial discussion and/or poor listening /30
Suggestion 1: Use active listening /31
Suggestion 2: Ask questions of the right type and level /34

Possible cause 6: Unco-ordinated effort — students are engaged in different tasks /34
Suggestion 1: Break the issue or problem down and focus everyone on the same part /34

## Chapter Three: Goals are Unacceptable /36

Possible cause 1: Students' experiences and values make them reject the teacher's goals /36
    Suggestion 1: Make your learning goals relevant to those of the students /37
    Suggestion 2: If you can't make your case, accept rejection — for now /38
    Suggestion 3: If you cannot convince your students of the value of the material, quit /40
    Suggestion 4: If you cannot convince *yourself* of the value of the material, quit /41

Possible cause 2: Teachers and students perceive the course goals differently because of their different intellectual frameworks /41
    Suggestion 1: Take into account different stages of intellectual development /41
    Suggestion 2: Match the students' level /42
    Suggestion 3: Use plus-one-staging /43
    Suggestion 4: Combine support with challenge /46
    Suggestion 5: Use metaphors /47
    Suggestion 6: Give it up /47

Possible cause 3: Teachers and students are not pursuing the same goals because the students are avoiding the real issues, which they find difficult or painful /47
    Suggestion 1: Make it clear that you support the students /48
    Suggestion 2: Divide students into groups of two or three for intensive discussion or buzz groups /48
    Suggestion 3: Encourage speakers to be concrete and specific /49

Possible cause 4: Teachers and students are not pursuing the same goals because the *teachers* are avoiding the real issues, which they find difficult or painful /49
    Suggestion 1: Invite a peer to review your class /49
    Suggestion 2: Separate your personal reactions from your professional ones /50

Possible cause 5: Teachers and students are not pursuing the same goals because there are hidden agendas /50
    Suggestion 1: Check your perception /51
    Suggestion 2: Confront /51

Possible cause 6: Students perceive the group activity as a waste of time because they think it is irrelevant /52
    Suggestion 1: Align the goals of the course with the evaluation /53

Suggestion 2: Discuss the goals and exam with your students /54
Suggestion 3: Write the objectives on a flip chart /54
Suggestion 4: Brief the small group leaders /54
Suggestion 5: Write the exam and the goals first, then plan the group activities /55
Suggestion 6: Explain the lecture/discussion co-ordination /55

**References for Part One /55**

# 1/Goals are Unclear

*"I never knew the whole year what was going on or where the teacher was heading. It was all so vague. There was no flow or direction. Everything jumped all over the place. He never said what we were doing or where we were going. I survived by copying down some key words and reading sections of the text that seemed relevant. I faked it."*

Unclear goals are frustrating for both teachers and students. Students thrash around in confusion, and teachers, often unaware of that confusion, face unresponsive classes without a clue as to what is happening. This picture of confusion occurs over and over again, and it appears to have two common causes. The first is a simple failure to establish the goals of the group; the second is digression from those goals.

## Possible cause 1: Failure to establish the goals of the group

An economics professor and her teaching assistants conducted several tutorial sessions in conjunction with her lectures. Year after year, she received lower ratings on student evaluations than her assistants. She was really sore about it. She said that she felt burned out, that her teaching assistants received higher evaluations because they were younger and more in tune with the students, and that that was all there was to it.

This was the second year she had taught the particular course she called me in to discuss. We talked about the structure of her tutorials and students' responses to them. At first, her goal had been for the tutorials to provide an opportunity for students to ask questions. When they asked very few questions and the sessions went dead, she changed the goal and, instead, she asked the questions. At the end of the year students gave her a very low evaluation. They accused her of using the tutorials to "grill" rather than help them. One even wrote "sadistic" on the questionnaire.

The next year, before she called me, she tried a third goal for the group: she used the tutorial to reinforce the main points of her lectures. Were the students happy? They made it clear that they considered the tutorials a relatively painless waste of time. They perceived her as wandering around the topic without any focus. She was fed up. She wanted a sympathetic ear more than educational advice. She didn't really think anybody could do anything to help.

Her understanding of the problem grew out of her concept of teaching as something you do to students. The performing arts may be like this, but teaching and learning should not be. What I offered, instead of another goal for the group, was an alternative concept of teaching as a process of co-operative interaction.

To me the significant fact was that, through all of these changes, she had never included the students in her efforts to find suitable goals for the tutorials. She had struggled privately and then acted upon rather than with the students. The point is that, although none of her goals had worked, in fact, any of them could have succeeded if both teacher and students had known about and agreed to them.

One more point about goals. There is a common myth that students will praise any teaching session in which they have a good time. Some teachers imagine that if they are entertaining, the students will be happy. These teachers are soon disillusioned. If students enjoy themselves, they may appear satisfied, and they may even be satisfied — for a while. But afterwards, when they think about what they learned and compare it with what they feel they should have got out of the class, they criticize and stay away. They want and need more, and part of that more is clear objectives.


## Suggestion 1: Set goals for the course

The first thing a teacher needs to do, before this kind of confusion or frustration arises, is to make sure that the students understand the goals of the course.

One of the group leader's functions is to ensure that a set of mutually agreed-upon goals is established early in the course, preferably at the very first meeting. The goals should be specific enough to guide the actions of the group and to serve as criteria with which to measure the group's success.

There are ways to broach this subject which will engage students in constructive negotiations with you. You might say, for example: "Let's spend a few minutes deciding how we might use the time in our discussions." This is highly preferable to: "I want to spend a few minutes telling you the purpose of this session."

### Suggestion 2: Negotiate goals for the course

If at all possible, students should take part in deciding the goals of the group. People take more responsibility for goals and accept them more readily when they have helped to choose them, and the goals students have helped to set are often better than ones a teacher alone comes up with.

### Suggestion 3: Be prepared to negotiate difficulties that may come up

**1.** Sometimes it becomes evident that *no one goal will please all the students.* If that happens, you may want to say something like, "I gather from your comments that you disagree as to how we should use our tutorial time. Some of you would like to review points from the lectures, others would like me to answer questions about areas you are having trouble with, and still others want to discuss new issues stimulated by the material. Splitting the time may be the answer, but those who want to discuss new issues are saying that lecture review is boring. I appreciate that people taking this course have different academic backgrounds, but I personally would not like to see our activity reduced to the level of the least prepared student. I would hope, rather, that students with less background would be drawn to a higher level by taking part in the interaction. How about beginning each hour with a brief — say 15-minute — period during which any of us can help answer questions about the lecture material, then using the rest of the time to discuss issues? Shall we try this for the first few times and then see how well it is working?"

The economics teacher above did this, and her students seemed to accept both her summary of their dilemma and her proposal for reconciling the various needs. The next class was taken up almost entirely with discussion of new issues because no one raised any questions. By the third class, she had forgotten about the arrangement and some of the students complained afterward that they hadn't had the agreed-upon question period. At the fourth session she kept to her plan, making room for the question period whether there were any questions or not. There is an important message here: you have to stick to what you say you will do. It takes a few sessions to get used to a new structure.

**2.** Sometimes *students disagree with the teacher about what the goals should be.* The problem is often avoided by bearing in mind that the teacher is not an adversary of the students but is there to help them learn the material. If the group process is not helping students, change it. Of course, sometimes students don't know what helps them learn, and sometimes they simply want an easy time. However, these occasions are rare in adult learning. Most students assume that the teacher has a better grasp of the material than they do and will accomodate to the teacher who provides a clear and reasonable rationale for the plan he or she presents.

**3.** Another difficulty arises when *the decision about objectives takes up too much time.* Negotiation can go on forever. One skilled teacher handled this problem with, "It's obvious that it is taking us more than a few minutes to come to some agreement on objectives and priorities. In my experience, it has been worthwhile to discuss the agenda even if it takes most of our first meeting. We do have 14 weeks together. One fourteenth of our time is not too much to invest if it will encourage the mutual understanding and agreement that will enable the group to co-operate. Does this make sense based on your experience with small group discussion courses?"

In a once-only session, time is very short. You cannot spend much of it negotiating objectives. One teacher, when discussion bogged down, said: "We have only an hour to discuss the issue and we have already used up a quarter of that time trying to agree over the goals. If we go on much longer we'll not have much time for discussion. I have a suggestion — let's get into the topic for the next 15 or 20 minutes, just to get some of the facts about acid rain and the major policy statements of the governments on the table. And then, with the facts in front of us, it may be easier to decide whether to clarify the issues or to analyze the empirical studies."

### Suggestion 4: Establish goals for each meeting

Although the goals of a course may be negotiated only once, it is always a good idea to strike an agenda *for each meeting.* This can be the briefest reminder of the established agreement. For example: "Today we will follow the usual procedure: first briefly describe the case and then everyone will have a chance to present their positions. Who would like to summarize the main points of the case?"

### Suggestion 5: Include criteria for success

Goals should include standards of success against which to measure the progress of the group. It may be useful to enlist the help of one of the learners to monitor the progress of the group toward these goals. Here is an example of a teacher setting standards of success for a learning group: "We said last week that we would each speak more briefly so that more of us would have a chance to speak. Does someone want to keep track of length of speaking times during the first 15 minutes so that we can compare it with last week?"

### Suggestion 6: Modify goals if necessary

Sometimes a class aspires to unrealistic goals. The teacher might then say, "This course won't give you a complete understanding of Kant's philosophy since that would take more time than we will devote to Kant, but let's understand his concept of causality."

# Possible cause 2: Digression from goals

Sometimes the problem is not setting goals but, rather, sticking to them. I am a major offender here: causing confusion by digressing from the course plan is one of the most frequent criticisms I receive. At the beginning of the course I pass out a detailed course outline, including questions to guide discussion, exercises for class preparation, and readings. After all, we educators have to set an example. Then I ignore it.

One student said to me: "The course outline is very interesting but we don't stick to it. I used to prepare by reading the articles and thinking about the questions you hand out, but we go off on a tangent and never get to the questions so I don't bother anymore." That certainly made me think again about how I was using my outline and what good it was doing.

I have discussed this problem a lot with students and colleagues, I have thought about it a great deal, and I have come to the conclusion that I have always been uncomfortable with outlines because they strangle the spontaneity that keeps me alive in a class. Realizing this was a great help. I now make clear from the start how we are going to use the outline. I ask each student to read and report briefly on one article. After all the ideas are raised, the discussion starts spontaneously — in an unpredictable direction, but always touching the main concepts. We use the questions in the outline only if the discussion falters or strays.

## Suggestion 1: Precirculate questions or issues

The group will be less likely to digress if everyone has prepared a common set of readings or thought about a common set of issues or questions. Remember to refer to these readings or issues at the beginning of the session. It is not necessary to stick slavishly to them but if you want to deviate, explain your reasons and gain the students' agreement. Otherwise, those who have prepared may feel that they have wasted their time. In my own teaching, I make sure that every student who has prepared a summary gets a chance to present it, but the presenters decide the order in which they want to speak: "Who prepared readings for today? Three, four, five. Okay, briefly summarize the highlights of each article to get the information on the table before we begin the discussion. Who would like to start?"

## Suggestion 2: Get right into it

Reaching agreement on group goals is important, but discussing the goals is not so exciting as pursuing and achieving them. Get into the topic as soon as possible.

A philosophy teacher provoked students from the very first few seconds of the class, before backing up the set goals for the session: "Good morning. Have you had a chance to read Plato? Good. Do you think he was a fascist? [Looking at individual students and asking the question again. Students begin to react.] Really? Do *you* think he was a fascist? Do *you*? Do *you*? This reminds me of the device that TV detective stories use to "hook" you before they screen a series of commercials. The murder takes place in a few lurid seconds, then the commercials cut in. The idea is to get you to stick around to find out who dunnit.

## Suggestion 3: Incorporate students' agendas into the class goals

Students sometimes have issues of their own. A useful way to encourage them to raise these issues at the outset and to give the issues legitimacy is to put them on the agenda. "Before we look at the agenda, does anyone have anything to add? Yes, Edith, thank you. With Edith's issue added to the list, we have three items. Where would you like to begin?"

## Suggestion 4: Restate the agenda or summarize

Restating the group's goals or summarizing progress toward those goals can return you and your students to the topic. Periodic summaries are particularly useful to rein in a discussion which has strayed off topic: "We started with the MacDonald case, but for the last ten minutes or so we have been discussing the changing roles of 'line' and 'staff' management. That's okay, but we need to clarify these terms. I'll summarize what we have said and then restate the case. Then we can move on."

Summaries are not without pitfalls. If the summary is viewed as a judgment rather than a service to the group, it may threaten or stifle the group members. To avoid this danger, learners can be encouraged to take turns summarizing for the group. At first, of course, they will need to be cued — "It sounds as though we could use a summary of where we are and where we are going. Does anyone want to take a shot at it?"

## Suggestion 5: Paraphrase

While summarizing clarifies the group's position, paraphrasing clarifies the position of an individual speaker. It is a useful strategy not only for the group leader but for any group member who is unclear about what is being said. For example, a student says, "There's no way that recycling will work." The teacher questions, "Do you mean technologically, it can't work?" "No," comes the answer, "it's technically possible, but it's too costly." "So people have other priorities?" "That's right, the problem isn't important enough to the average person."

## Suggestion 6: Use a flip chart or chalk board

A flip chart (newsprint pad) or a chalk board can be used to list group goals, to summarize, or to record and display the progress of the group. A flip chart has the added advantage of allowing successive records of the group's transactions to be preserved and taped on the walls for display.

Whenever I have observed a teacher using a flip chart, either to remind the group of its goals or to record the group's progress, I have been surprised at how often people glance at it and refer to it. The visual display helps in the difficult task of keeping several individuals in the same stream of thought.

## Suggestion 7: Identify irrelevant remarks

An irrelevant remark can throw the group off track. One way to keep the discussion on track is to identify irrelevant remarks for what they are. This must be done in a manner which recognizes, rather than embarrasses, the speaker. Obviously, this suggestion must be tempered by the realization that a coherent discussion ought to be able to withstand the occasional irrelevant comment; to jump on every stray comment would be tyrannical and counterproductive. The time to identify the irrelevant remark is when it is in danger of leading the class down a side path away from the agenda.

In a course on 19th century British philosophy, a psychology major began to discuss the concept of guilt in connection with Mill's notion of social conscience. The teacher did not want to discourage the student from trying to integrate his knowledge, but she also did not want to be drawn away from teaching the philosophy of Mill by a student who may have been more interested in Freud than Mill. The task is to support the *student* but identify the *remarks* as irrelevant. The teacher said, "The concept of 'guilt' is, of course, extremely important to such theorists Freud and Buber, but Mill did not use it in his analysis. A discussion of guilt as a way to generate social conscience may draw us away from Mill. Mill talked about the development of social conscience. Let's clarify what he meant by that first, and then we can see the relationship between his terms and more recent concepts such as 'guilt' in Freud and Buber."

## Suggestion 8: Evaluate the group product or process (but not the persons)

A physician conducting a small clinic group might say, "We have only 20 minutes left and we are still on physical findings. Let's get on to the lab results so that we can leave some time to discuss the treatment plan." She or he should not say, "You're a very slow group. We should have gotten beyond physical findings by now."

## Suggestion 9: Give praise when it's due

When things are going well, say so. For example, "I would like to give the group some feedback. I really appreciate our discussion. It seems to me that you are making the best use of the diverse backgrounds that you all have. Everyone jumps right in when they can contribute something to the topic and lets others talk when they have nothing to add. The result is a very rich interaction."

# 2/Goals are Unattainable

*"The idea is that we all talk, and we want to. But the presenters go on and on and then it's over. The rest of us can't get a word in edgewise. It's like being in another lecture."*

Once class goals are clear, the teacher must help students attain those goals. A teacher of language skills, for example, must include an opportunity to practise speaking. In other words, group activities must be appropriate to group goals.

## Possible cause 1: Wrong group structure and process

The teacher and members of a small group are often in perfect agreement about the group's goals. They know what they want to do and they all want to do the same thing, but despite this they never get it done because they don't go about it the right way.

The seminar I have in mind was on enzyme kinetics. The students hadn't understood the lectures and the book had been no help because it contained a lot of X's, which is exactly what the students had not been able to cope with in the lectures.

The students felt that the seminar would be an excellent opportunity to find out what the X's were all about, and the lecturer thought it would be an excellent chance to explore the students' problems with the material. The scene seemed to have been set for a satisfying and productive interaction. It wasn't.

The problem was that the professor had the fixed idea that small group means discussion. He opened the group with, "Let's discuss this. Who would like to start?" The response was a defeated silence. You have to understand at least a little about a subject to be able to express what it is you don't understand, and these students were too mystified by the whole topic even to attempt to discuss it. What could the teacher have done?

There are many different types of small groups to choose from. The more alternatives you are aware of, the more likely it is that you will be able to find an effective one for your objectives. The enzyme kinetics teacher had only one tool in his tool box. He used a discussion group when he probably should have conducted a tutorial. Discussion groups belong to a family of groups whose special purpose is to foster interaction. Tutorials belong to a different family of groups which are designed primarily to relay new information. A third major category of groups comprises those designed to help members understand the feelings and points of view of others. These three categories include most of the types of learning groups. The groups that foster interpersonal understanding will be taken up in Suggestion 2, and in Part Two.

Several books describe different types of learning groups and their uses. Bergquist and Phillips (1975) describe 13 different small group structures in their *Handbook for Faculty Development*. McLeish, Matheson, and Park (1973) in *The Psychology of the Learning Group* present the pros and cons of nine different group structures.

## Suggestion 1: Familiarize yourself with the many types of groups that provide information, stimulation, or provocation

Group structures in this category are designed to bring information to the group. The problem here is not so much that the members need encouragement to participate, but that, without new information, they have nothing to talk about.

**Tutorial.** The tutorial is a hybrid. It resembles a seminar in that it addresses a topic set by the teacher, but it is typically more narrowly focussed than a seminar. For example, a tutorial might consider the differential equations that had been assigned the week before. But unlike a seminar, no one presents. The agenda is driven by student questions which the tutor usually answers. In some sense this is an ideal educational arrangement since it clarifies the topic and is completely student driven. The trick is to foster the right kinds of questions. A problem set or handout could accomplish that. Or an incomprehensible lecture.

**Seminar.** The essence of the seminar is that someone, or several persons, makes a presentation which then is followed by discussion and questions. The seminar would not be my choice for the enzyme kinetics problem because the students didn't understand the material enough to present it. Seminars can be used very effectively in literature courses when one student interprets a text and discussion follows, or in courses like psychology where students present reviews of the literature and questions follow. Though the nature of the presentation may vary enormously, its purpose is always to provide members with a common starting point for questioning, clarification of ideas, or discussion.

Preparing a subject for presentation is one of the most effective ways to learn it, and seminars are useful learning experiences for the presenters. It is less certain that other group members will find the seminar a useful stimulus for their learning. Seminars are better than free group discussion when information is required in order to stimulate questions, discussion, and learning. But if presenting the information inhibits the very interaction it is meant to stimulate, then it has no advantage over a didactic lecture. The organizer of a seminar, therefore, must be ever watchful that the presentation stimulates, rather than inhibits, interaction. The following guidelines might be useful:

**1.** Limit the presenter to a quarter to one half of the total time available, to leave plenty of time for questions and discussion. Suggest to the presenters that they should not try to anticipate and answer all of the questions that might arise from their talk. Rather they should encourage and be prepared for questions.
**2.** Suggest topics to the presenters or at least edit their topics so that the material they present is relevant to the course objectives.
**3.** Make sure that all students prepare for the topics, not just the presenters. The presenter might select a couple of significant articles to precirculate a week in advance.
**4.** Give the group members a formal role in providing feedback to the presenters.

In the larger world, discussants criticize a presentation, praise it, elaborate an aspect of the theme, compare it to other ideas, and/or apply it to their own specific situations. For the prupose of learning groups it is useful if discussants restrict themselves to constructive comments, raising points which engage the presenter in a dialogue, rather than ones which embarass or intimidate him or her. Discussants could, for example, apply the presenter's ideas to their own context or compare his or her ideas with their own framework.

**Demonstration.** A demonstration can also provide the necessary information or stimulus for learning. Imitation is a powerful method, especially for learning a practice such as teaching, health care, or manual skills, because the students can see much more than the teacher can explain. The teacher should practise first while the student watches, because it is important that students see correct practices. Video feedback is useful to show students how their actions diverge from the model.

The interesting thing about imitation learning is that its major strength is also its drawback. Students observe so closely that they may learn habits of the teacher which are incidental to the practice being taught, like scratching your head! In fact, they can be so caught up in such irrelevant mimicry that they lose the main point, like little kids playing school. The child who takes the role of teacher bosses everyone — gives permissions to go to the washroom and write on the chalkboard — but there is no content. It is important, therefore, that teachers vary their demonstrations or get other teachers or students to display variants of the demonstration so that learners can extract the important aspects out of demonstration and separate out the unnecessary details.

**Pyramid Plan.** Panel discussions symposia, and demonstrations share the disadvantage of being expensive in teacher or expert time. Even seminars are time consuming if teachers need to assist the presenters. There are times when such heavy commitment of teacher time is not possible and yet, because of the complexity or subtlety of the subject matter, the group needs expert input.

The pyramid plan is a common solution to this difficulty. A team is formed in which more senior students stimulate discussion and answer questions for the junior ones.

In a psychology department, this team might consist of six undergraduate students from first year, six from second year, two from third year, who would be assistant leaders, and the group leader, a fourth year student. Pyramid groups tend to score higher than ordinary classes on such measures as attitude, scientific thinking, use of the library, intellectual orientation, resourcefulness in problem solving, and number of students continuing as majors (McKeachie, 1983).

### Suggestion 2: Familiarize yourself with the types of groups that encourage participation

In the introduction I made the point that it is inherently easier to foster interaction in small groups than in large ones. This principle applies to small groups of various sizes and structures. The

20

smaller the group, the easier it is to stimulate interaction. This suggestion explores the variations on the theme of participatory small groups.

**Free Group Discussion.** This most common type of participatory group is structured by pre-planning the agenda, setting topics, and assigning material to be covered. The group leader encourages everyone to participate and ensures that the group does not range too far from the agenda. Discussion then ranges relatively freely, within the bounds of the topic, and may be further controlled and focussed by the use of questions or a list of issues, or by following some step-by-step procedure, such as that found in clinic group teaching: history, physical examination, diagnosis, and treatment, by solving a problem (problem-solving group), or taking up a case (case discussion).

**Buzz Groups.** Here, the small group is subdivided into groups of two to six persons. The groups are given a task, a time limit, and a student recorder who documents and reports their progress to the larger group. It is essential that each group's task be perfectly clear, that it be relevant to the objective of the larger group, and that contributions of the buzz groups be integrated into the larger group afterwards. If the task is unclear, or the relation to the group work is fuzzy, the groups will feel that they are wasting their time.

Buzz groups can be used during a lecture to draw out questions or to increase student involvement. They lose some richness because of the reduced variety of members, but the real advantage of dividing into buzz groups becomes apparent when they reconvene into the larger group: after a brief period in the smaller group, individual members are less timid about speaking out, and, having tried out their ideas in a safer group, have polished their rough thoughts. The main purpose, then, of buzz groups is to improve interaction in the larger group, not to replace it. For this reason, I would use buzz groups for no more than a quarter of the time available. I would also break from the common practice of one person's reporting to the larger group. At formal meetings, this is necessary, but in a learning group it would be preferable to get more students to talk. That, after all, is the idea of buzz groups in the first place.

**Learning cells.** Learning cells — co-operative learning arrangements of two or three students who read material, answer set questions on their own, and then discuss their answers with the group — maximize active participation. The teacher should review the questions and occasionally observe the process to ensure relevance. Members in the group should be rotated for variety and interest (Milne, 1984).

**POPS.** In a variation of the learning cell technique (Bergquist

& Phillips, 1975), each student reads a different assignment. They then explain the material to each other and discuss the questions. This variation has been further developed (Small, 1985) into Patient Oriented Problem Solving (POPS), a system which helps students learn material and solve problems by working together. POPS has three objectives: to help students learn to apply basic knowledge to the solution of clinical problems; to encourage students to locate information necessary for solving problems by utilizing sources that are available to health care professionals throughout their careers (e.g., textbooks and peers); and to encourage students to work together and, in doing so, to develop the ability to evaluate colleagues' opinions, thought processes, and diagnoses.

The POPS process is straightforward. All the students read a list of behavioral objectives and take a short pre-test. Then the class is divided into small work groups comprised of four students. Each of the four students receives a different set of materials related to a common theme or topic. The students then go off on their own to study the materials. After an hour they reconvene, within their groups of four, to share their information. They teach one another about the material they have learned in order to answer a set of study questions prepared by the POPS designers. Finally, there is a test of the information which students take individually. Since the students are aware that the test will be closely related to the study questions, they are motivated to prepare answers thoroughly. Indeed, peer pressure is usually exerted on students by one another to prepare thoroughly and therefore teach well.

**Brain-Storming Groups.** Brain-storming is a group process in which members "storm" a problem with ideas. Although it was originally used for problem-solving groups, it can easily be adapted for use with educational groups to coax creative ideas out of participants who may be reluctant to speak because of fear of criticism. The key to brain-storming is that no criticism is allowed of contributions. Any ideas are accepted and written down. Wild ideas are particularly encouraged because they may break up mental blinders and lead to other creative and more practical ideas. After the session the ideas can be subjected to criticism.

While this structure is too intense to be tolerated for long, it is highly creative and can lead to unexpected avenues of exploration.

**Debate.** A debate requires a controversial issue on which group members can take opposing sides. The gain in floor time for group members results from the formal nature of the debate (argument, opposing argument, rebuttal) in which everyone is assured a chance to speak. More individual involvement can be gained if the groups develop their arguments separately before the debate. In a group of fifteen or more, it is possible to create three or four "sides" to the debate rather than two.

Creating more than two sides is useful for another reason. Debating tends to polarize issues and thereby miss shades of gray and compromise positions. With several sides in the picture, some of the students can take the compromise positions.

Another unhappy tendency of competitive situations is insensitivity to ideas and feelings of others. Debaters are so busy presenting their own views and trying to "win" that they forget that the purpose of the exercise is to understand the various positions. One way to get around this problem is to assign roles to the various groups. The best example I ever saw of this use of the debate method was by a professor of forest policy. He divided a class of 40 into groups of 10. One group had to take the position of the government, another of the conservationists, a third the forest industry, and the fourth the people living on the forested lands. In case they got too carried away with talking and not listening to each other, he made it clear that the exam would ask them to present all four positions. The atmosphere was closer to co-operative learning than competitive debating, but the debate aspect did seem to add a certain levity to the exchange, especially when students began to recognize that they were accusing one another of hidden intentions in much the same way as the real players in the real world. In short, this kind of role play is probably superior to a straight debate for learning purposes because it adds the dimension of coming to know the feelings of a real group.

### Suggestion 3: Familiarize yourself with the types of groups that help members understand the feelings or points of view of others

The usual purpose of the learning group is to facilitate the learning of a subject matter external to the group, such as history, physics, or languages. The focus, therefore, is usually not on the emotions or personalities of the group members as it would be in a therapeutic group. However, there are times when emotions and personalities are a subject of study in themselves or when they need to be dealt with in order to move on to the external issues.

**Role Playing and Simulation.** Attempting to enact the role of another enables the actor to *feel* what it is like to be in the other's position and to understand her or his point of view. In the example of the forestry class given above, when students identified with various political factions in the controversy over use of forest resources, they experienced directly the emotions of various political groups. They also had a lot of fun.

Simulation techniques are role enactments in which the roles are chosen to reproduce or simulate some role in the real world (a jury, terrorist group) in order to apply the ideas of the subject to a concrete situation and to facilitate understanding of the real world actors.

The effectiveness of role playing can be destroyed by endless discussion of the relevance of the role. The idea is to get right into the role and identify the feelings that you may share with the person or group whose role you are enacting. Sure, it's a little phony, but if you can get right into it, the feelings generated will be similar to those of the relevant people.

Another problem with role playing is people's reluctance to act in public. One way to overcome this inhibition is for the teacher to show the way by taking the first role. In one particularly successful session, the objective of the workshop was to help teaching assistants with their teaching difficulties, but they were much too inhibited at first to act out their problems. However, they were quite willing to describe those problems to the senior teacher and undergraduates, who then did the acting. After a problem was portrayed, the teaching assistants were asked to suggest ways to deal with it. Eventually, when everyone felt more relaxed, the teaching assistants began to do the acting themselves. In summary, they were gradually drawn into participating in the role enactment by the example of the senior teacher (Tiberius, Silver, Fleming, Hoffman & Cappe).

**Role Reversal.** Role reversal is a powerful variant of role enactment for use in interactions between two persons or groups. Take, for example, the teacher-student situation. As teachers' memories of their own student days fade they find it increasingly difficult to understand their students' points of view. A common — and cynical — misconception of many teachers is that students are interested only in grades. The truth, I believe, is that students' primary concern is for survival, and grades are of primary importance to them. However, once that need is satisfied, their motivation quickly switches to interest in the subject, desire to be successful in their future work, their own personal growth, or whatever. Teachers forget how preoccupied they once were with passing the course.

An interesting experiment in role reversal was administered to my colleagues and other international visitors by the leaders of a faculty development workshop at the University of Göteborg in Sweden. With straight faces, the group leaders administered a test to the participants in the rather severe atmosphere undergraduates might find typical but which is considered an unacceptable effrontery when done to peers. It was an exciting but risky way to begin a conference on teaching improvement. The participants with whom I spoke said that the test angered them (Pascal, 1989). The discussion that followed was no doubt envigorated by the stinging memory of the exam; the teachers who objected to the exam were forced to ask themselves what they were doing to their own students. On the other hand, some teachers learned nothing from the experience, they were simply angry at the group leaders for putting them through it!

**The fishbowl or concentric circles.** In the fishbowl or concentric circle format, a few volunteers agree to interact in an inner circle while the rest of the group observe from an outer circle. This is a powerful means of gaining insight into the subtle emotions and dynamics of group interaction. The outer group invariably note aspects of the group process that escaped the notice of the inner group, while the inner group can usually share feelings about being in the action that escaped the outer group because of their remoteness from it.

Fishbowls have been used simply to stimulate discussion by breaking down the number, but I do not agree with this use of the fishbowl since it leaves the larger number in the outer ring silent and uninvolved.

**Structures for other specific purposes.** The three categories described above include most group structures. There are occasions, however, when your aims would be served by the use of an activity designed specifically to foster trust, to help people cope with anger, or to build team spirit and collaboration in an organization. Such specific structures or plans are a temporary departure for a class which is normally organized as a discussion or seminar.

Although it is difficult for busy teachers to structure such experiences and test them, we are fortunate to have available a comprehensive resource for just this purpose. I refer to Pfeiffer and Jones's nine-volume *Handbook of Structured Experiences for Human Relations Training* and the 12 volumes of the *Annual Handbook of Structured Experiences*. Let me use an example to illustrate the use of these books.

Certain members of your group are being pushed into pigeon holes by other members because of views they have expressed, and you want to find a structure which will enable your group to experience the pressures of role expectations. What you are dealing with here is a type of stereotype: the individual who supported an unpopular view in the first class is now being viewed as a rebel in every class and can't seem to shake the label, so you would like to raise group awareness to these kinds of pressures. First, you look through the *Reference Guide to Handbooks and Annuals* which organizes the activities from all 21 volumes. While a few categories appear to contain relevant material, "Values Clarification/Stereotypy"stands out. In that category you will find an entry called "Headbands: Group Role Expectations," followed by its author, a brief explanation of its goals, the approximate running time of the activity, and the volume and page number of detailed description.

In that description, you will find instructions for headbands on which are written a role and an instruction to others in the group. For example, the headband might read *Expert: Ask my advice*, or *Insignificant: Ignore me*. The headbands are placed on volunteers so that everyone but the wearers can read them easily. The facilitator provides a topic and instructs each member to follow the instructions on the headbands when they respond to the volunteers.

After about 20 minutes the facilitator stops the discussion, asks the volunteers to guess what their headbands said, and then take them off and read them. The facilitator then asks a number of questions designed to raise the students' awareness to group pressures: Was it difficult being yourself under group pressure? How did it feel to be misunderstood? How did the experience alter your group behavior?

The Pfeiffer and Jones books describe hundreds of such activities, not all of which require as much involvement as this one. Some of the groups require intensive leadership, while other groups work entirely on their own outside the regular class to support and help one another (self-help groups) or produce a report to submit to the class (syndicate groups).

**Suggestion 4: Use more than one type of group if appropriate**
Keep in mind that it is not necessary to stick with one kind of group throughout the course or even throughout one meeting. A seminar may serve to raise issues which are then discussed by the entire group using an unstructured format. A large discussion group may be broken into dyads or triads to increase involvement.

**Suggestion 5: Consider projects that take place outside the group and report back to it**

Restructuring a group to suit its objectives can be extended to include outside activities. Individual students can write brief position papers (a paragraph or two stating their position on a particular article) or keep notebooks of their experiences related to the learning. The results of such exercises then become part of the group process when students share them with the group.

Groups which function largely outside the classroom include case study groups or project groups. If members feel forced to participate with others who contribute little to the effort, they will become resentful and angry, but when they function co-operatively, these kinds of groups are exciting to belong to.

### Suggestion 6: Practise

You may never try any of these techniques when a group you are leading is in trouble if you haven't first practised under more relaxed conditions. We tend not to take risks when we are under stress. So try out some of these forms just for variety, just for the fun of it, on a class that is going well. True, if it ain't broke, don't fix it, but when it ain't broke may be the perfect time to play with it.

### Suggestion 7: Discuss the group structure in class

Group members are often unaware of the structure of their group. It is important to raise the issue in order to clarify the relationship between the objectives of the group and the group structure. Moreover, students usually do not know about alternative structures which may be useful. And group process is invigorated by the sense of ownership that flows from having influenced the shape of the group.

## Possible cause 2: Students are not active enough

Although teachers of such subjects as languages, nursing, or fine arts are usually aware of the necessity for active participation, most teachers tend to forget the necessity for active involvement and practice of skills like problem solving, critical thinking, and articulation.

The first time I encountered this phenomenon, a group of teaching assistants in sociology were complaining about how slow their students were. "They can't put two sentences together that make any sense," was a common criticism. But when did they have an opportunity to practise putting two sentences together, or even to pronounce the sociological terms? They listened to lectures and read their text, and the small group sessions were not small enough to allow them much floor time.

## Suggestion 1: Use learning cells

The learning cell and its variants offer formal arrangements whereby groups of three or four students teach one another and practise speaking the language of the subject, problem solving, or thinking. Ironically, in passive learning formats the teacher gets more practice than the learner. Learning cells are useful for practising a subject matter where a monitor is not necessary — for giving explanations or articulating arguments.

## Suggestion 2: Use helping trios

Helping trios are ideal arrangements for practising communication skills. Three is the minimum number which will allow a speaker, a listener, and a monitor: while the speaker and listener focus on the content of the communication, the monitor is free to observe the process. For example, in a lesson on interviewing, while Sarah interviews Jim, the monitor observes the process with an eye on the teacher's handout providing the guidelines for good interviewing.

## Suggestion 3: Arrange practice sessions

Language students can practise by speaking and writing. Fine art students and health care students can approximate what they will be doing when they graduate. But how is history or philosophy practised? Before exercises can be arranged for subjects such as these, whose outcomes are knowledge and understanding rather than actions, the subjects must be examined to find out precisely what it means to "do" them. Most books on behavioral objectives list verbs describing educational outcomes in specific terms. Such lists can help teachers who are shopping for the precise verb to describe the action of their subject — "interpret, distinguish, apply, demonstrate, conclude, compare, restructure" (see, for example, Gronlund, 1970; Kibler, Barker, & Miles, 1970; and Mager, 1975).

Once you have specified the precise verb, you will find it much easier to develop an exercise that allows your students to practise. For example, a teacher of moral philosophy may ask her students to prepare and defend a position paper on an ethical issue for each small group discussion. A history teacher might require his students to list the evidence for and against a historical statement.

# Possible Cause 3: Distortion caused by evaluation of group performance

It is a common practice to evaluate student performance in the small group as an incentive for participation. Encouragement of participation will be taken up in detail in Part Two, but here it is important to mention the potential of evaluation of student performance for distracting the group from the real goals of the course. When the group performance is evaluated students often move into what Barnes (1975) has called "performance mode" where they are more concerned with what they are supposed to say to get a good mark or to impress the teacher than with the meaning of the material. The alternative is "disclosure mode," in which students feel free to disclose and deal with their ignorance.

### Suggestion 1: Evaluate the product of the group rather than its participation

Obvious examples of group products are co-operative efforts such as joint research projects or laboratory exercises. But the product of the group can also be individual, for example each student can gain understanding of concepts or ability to solve problems as a result of group interaction.

### Suggestion 2: Reduce anxiety about the exam

I have done this by administering a multiple choice test to evaluate the minimum standard for the course. As one of my students said to calm down his anxious friend: "What are you worried about? You can't fail the course if you pass the multiple choice test and it's a Mickey Mouse test. He just asks you the basic stuff. If you want an 'A,' that's different. You have to pass in an 'A' paper." I couldn't have put it better.

# Possible Cause 4: Poor time planning

Discussions can be frustrating if the time for the session runs out before the discussion gets anywhere.

### Suggestion 1: Consider time in planning

After teaching the same subject over and over, you learn how long different activities take. For example, it takes about five minutes for each student to present a brief synopsis of an article, but if there is some class reaction to each article, it may take 15 minutes.

Consider time when you are planning the number of articles or the number of problems you will be able to take up in a class. If you do, you may find yourself cutting the number down to leave more time for discussion, or suggesting that the students indicate the most difficult problems.

Don't forget to plan for — and take — breaks. Students are often too polite to let you know that you have gone into the break, but they may become resentful or restless if you do.

### Suggestion 2: Remind the group of the schedule

I have a target time of about half an hour for the part of the class in which students present their brief reviews of articles. If the presentations or follow-up question periods exceed the half-hour limit, I remind the group that we need to get all the data on the table before we discuss the material in depth. Besides, until all the articles are presented some of the students are not fully participating because they are either waiting for their turn to present or politely waiting until all of the presentations are made before they raise more general issues. Once the presentations are out, everyone is on an equal footing, and discussion can begin.

### Suggestion 3: Assign preparation tasks

Some teachers assign position papers, a paragraph or two in which students present their reactions to the readings, their views, or, in the case of factual material, describe any problems they had in understanding the material. Other teachers run courses as a series of question and answer sessions. Students develop written questions about material they do not understand, the class period is used to answer them. In my own education course, I ask students to present brief reviews of papers. This connects each student with something in the literature and provides the class with a basis of discussion.

## Possible Cause 5: Superficial discussion and/or poor listening

Examples in this category often reflect a cruel irony in which a teacher's kindness and thoughtfulness backfire. The most memorable of these was the conscientious French literature teacher who was considered brilliant in both criticism and creative writing. Far from being arrogant, she was keenly aware of the advantage her years of study gave her over undergraduate students, and was prepared to be very patient with them. She therefore did not question students or intervene with her own comments. She remembered from her own undergraduate years how teachers humiliated students by incessant grilling and correcting. Instead, she bore every comment with calm acceptance.

Here's the ironic part. The students I interviewed from her class said that she was well meaning but not very bright. The class was confusing and frustrating because the students didn't know what they were talking about and no one could understand anyone else. They thought she let the class become a bull session because she had a superficial understanding of the subject herself. I felt like telling them how ungrateful they were, that they should take some of the responsibility, and so on. But that would only have made it difficult for me to find out what was really going on. Instead, I discussed the issue with them for almost half an hour until I began to understand what had happened.

This is how I now perceive it: students, who by definition are not experts in a subject matter, often cannot speak clearly or coherently on the subject. They are practising the language of a new field. Although they make honest efforts to be understood, their contributions are often too abstract, complex, superficial, or poorly stated to be clear to the rest of the class.

If students are not secure enough to challenge one another, and if the teacher is reluctant to intervene or question, the discussion becomes muddy, superficial, or irrelevant and the discussion degenerates to the point at which no one is really listening to anyone else.

## Suggestion 1: Use active listening

Active listening means more than just hearing someone else's words. It means taking some of the responsibility for the communication by taking an *active* role as a listener. It means *helping* the other person communicate by asking follow-up or probing questions, by paraphrasing, by summarizing, and by connecting what they say to the subject.

**Follow-up questioning or probing.** The listener asks a question not to challenge the speaker but to get the listener to elaborate. The probe should express acceptance and empathy.

**Paraphrasing.** A paraphrase is a kind of feedback to the speaker of the effect of her or his message. In paraphrasing you express, in your own words, what you think the speaker was trying to say. Use concrete and descriptive language if you can. It doesn't matter if you are wrong. The idea is to let the speaker know your exact interpretation so that he or she can then restate this point in a clearer way.

**Summarizing and Connecting.** A summary of a discussion can often be put in the context of the goals of the group, so that it becomes a kind of report on the accomplishments of the group.

Here are some nonsequiturs that came up in the French literature class:

Teacher: "Did you recognize any common themes or have any feelings about today's writings that you want to share?"

Roger: "Both Sartre and Camus were writing about death. It was actually pretty depressing to read this stuff."

Alice: "I don't think they were depressing at all. They are dealing with choices and life is choices."

Kim: "Well, existentialism is a philosophy of engagement, of choosing. Sartre is telling us to choose?"

Without active listening this discussion might never get off the ground. Or, what's probably more to the point, it will never touch ground. Here is a sample of use of some of these active listening techniques on the same dialogue.

Roger: "Both Sartre and Camus were writing about death. It was actually pretty depressing."

Teacher: "They made you sad." [empathizing with Roger, accepting his feelings]

Roger: "Yeah."

Teacher: "I can certainly understand that. Can you take one novel and give us an example of what you found depressing." [probing, trying to get him to become a little more concrete]

Roger: "In *No Exit*, everyone is dead looking down at earth and talking about the past."

Teacher: "Did that make you sad because they were dead or because of what they are saying?" [probe]

Roger: "Well, it didn't really bother me that they are dead because they weren't built up in the story as characters or anything. No, it's more what they are saying. They were so tormented."

Teacher: "That's for sure."

Alice: "I don't think they were depressing at all. They are dealing with choices and life is choices."

Teacher: "What do you mean by 'dealing with choices'?" [this follow-up question fails to draw elaboration from Alice who replies by redefining "dealing with"]

Alice: "They had to choose which way to go in life."

Teacher: [Summarizing and connecting] "Roger's example has us in the room where they were discussing their lives on earth. [paraphrasing] You are saying that they were talking about their choices?"

Alice: "That's right. They were discussing choices they had made back on earth."

Teacher: "For example . . ." [looking at Alice]

Alice: "For example when the guy kept saying that he chose to leave the revolution only to get help, and that he wasn't deserting the cause."

Teacher: "Let's stay with that situation for a minute. Garcin was tormented because he was thinking about the choice he made back on earth to leave the revolution to get help, rather than stay and fight. It sounds like he made a sensible choice. [summary] What is tormenting him?" [question]

Kim: "Well, existentialism is a philosophy of engagement, of choosing. Isn't Sartre is telling us to choose?"

Philip: "Garcin did choose, but he's worried that he has made the wrong choice."

Teacher: "What's tormenting him? That he failed to choose? Or that he made the wrong choice? Or what?"

Philip: "Well, he looks pretty bad and Inex is sure not letting him forget it."

Alice: "That's right. He's happy with his choice but he left himself open because no one knew he was going for supplies, so I agree, that he looks pretty bad."

Teacher: "So, we have one person tormented by another because his actions and his intentions seem to the other person to be at variance, even though, in his own mind, he feels that they are not, and that he is not 'in bad faith,' in Sartre's phrase. One of the points that Sartre is making in this play is that hell is other people. And, of course, the theme of aligning your actions with your intentions is a common one in existentialist literature." [summary]

### Suggestion 2: Ask questions of the right type and level

It is important to pay special attention to the type of questions you ask and the kinds of responses they elicit. Ray Rasmussen (1984) lists four types of questions:

**Structured versus unstructured.** Our literature teacher used a structured question when she asked, "What is tormenting him?" An unstructured question might have been, "What's going on here?" The structured question, by narrowing the focus and providing the context for the answer, can prevent the kind of drifting that is the subject of this chapter.

**Convergent versus divergent.** Divergent questions indicate that there are a number of possible answers to the question. Convergent questions require a single right answer, making it risky to answer. In the dialogue above most of the questions were convergent because they were follow-up questions, whose intention was to focus, to bring the dialogue to the concrete level. But, when the teacher began her discussion, she was wise to begin with the divergent question, asking about common themes and feelings in today's readings. A convergent question might have initiated a period of awkward silence.

**Low-level versus high-level.** A low-level question can be answered by rote recall from memory. A high-level question requires analysis, synthesis, or evaluation. An example of a low-level question from our dialogue would be, "Which of the characters in *No Exit* was concerned about acting in bad faith?" This kind of question might elicit tracking responses from students rather than thinking responses. They will try to psych out the questions from the context rather than think about the topic and develop their own ideas. As soon as students begin to look outward instead of inward for their source of ideas the discussion begins to become meaningless.

**Single versus multiple.** Pursue one question at a time.

# Possible Cause 6: Unco-ordinated effort — students are engaged in different tasks

Students who are at different levels of ability, preparation, and motivation find it frustrating to listen to questions and concerns which do not interest them. This frustration leads to a feeling of wasting time.

### Suggestion 1: Break the issue or problem down and focus everyone on the same part

The problem-solving literature (Maier, 1970) advocates breaking a problem down into smaller parts and focussing everyone on one at a time. This approach can be extended to the learning group. If the agenda is clear to everyone, students will have the option of entering the discussion when they feel it is appropriate. For example, a teacher might set up a schedule in which the first hour is used to clarify concepts and the second hour is used to solve problems. She may then invite students to come for the second hour only if they understand the problems or leave after the first hour if they have no difficulties.

# 3/Goals are Unacceptable

*"What the blank does Shakespeare have to do with chemical engineering?"*

The groups in this chapter reject the group's goals because they are either unwilling or unable to accept them. I have identified five possible causes, each of which is illustrated with examples from my consulting.

## Possible Cause 1: Students' experiences and values make them reject the teacher's goals

Our medical genetics course used to have the distinction of receiving the lowest student ratings of all courses in the second year. The teacher, an internationally respected authority in the field, had exhausted himself trying to make the material interesting. With strange calm this otherwise passionate researcher explained that his students saw the course as irrelevant: "They feel that the purpose of a medical education is to help them become excellent practitioners, and they see my course as irrelevant to practice. In some sense, of course, they are right. Only a few diseases of genetic origin can be treated. The students' orientation is toward learning how to treat patients."

I asked him if some aspects of the course weren't relevant to general practice and would therefore interest students. He said that there were, but the practical end of it was mainly the counselling of patients who have genetic problems in the family.

## Suggestion 1: Make your learning goals relevant to those of the students

If possible, explain how pursuing your goals will help students get what they want. Several years after the conversation described above, I was astounded to see very high student ratings for the genetics course. I phoned the new teacher of this course to ask what she had done. I expected to find someone extremely charismatic who had overwhelmed the small group with her interpersonal skills. Not at all. She was very serious and analytical, and as passionate about scientific genetics as the previous teacher had been. The only difference is that she applied her analytical skills to the problem of the discrepancy between her goals and the students', had come to the conclusion that the aspect of medical genetics that most of the students would use in the future was patient counselling, and had set up her assignments accordingly.

Students were asked to imagine that they were family doctors and were confronted with a patient who needed advice on a genetic problem. Their task was to explain, in nonmedical language, what the patient needed to know. I subsequently talked to two groups of students from her class. They were fascinated with the problem method: "Asking us to explain the material to a patient who had no background in genetics is very useful in helping us understand it"; "It is a wonderful concept"; "It is difficult to do but very useful."

I increasingly observe teachers who attempt to meet students' need for relevance before a problem arises. If you want to try it, I suggest an informal approach. Ask students how they feel about the subject. Let them volunteer information, don't pressure them. Follow each statement with a few questions. It may even be useful to ask a colleague or teaching assistant to chat with students who might be too shy to tell you that they find the course irrelevant.

The horrible technique of asking each student why he or she is in the class is becoming increasingly popular with teachers who have taken teaching improvement workshops. This tactic is supposed to draw students out and uncover their values, beliefs, and interests as they relate to the subject matter. The only thing I have to say about this technique is: don't do it. Student answers are frequently either contrived or less than inspiring. In some classes, the only reason the students are there is because they have to be. And teachers' doing exactly what they had planned without taking any notice of students' desires generates mistrust.

Teachers also run into trouble when they try to link course goals and student goals but simply don't know their subject matter well enough to make those links adequately. The medical genetics teacher was not only a bench researcher, she was a genetic counsellor as well. But what if she had never done any genetic counselling? The small group teacher must be able to leave her planned material in order to "go with the flow" of the discussion and the interests of the students.

A history teacher I knew put it very well: "After I have lectured on the same subject about five times I get to the point at which I can teach it to a small group. This is because each time I lecture I organize the lecture from a slightly different point of view to keep from getting bored. Then, from whatever angle students in the small group approach the subject, I can follow them and make the appropriate connections with important concepts and ideas." His students found him truly astounding. They used to joke about it. One student told me: "It's amazing. No matter what we raise from readings, he can connect it to balance of powers." I asked students if they felt manipulated by this. They said not at all, that they felt there was nothing sneaky in his approach since everyone knows that the course is about balance of powers, and in a sense, it is the teacher's job is to show them that the concept is not just hot air but a useful idea that connects with things that students are interested in. Dr. J. was not covertly manipulating the discussion toward balance of powers; he was overtly demonstrating that you can't talk about modern history without talking about the balance of powers; he was making his case by connecting the concept to everything that was said. The students saw his teaching strategy exactly as he intended it, as a reflection of the intrinsic nature of the subject rather than a teaching ploy. While this teaching strategy might pose ethical problems for elementary school children who might not be aware that the teacher's point of view is just a point of view, it ought to be safe to use, from a moral point of view, in higher education. Still, it might be useful if the teacher would let students know that she or he is consciously trying to interpret the issues from a balance of powers point of view, or Marxist, or behaviorist, or whatever the concept.

### Suggestion 2: If you can't make your case, accept rejection — for now

If you cannot or will not find ways to define the course goals in terms of the individual interests of students, then present them with the best defense of your goals that you possibly can, and be prepared for most of the students to reject it. If students don't think that your goals for learning are worth pursuing, they will probably not be convinced by the case you make. But your efforts will have served two purposes: you may stimulate those few students who are inclined to pursue your view of the course, and you will convince the students that, at least, you are sincere in your belief that the goals of the course will benefit them. Do not underestimate the importance of this second point. One of the most common assumptions for students to make, when they fail to see the value of their teacher's goals, is that the teacher did not care enough about them to consider their needs. They tend to view such teachers as indulging themselves in their own research interests at the students' expense.

Particularly in professional schools, the teaching of any subject not directly related to the major field is plagued with student rejection, whether the subject is biochemistry in medicine, statistics in social sciences, or writing skills in engineering. The example here is from a forestry seminar in research methods.

The students were not amused. Many of them saw the forester as a romantic symbol of the Canadian North. The job required physical stamina, knowledge of the woods, and superlative skill at driving a pickup truck through the bush while wearing heavy boots. Scientific forestry, on the other hand, was an insidious plot to urbanize the last remaining occupation for the free outdoor spirit. The teacher seemed more at home with a computer than an axe, and the students roundly rejected both him and his course.

He was unemotional when we spoke about what I saw as nearly open rebellion in his class. He told me, "Forestry is changing. It has to be put more on a scientific basis. Fifty years ago the profession was concerned with exploiting the forest in the most efficient way as if it were some kind of limitless resource. Today the emphasis has to be on management through increased understanding of trees, their habitat, soil, diseases. In short, we are not running a four-year university course to teach people to drive a pickup truck. The emphasis will be on soil and plant science and on the social side, and on policy making."

He went on to say that every year he puts this view to the class and every year he gets less flack about it. "For one thing," he said, "the word is getting around, and among the new applicants there are fewer every year who have an axe in their closet. For another, they know that I am not just telling them this to rationalize my own interests. They know by the way that I say it that I'm telling them the way forestry is going. Some of them respect that, and they can meet the challenge. Others drop out."

## Suggestion 3: If you cannot convince your students of the value of the material, quit

I'm serious. Don't try to teach anything to students if you cannot convince them that it is beneficial for them to learn it.

There is a widespread misconception that a skilled teacher can teach anything to anyone at some level. Like most misconceptions there is enough truth in it to sustain it, but it isn't true in general. The true part is that most of the time teachers can find a way either to match the students' motivation or to stimulate new motivation in support of course goals. Students are not a random selection of people herded at gun point into a class, at least not in higher education. Engineering students, for example, who are required to take a writing skills course, may reject the goal at first but can usually be persuaded of its value.

But teaching can take place only if participants agree on a number of assumptions. For one thing, the teacher and learner have to agree that the subject is worth learning. If either one ceases to value the subject, teaching and learning become a hollow game. To continue teaching under these conditions is to invite burn-out and to be perceived as a fake by the students.

The teacher of a sociology course was acutely aware that her discipline surveyed general statements while her students were concerned with particular problems. She invited a physician to class in the hope that he would be able to confirm the relevance of her material to nursing practice. At one point in the discussion she introduced some sociological data on how different ethnic groups regard their bodies. Some groups, for example, believe that injections are stronger medicine than pills. This belief, she suggested, should be taken into consideration in dealing with patients of that group. The teacher then turned to the physician for confirmation. He winced and twitched for a few painful seconds and then confessed that he just didn't work that way. He asks patients how they feel about injections and pills. He can find out much more that way than by reading volumes about the sociological characteristics of groups to which the patients belong.

This confirmed the student nurses' suspicions that sociology was irrelevant to real clinical problems. They were interested in generalizations only if the generalization provided them with strategies for interacting with patients that are superior to other strategies — such as asking questions. The course continued dismally.

### Suggestion 4: If you cannot convince <u>yourself</u> of the value of the material, quit

To lose faith in what you are teaching is the straight road to burn-out. The fuel that drives teachers is the belief that they are contributing something valuable. My saddest memories as an educational consultant are those times when teachers have voiced doubts of the value of their subject to students.

## Possible Cause 2: Teachers and students perceive the course goals differently because of their different intellectual frameworks

A behavioral science teacher who conducted small seminars of medical students tried to facilitate a discussion of the literature on patient compliance (the extent to which patients do what their doctors tell them to). She hoped to stimulate student discussion around various points of view in the literature, and to examine evidence for each point of view. Several students expressed their dissatisfaction with the task. They complained that there was no point in a bull session when they needed a clear cut list of "do's and don't's." As one angry student put it: "Why can't she give us a clear picture? We would rather spend our seminar time talking about how to handle patients, instead of wasting time arguing with one another about the literature."

Although the objective of clarifying the points of view in the literature is certainly a valid one, it did not suit the orientation of these students. Perhaps the teacher's goal failed to match the students' intellectual position or stage.

### Suggestion 1: Take into account different stages of intellectual development

A practical approach to intellectual development is to consider various developmental positions in three major stages (see King, 1977; Kitchener, 1977; Perry, 1970).

During the first or "dualistic" stage, people view themselves as receiving "truth" from those in authority. Dualistic students believe that there are "right" answers to their questions and that their teachers, who are the experts, know them, or *should* know them. They become frustrated if the teacher will not give them clear-cut answers. They have difficulty handling conflicting views, and even more difficulty producing their own view out of the conflicting views.

The second stage is intellectual "relativism." During this

developmental stage students begin to realize that there is more than one right answer to a question and they become more tolerant of people with different viewpoints. Truths are seen as emerging from their own thought and experience as well as from external sources.

A final series of developmental changes reflects intellectual "commitment." People begin to orient themselves among multiple perspectives by means of their own choices. Students begin to realize that the teacher has to interpret conflicting claims in the literature and that students have to do this too. They begin to realize that anwers to questions depend on one's framework. In this final position students are able to take a stand about an issue based on their own values, experience, and knowledge, and they can make probabilistic judgments, that is, after weighing evidence for and against a conclusion, they can conclude, "Even though I can't be certain, it appears from the evidence that. . . ."

One of the most common teaching situations is one in which dualistic students are taught by a teacher who makes probabilistic decisions. The behavioral science teacher, for example, tried to encourage her students to develop their own points of view based on their understanding of the literature, their values, and the particular style of medicine that they would like to practise. Ironically, the students perceived her as incompetent or uncaring.

Even if developmental schemes do not influence your teaching behavior directly, they can be comforting to teachers who cannot understand why they are perceived so differently by various students in their classes (Perry, 1970). Instead of bouncing from pillar to post trying to please everyone, the teacher who understands the developmental basis of this misunderstanding can concentrate on learning "where the students are" intellectually, and attempting to reach them.

## Suggestion 2: Match the students' level

According to developmental theory, students tend to be more satisfied and to learn more efficiently if they are taught by a method which is matched to their level of development. David Hunt, an educational psychologist at the Ontario Institute for Studies in Education, working with a developmental theory similar to the early stages of Perry's, gathered evidence showing that matching the students' level of conceptual development leads to increased satisfaction by the learner and increased efficiency of learning (1971; Hunt & Sullivan, 1974). According to Hunt, students who are at a low level of conceptual development prefer a greater degree of structure in their learning environment (as reflected in teacher-centred methods like lectures) whereas students who are at a high level of conceptual development require a low degree of structure in their learning environment (as reflected in student-centred methods such as independent learning and discovery learning).

How do we use developmental ideas in small group teaching? It is neither practical nor ethical to test all the students on various developmental dimensions, personality and intellectual, create homogeneous groupings of students, and then teach them by some matching optimal strategy, a strategy which considers both their present and future needs. At least one psychologist (Jackson, 1970) has argued that there is not much value in studying interactions between students and different teaching methods because teachers cannot make use of them in the present educational system.

On the other hand, although facilitators of small groups may not be able to match their teaching method with the developmental level of the group as a whole, small groups may allow opportunities for matching on a micro scale (Cronbach, 1967). The face-to-face interaction of a small group may provide teachers with sufficient information about individual students to enable them to understand those students' limitations and capabilities and to respond in ways that are most helpful to their learning. The teachers' ability to discern such student differences and to construct appropriate responses depends on their understanding of the relevant dimensions involved. This kind of microadaptation would be exemplified by a teacher providing a rule about the length of the essay assignment for a student who felt uneasy about the general guidelines.

One of the most important dimensions on which teachers can learn about their students in order to be more sensitive to them is their attitudes toward working in small groups (Hunt, 1989). Do they enjoy or value the small group process? If not, then everything else is beside the point. Teachers can easily gather sufficient information from students about a dimension as simple as whether students value the small group. And they can be sensitive to the information that they gather.

## Suggestion 3: Use plus-one-staging

Although matching students' developmental level may benefit them in the short run, it may harm them in the long run. Teaching styles that are matched to learning styles may be both comfortable and profitable for students' short-term learning, but may fail to challenge students to develop intellectually.

It is to this problem of fostering long-term development of

students by challenging their preferred method of learning that this and the following suggestions are directed. The ultimate goal is to encourage learners to grow in a direction that expands their ability to learn in different ways, that is, their learning flexibility.

Students can be challenged to stretch to a higher developmental stage but the challenge should not be overwhelming. This method of moderate challenge based on the present developmental stage of the student is called plus-one-staging (Widick, 1977). For example, dualist students should be challenged with multiple perspectives but not be required to make commitments based on their values, or styles.

Janet Schmidt, a counsellor, and Mark Davidson, an educational psychologist, both working in Minnesota, have provided (1983) detailed instructions to the teacher who would like to use a plus-one-staging approach. Some of these are paraphrased below.

**To challenge dualistic thinkers** to appreciate points of view:
**1.** Challenge cliches. In teaching about patient compliance, the teacher might say, "Is it always patients' fault if they do not follow your advice? Can you think of instances in which the patient either does not follow your advice through no fault of his or her own, or might choose not to follow your advice?"
**2.** Legitimate alternative points of view. For example, "Have you thought of any reasons in favor of the point of view you are rejecting? Does the alternative explanation have any advantages?"
**3.** Require evidence in support of opinions. For example, "What is the line of thinking that led you to that point of view? What is the evidence on which you support your conclusion?"
**4.** Reinforce students' appreciation of competing points of view. For example, "Are you aware of the disagreements between authors in the field?"
**5.** Legitimate students' own experience and judgment in reaching conclusions. For example, "That's what the text says, but what do you think, based on your experience, independent of the text?"
**6.** Support students in their growing awareness that it is okay to change their minds based on rational argument. For example, "I noticed that your position has shifted away from clear cutting in the lumbering industry. What kinds of things influenced your decision?"

**To challenge relativist thinkers** to move from a position of merely understanding and accepting the existence of different points of view to a position of evaluating them on the basis of evidence and their context:

**1.** Encourage students to appreciate that some points of view are logically preferable to others. For example, "Comparing the two essays, who do you think has made the better case? What kind of evidence or logic influenced your decision?"

**2.** Encourage students to consider the relevance of the context in evaluating a point of view. For example, "Would you come to the same conclusion if a very young patient didn't comply with your advice?" "What about an older person, with poor hearing?"

**3.** Encourage students to appreciate why authorities disagree. For example, "Why do our two authors disagree with regard to their projection of the economy? Aren't they gathering the same statistics? Do they have the same assumptions about people? Do they use a different form of argument to arrive at their conclusions?"

**4.** Identify the criteria on which judgments are made between conflicting points of view. "Why do you consider Hofstadter's definition of indoctrination a good one? What makes a definition good?" Or, "If you count the number of arguments each author raised, Davidson wins. He provides ten while Axelrad provides only six. Does this mean we go with Davidson? If quality of argument counts as well as quantity, then we have to describe what makes a high quality argument. What kinds of arguments are we more willing to accept?"

**5.** Emphasize that not all evidence is equally valid. For example, "Why are you more willing to accept the pollution statistics of the ecology professor over those provided by the paper mill? What is it that gives you confidence in evidence?"

**6.** Help students achieve sensitivity to the domain in which evidence is valid. "How useful is scientific evidence in proving religious faiths?"

**7.** Divide an argument into component parts. "You agree with all Sumner's assumptions, but you don't agree with his conclusion. Let's examine the structure of his argument to see where you begin to fall out with him."

**To challenge probabilistic thinkers** who are beginning to understand the process of making judgments among multiple points of view to rethink their decisions as conditions change and new information comes to light, and to take responsibility for their own learning:

**1.** Raise the possibility of basing decisions on uncertain information. For example, "Although you are faced with a situation in which none of the facts are 100 per cent certain, you can still come to a conclusion."

**2.** Help students understand the difference between reasoned judgment and fixation. For example, "You have come to a rather firm conclusion based on your present thinking; what conditions would influence you to change your mind?" "If your decision is a result of a reasoning process based on evidence and logic then any changes in the facts or assumptions might lead to a different interpretation of the problem and a different decision."

**3.** Focus on the student's own reasoning process. "Which of the assumptions carries more weight for you, the assumption about possible harm to the public or about possible destruction of the reputation of the official?"

**4.** Encourage well-reasoned, probabilistic statements. For example, in response to a student's saying, "It appears from my interpretation of the little available evidence that prejudice decreases as a result of proximity," the teacher might reply, "Your statement is quite sophisticated. It implies that you are basing your decision on the evidence but are nevertheless aware of the inadequacies of the evidence. You are giving your best decision, for now."

### Suggestion 4: Combine support with challenge

Teachers should use support as well as challenge in their encouragement of students toward a higher stage of intellectual functioning (Sanford, 1966). There should be enough challenge to encourage the students to stretch to the next stage of development but the challenge must be accompanied by emotional support because reaching beyond one's stage of development is uncomfortable and psychologically risky.

Janet Schmidt and Mark Davidson (1983) have provided some concrete suggestions for the kind of support you could provide students. They recommend that teachers:

**1.** Demonstrate respect and tolerance for the points of view of others in their own actions and thinking;

**2.** Appreciate the struggle students go through to stretch intellectually;

**3.** Introduce challenges gradually, not require dualist students to make personal, probabilistic decisions;

**4.** Encourage co-operation and trust among class members;

**5.** Disclose their own appreciation of multiple viewpoints or personal choices and their own continuing struggle to grow intellectually;

**6.** Empathize with students concerning the anxiety of appreciating multiple viewpoints, facing situations that are uncertain, or making wrong decisions;

**7.** Help students recognize that they are not alone and that their fellow students are going through a similar struggle;

**8.** Treat students as future colleagues who are going through struggles that everyone else has gone through.

### Suggestion 5: Use metaphors

Seek a metaphor which connects the material you are teaching with an area in which students are more intellectually developed. For example, the behavioral science teacher might draw a comparison between the literature on patient compliance and a difficult clinical decision in which there are several points of view. Students who may have already reached the stages of multiplicity or commitment in their clinical thinking can use their understanding in one area to bridge to another.

### Suggestion 6: Give it up

It is important to remember that not everything is teachable to everyone. If students are only able to seek the one "right" answer, you are not going to be able to engage them in probabilistic judgment. Students who are new to a subject, or not physically well, or stressed, may shift to a dualist position even if they are normally at a higher stage, and both age (Lawson, 1980) and years of education (Strange, 1978) are important in the development of reflective judgment. If your subject and goals require relativist thinking, then you may have to give up teaching your subject to some students until they gain more experience or until circumstances in their lives improve.

## Possible Cause 3: Teachers and students are not pursuing the same goals because the students are avoiding the real issues, which they find difficult or painful

A professor of environmental geography was trying to engage her students in the subject matter by connecting the main points of her argument with the lives of the students. She wanted to address the question, Why are most people not involved in environmental societies or in recycling waste? She began by asking students if they were members of the Sierra Club or whether they recycled their newspapers, tins, or bottles. The method backfired. Instead of students feeling involved in the issue because of its connection with their own lives, they became defensive and evasive.

## Suggestion 1: Make it clear that you support the students

Teachers must make it clear that they support their students. The geography teacher's aim was to use personal data as a starting point so that the discussion would be more meaningful to students. She certainly didn't intend to put down the students. Instead of asking questions that may be embarrassing she should have asked questions such as the following:

Teacher: "Do any of you live in North York?"

Student: "I do."

Teacher: "Their recycling program was the first one in the Metro area. How is it going? Are many households using the blue boxes?"

Or, she might ask:

Teacher: "Do you know anyone who doesn't recycle?"

Student: "I do [laughing]. My parents."

Teacher: "Do you know why they don't?"

Because the student volunteered to disclose the information about her parents, there is little danger of her feeling bullied. If the teacher had asked students whether their parents recycled, she may have provoked defensiveness.

## Suggestion 2: Divide students into groups of two or three for intensive discussion or buzz groups

Students may find issues difficult because of the potential embarrassment of discussing them in front of other students. One way to overcome such inhibition is to encourage students to talk to one another. Talking with peers is encouraging because students find out that they are not alone in their fears and feelings or that their worst assumptions were not true.

After such a buzz group one student confessed that he was very glad for the chance to talk to others. When all the hands went up except his own in answer to the question, "Do you recycle?" he had felt like crawling under the table. But by talking to others he learned that he was the only one who lived in a part of the city in which the recycling program has not yet started.

I face this problem in my own work whenever I attempt to gather information from a group of students about their study habits. They generally speak without hesitation about the merits or faults of the teacher, but often go silent when asked about themselves. But once someone breaks the ice and admits to not reading the material before the lecture, for example, others find the courage to speak about it, too. It is this facilitating effect of conversation that has convinced me to use small discussion groups to gather information from students.

### Suggestion 3: Encourage speakers to be concrete and specific

If the topic is difficult or painful, students might become evasive. They might begin to talk in abstract or general terms. Students in the geography class might begin to speak of recycling and support of environmental causes after support and some warming up by interaction with other students, but they are not likely to be very specific at first.

Gary: I recycle whenever I can.

Prof L.: And when is that?

Gary: [Laughing] Never.

Prof L.: Let's explore some of the reasons why we don't recycle, because they may be similar to the reasons why, as a society, we don't recycle.

Megan: You really don't have time.

Prof L.: Who really doesn't?

Megan: We don't. Students. I don't, a lot of the time.

Prof L.: What does recycling involve in time? Does anyone know, precisely?

Barb: You have to wash the cans, take the labels off, wash them, for one thing.

Prof L.: Do you have to? Does anyone know the rules for recycling of metals by the city?

# Possible Cause 4: Teachers and students are not pursuing the same goals because the teachers are avoiding the real issues, which they find difficult or painful

It is extremely difficult to perceive your own avoidance of topics you find difficult or painful. Unhappily, even students are seldom able to detect when the teacher is avoiding a topic, because students rely on the teachers to define the subject matter. The problem of teachers' bypassing important goals is one which the peer observer is uniquely constituted to solve.

### Suggestion 1: Invite a peer to review your class

Invite a colleague who is familiar with your subject area to observe your class and to read your course outline and materials. If she or he agrees, ask for comment on the appropriateness of the content and for particular note of anything you might have left out of the course because of some bias or personal discomfort of which you are unaware. This very process helped me to find out that I was short changing the organizational and institutional approach to faculty development in my course which is supposed to be a survey of *all* the tools of the faculty development consultant. The truth is that I found the organizational issues boring and I was not very knowledgeable in that area.

### Suggestion 2: Separate your personal reactions from your professional ones

If you are aware of avoiding certain topics, then there are steps you can take to overcome your inhibition about them. Many professors have blocks about women's issues, sexual issues, or race issues, for example. These teachers are frequently unable to approach the issue professionally. One teacher found that talking to the group about the conflict was very helpful. He told the group about his dilemma. As a psychologist, he said, he can examine the literature on child pornography dispassionately; but, as a person, he finds himself slipping into value judgments and anger. That disclosure seemed to relax him enough to be able to continue to talk about the subject in the two frames of mind.

## Possible Cause 5: Teachers and students are not pursuing the same goals because there are hidden agendas

The associate dean of a community college invited me to run an all-day workshop on large group teaching. The group was resistant from the start. After an hour, the resistance had escalated to outright hostility, and group participants were actually making sarcastic remarks at my expense. I made the usual egocentric mistake of all presenters: everything that happens is my fault. What I was doing wrong? Why weren't we getting anywhere?

It was particularly embarrassing that my Ph.D. thesis supervisor, whom I had not seen for years, had asked to observe one of my workshops because he had heard that I am very good at it and was going to have to run one soon himself. This man, whose good opinion is very important to me, was sitting there and nothing was working!

I called a break, a good workshop technique in situations like this. The washroom is not a place for long conversations so I remember this one almost verbatim:
Ed: They sure are hostile. What's wrong?
Me: I don't know.
Ed: What are you going to do?
Me: I'm going home.

When the group reconvened I said to them that I was puzzled by some of their behavior. I mentioned specific sarcastic comments. I said that I didn't know what was happening, but that for some reason it just wasn't working and I then asked if they had anything to say about it. The teachers were surprised at my response. At first they denied that anything was wrong; the attitude was, "Everything's okay. Let's just continue with the workshop and get it over with." One participant volunteered that I had been set up and that it wasn't my fault so I shouldn't bother to get into it.

I told them that I didn't think it would be very productive to continue under the circumstances, and that I was going to cancel the workshop. This really surprised them. They had expected to be able to carry on, ignoring their feelings. One participant said that she felt she could talk a little more freely since the dean had left during the break. Bit by bit the story came out: the dean had written them informing them of an impending reduction of ten per cent in staff over the next year. Class size was to be increased, and someone was being invited to teach the remaining teachers how to teach in large groups. Great. I was part of the dean's hatchet crew.

They told me that everyone felt obligated to attend the workshop out of fear of being fired themselves, yet no one was happy about taking part in a workshop for the purpose of helping to fire their colleagues. Everyone was participating in the workshop in a perfunctory manner, physically present, but at best unwilling to put energy into it, and at worst openly hostile.

## Suggestion 1: Check your perception

My first response was to check my perception of the behavior that I perceived as hostile. It could have been the case that they were not hostile at all and that my perception of hostility came from my own state of anxiety in wanting to impress my thesis supervisor.

But misperception was not the cause in this situation. Instead, I was correct in assuming that something was wrong but that the participants were not willing to disclose it. Finding out that my perception of hostility was accurate enabled me at least to try to work with a real issue rather than an imagined one.

## Suggestion 2: Confront

Confrontation has a bad name in modern interaction theory, but there is a place for it if you think of it as a method of calling attention to the problem. Confrontation communicates that this is a serious problem that cannot be ignored. My willingness to cancel the workshop — it was not an idle threat — conveyed the clear message that we could not pretend to have a workshop on teaching improvement in a hostile climate.

## Possible Cause 6: Students perceive the group activity as a waste of time because they think it is irrelevant

There is an old Italian story about a man who went out looking for firewood. He came across a purse full of money but passed by without picking it up. Later, his wife was upset with him for not bringing the purse home. But the man said, "When I'm looking for wood, I'm looking for wood. When I'm looking for purses, I'm looking for purses." I often think that both teachers and students are like that man. They have definite expectations, and if these are not fulfilled, they tend to overlook any other value a session may have. Students may reject the goals of the small group because the goals do not fit with what they perceive to be the more important aspects of the course, notably the exam.

A professor of political science asked me to attend his lectures and tutorials. He had the brassy voice of a drill sergeant which blared out from through a great arch of mustache. He carried a pile of paper wrapped in some ancient battered leather, the remnants of a briefcase which he clutched tightly under his arm to save it from complete disintegration.

After talking to him for a few minutes, I began to sense that he was rather proud of his program and that it was congratulation rather than evaluation that he sought. Well, there's nothing wrong with that, and as a matter of fact, when I attended his first lecture, everything seemed to be going rather well. He was a forceful, clear speaker, and the students asked relevant, probing questions.

I then attended a tutorial. Again, all seemed well. The students listened, and asked and answered questions. When I met the students afterwards I fully expected a complete positive assessment of the course. But at the first invitation, they blurted out, "We're not getting anywhere. The tutorial sessions are a total waste of time." They explained that, although the discussion was often lively, it was irrelevant. "We don't really talk about the stuff that's in the lectures. It would be okay if we didn't have anything else to do. The discussion about antagonism between the judicial and legislative was interesting but I don't even understand the Constitution and the Constitution is sure to be on the

52

exam." In contrast, the teacher considered the small group discussions extremely relevant: "This [the small group sessions] is where we get into really interesting stuff. They're bright students, who can take an idea and run with it — like today's discussion of judiciary versus legislative powers. It's really exciting."

Students' first priority is to fulfill the requirements of the course, to pass the exam or complete a paper, and to them what matters is whether the teaching helps them to do this. Even if they get some temporary enjoyment from sessions which seem unconnected to the goals of the course, they will in the long run find these sessions frustrating and confusing. The exam is the priority of the course, and they see lectures as the major preparation for the exam. Therefore, the lecture becomes "the course" and the small group discussion is an "add on," an optional component. If the "add on" is not seen to be supporting the lectures, and thus the exam, then it is a waste of time.

In short, I am saying two things: first, the various components of a course should be aligned for maximum learning effectiveness and learner satisfaction (Cohen, 1987); and, second, the exam usually calls the tune. If the exams supported the small groups rather than the lectures, students would trash the lectures and the problem would be one of bringing the lectures into alignment with the small groups.

## Suggestion 1: Align the goals of the course with the evaluation

All components of a course should be aligned with one another, with the objectives, and especially with the exam. Further, I recommend that you begin with the exam, and then align the other components with it. Or, if the course is one of those rare ones in which the exam is clearly not the main focus, be sure to align the exam to that other focus.

The small clinic groups in medical school, during which students learn interviewing and medical problem-solving skills with patients, are enormously popular. In one department, the exam at the end of the clinic was a multiple choice exam that bore little relationship to what the students were learning in the clinic. It was remote from real experience and out of context, and in this case the students attacked the exam and not the small group experience.

If the main purpose of a clinic group is to teach clinical skills, then devise a brief oral exam in which clinical skills are evaluated or a multiple choice exam which reflects clinical judgment of the common problems seen in the clinic.

## Suggestion 2: Discuss the goals and exam with your students

It is useful to know how the students view the compatibility of the goals of the course and the exam. Even if you think that the goals are aligned with the exam your students may not. I recall a botany course in which, although hundreds of slides were shown, students paid little attention to them. The teacher was puzzled about this because the slides illustrated material which was relevant to exam questions. When I discussed the slides with the students, I found that they had a different view. They said that it was nice to see the slides, but it was definitely a luxury for the confident students who were caught up on their reading. They said that if students are in a panic about the exam, their best strategy is still to read the material in the notes, since the exam is multiple choice, and the information has to be produced in the form of words and concepts, not pictures. "Slides would only help us answer the questions if they showed slides during the exam with little arrows and asked us to name this or that. If that happened, we would pay attention to them in class."

## Suggestion 3: Write the objectives on a flip chart

The group needs a constant and present reminder of their immediate purposes against which they can check their progress and monitor the appropriateness of their process. I recommend a few statements of the objectives for the immediate session penned on a flip chart at the beginning of the session. Keep in mind that if the immediate goals of the group change as a result of group negotiation, those sentences need to be crossed out and new ones written in their place.

I am aware that the course syllabus or handout usually contains these kinds of statements of the objectives of the group and a rationale for use of a particular group process. But handouts are easy to forget about when they are out of sight, tucked away in a binder somewhere.

## Suggestion 4: Brief the small group leaders

Ideally, the tutorial or discussion leaders should sit in on those lectures which are relevant to their sessions so that they know what the students have heard and can make appropriate connections in the small groups. But this may not be feasible during these lean days when everyone is overbooked. It might be more practical to meet with the discussion leaders together once or twice during the year to discuss the purposes of the discussion sessions, the goals of the course, their own ideas, and their styles of teaching.

### Suggestion 5: Write the exam and the goals first then plan the group activities

Most of us do it the other way around. Beause we don't think about the evaluation until near the end of the course, our teaching is not guided by it. We tend to stray from the material that is essential to the goals of the course, and then return to it during the exam. This is a formula for poor grades, student anger, and frustration. If you write the exam questions first, you are more likely to align the curriculum with the exams.

### Suggestion 6: Explain the lecture/discussion co-ordination

You can't assume that the students are aware of the connection between the lectures and the discussion sessions even if it seems obvious to you as the teacher. They should be told the precise relationship of the discussions both to the lectures and to the evaluation. What are the discussions supposed to do? Follow up the main points of the lecture? Clarify and elaborate subtle concepts? Help students learn to solve problems? Demonstrate some of the phenomena raised in the lecture?

In these examples, I have assumed the usual situation in which discussion is used as follow-up to lectures (the main event). There are courses in which the small group is the main event and lectures are attended by the students only if they feel they will be valuable. According to this arrangement, series of lectures may be scheduled which students are not obliged to attend. In this kind of arrangement, students will tend to perceive the small group sessions as the meat of the course and may then consider the lectures irrelevant. But this reversal would occur only if the evaluation reflects the content of the small groups rather than the lectures. Ideally, the examination should be written in co-ordination with the tutorial leaders.

# References

Abercrombie, M.L.J. (1971). *Aims and techniques of group teaching* (4th ed.). Guildford, Surrey: Society for Research into Higher Education, University of Surrey.

Barnes, D. (1975). *From communication to curriculum*. Harmondsworth, Middlesex: Penguin.

Bergquist, W.H., & Phillips, S.R. (1975). *A handbook for faculty development*. Washington, DC: Council for the Advancement of Small Colleges.

Cohen, S.A. (1987). Instructional alignment: Searching for the magic bullet. *Educational Researcher, 16*(8), 16–20.

Cronbach, L.J. (1967). How can instruction be adapted to individual differences? In R.M. Gagne (Ed.), *Learning and individual differences*. New York: McMillan.

Gronlund, N.E. (1970). *Stating behavioral objectives for classroom instruction*. London: Macmillan.

Hunt, D.E. (1971). *Matching models in education*. Toronto: Ontario Institute for Studies in Education.

Hunt, D.E. (1989). Personal communication.

Hunt, D.E., & Sullivan, E.V. (1974). *Between psychology and education*. Hinsdale, Illinois: The Dryden Press.

Jackson, P.W. (1970). Is there a best way of teaching Harold Bateman? *Midway, 10,* 15-28.

Kibler, R.J., Barker, L.L., & Miles, D.T. (1970). *Behavioral objectives and instruction*. Boston: Allyn and Bacon.

King, P. (1977). *The development of reflective judgment and formal operational thinking in adolescents and young adults*. Unpublished doctoral dissertation, University Minnesota.

Kitchener, K.S. (1977). *Intellectual development in late adolescents and young adults: Reflective judgment and verbal reasoning*. Unpublished doctoral dissertation, University of Minnesota.

Lawson, J. (1980). The relationship between graduate education and the development of reflective judgement. A function of age or educational experience? Unpublished doctoral dissertation, University of Minnesota.

Mager, R.F. (1975). *Preparing instructional objectives* (2nd ed.). Belmont, CA: Fearon.

Maier, N.R.F. (1970). *Problem solving and creativity in individuals and groups*. Belmont, CA: Brooks/Cole.

McKeachie, W.J. (1986). *Teaching tips: A guidebook for the beginning college teacher* (8th ed.). Toronto: D.C. Heath & Co.

McKeachie, W.J., & Kulik, J.A. (1975). Effective college teaching. In F.N. Kerlinger (Ed.), *Review of research in education*. Itaska, Il: Peacock.

McLeish, J., Matheson, W., & Park, J. (1973). *The psychology of the learning group*. London: Hutchinson University Library.

Milne, P. (1984). *The learning cell: No. 1, Teaching Monograph Series*. Windsor, Ont: The Office of Teaching and Learning.

Pascal, C. (1989). Personal communication.

Perry, W. (1970). *Forms of intellectual and ethical development in the college years: A scheme*. New York: Holt, Rinehart & Winston.

Pfeiffer, J.W., & Jones, J.E. (1985). *Reference guide to handbooks and annuals*. San Diego, CA: University Associates.

Rasmussen, R. (1984). Practical discussion techniques for educators. *The Journal of the Alberta Association for Continuing Education, 12*(2), 38-47.

Rudduck, J. (1978). *Learning through small group discussion: A study of seminar work in higher education.* Guildford, Surrey: Society for Research into Higher Education, University of Surrey.

Sanford, N. (1966). *Self and society.* New York: Atherton Press.

Schmidt, J.A., & Davidson, M.L. (1983). Helping students think. *The Personnel and Guidance Journal, 61*(9), 563–569.

Simpson, R.J., & Galbo, J.J. (1987). Interaction and learning: Theorizing on the art of teaching. *Interchange, 17*(4), 37–51.

Small, P. (1985). *Patient oriented problem solving packages.* Gainsville, University of Florida: Upjohn.

Strange, C. (1978). Intellectual development, motive for education and learning styles during the college years: A comparison of adult and traditional age college students. Unpublished doctoral dissertation, University of Iowa.

Tiberius, R. G., Silver, I., Fleming, S., Hoffman, B., & Cappe, L. (in press). Teaching physicans about teaching: An experiential workshop. *Medical Teacher.*

Widick, C. (1977). The Perry scheme: A foundation for developmental practice. *The Counselling Psychologist, 6*(4), 35–38.

# Part Two/ Group Interaction

## Troubleshooting Guide

**Chapter Four: Lack of Interaction /65**

Possible cause 1: Lack of experience with learning in small groups /66
    Suggestion 1: Give students practical exercises /66
    Suggestion 2: Provide handouts on small group skills /67
    Suggestion 3: Encourage students to provide feedback on the effectiveness of their interactions /68
    Suggestion 4: Get someone to sit in on your class and comment /68
    Suggestion 5: Compare multiple perspectives /68
    Suggestion 6: Use audio-visual aids /70
    Suggestion 7: Use checklists to help observe the group /70

Possible cause 2: Overwhelming authority of the teacher /71
    Suggestion 1: Confirm your perception /71
    Suggestion 2: Talk less /72
    Suggestion 3: Point to your own mistakes /73

Suggestion 4: Beware the Socratic technique /73
Suggestion 5: Avoid argument by authority /73
Suggestion 6: Refrain from harsh or personal criticism,
sarcasm, or punishing remarks /74
Suggestion 7: Avoid evaluation /74
Suggestion 8: Resist premature closure /74
Suggestion 9: Pick up on students' comments /75

Possible cause 3: Students unrewarded for participation /75
Suggestion 1: Reflect on both content and process of the
group /75
Suggestion 2: Encourage students to reward one another /75
Suggestion 3: Compare entering tests with final tests /76
Suggestion 4: Display student comments on a flip chart /76
Suggestion 5: Reward student contributions by using
them /76
Suggestion 6: Remember who said what /77
Suggestion 7: Let learners arrive at generalizations
themselves /77
Suggestion 8: Foster choice in some aspects of the learning
situation /78
Suggestion 9: Explain the benefit of learning in small
groups /78

Possible cause 4: Coercing students to participate /79
Suggestion 1: Encourage intrinsic over extrinsic
motivation /79
Suggestion 2: If possible, don't assign grades for participation
or threaten in order to encourage participation /79
Suggestion 3: If you must evaluate participation skills, make
the objectives very clear /80
Suggestion 4: Coerced students cannot vote with their
feet /80

Possible cause 5: Lack of common background knowledge /80
Suggestion 1: Provide a common experience /81
Suggestion 2: Ensure the availability of course material /82
Suggestion 3: Provide both easy and more challenging
materials /82
Suggestion 4: Preview the readings /82
Suggestion 5: Do not review assigned readings in class
yourself /82
Suggestion 6: Have students review the readings in class /83
Suggestion 7: Assign brief position papers /83
Suggestion 8: Use student presentations /83
Suggestion 9: Compile a problem list /84
Suggestion 10: Investigate pressure from other sources /84

Possible cause 6: Confusion about the topic or about what people have said /85
    Suggestion 1: Facilitate organized and coherent communication /85
    Suggestion 2: Facilitate effective communication /86

Possible cause 7: Students don't know one another /86
    Suggestion 1: Encourage students to get to know one another by natural conversation /86
    Suggestion 2: Use get-acquainted games /88
    Suggestion 3: Remember students' names and use them /88
    Suggestion 4: Use name cards /89
    Suggestion 5: Deal with the title issue /89

Possible cause 8: Low level of trust /90
    Suggestion 1: Be perceived as someone concerned with students' welfare /90
    Suggestion 2: Be dependable and consistent /91
    Suggestion 3: Be willing to make disclosures and take personal risks /92
    Suggestion 4: Provide opportunities for students to co-operate and to trust one another /92
    Suggestion 5: Involve students in the process of teaching improvement /92

Possible cause 9: Fear of appearing foolish /93
    Suggestion 1: Encourage everyone to speak early /93
    Suggestion 2: Protect minority views /94
    Suggestion 3: Disinhibit students by your own example /94
    Suggestion 4: Respond tactfully to dumb questions /94
    Suggestion 5: Require that all students prepare all topics /94
    Suggestion 6: Encourage a non-threatening atmosphere /95

Possible cause 10: Group is too large /95
    Suggestion 1: Press for smaller classes /95
    Suggestion 2: Divide the class into smaller groups /95
    Suggestion 3: Divide the class into pairs for intensive interaction preliminary to an exercise /96

Possible cause 11: Inappropriate physical conditions /96
    Suggestion 1: Arrange the seating so that people can see each other's faces /96
    Suggestion 2: Use tables /97
    Suggestion 3: Sit at one end of the arc /97
    Suggestion 4: Use a flip chart or chalkboard /97
    Suggestion 5: Beware teaching in a lounge or office /97
    Suggestion 6: Know the names of the students /98
    Suggestion 7: Recognize and attempt to deal with distracting physical conditions /98

Possible cause 12: Interfering emotions /98
    See Part Three

**Chapter Five: Teacher Dominates Interaction /99**

Possible cause 1: Teacher talks too much /100
    Suggestion 1: Measure your proportion of talk /101
    Suggestion 2: Break the pattern of alternating between teacher and student /102
    Suggestion 3: Resist talking to only one or two students /103
    Suggestion 4: Wait a few minutes before you intervene /103
    Suggestion 5: Don't grab the reins /104
    Suggestion 6: Remember that listening is teaching too /104

Possible cause 2: Teacher's authority is overwhelming /104
    Suggestion 1: Negotiate objectives openly /104
    Suggestion 2: Provide the freedom to discover /105
    Suggestion 3: Have a student lead the class /105
    Suggestion 4: Try leaderless groups /106
    Suggestion 5: Resist answering questions /106
    Suggestion 6: Provide *one* answer, not *the* answer /107
    Suggestion 7: Avoid the kind of final statements that discourage disagreement or discussion /107
    Suggestion 8: Never talk just to display your knowledge /107
    Suggestion 9: Establish a friendly, a non-threatening atmosphere /107
    Suggestion 10: Try self-study groups such as POPS, learning cells, and pairing /108

Possible cause 3: Teacher tries so hard to inculcate certain ideas that there is no real connection with students /108
    Suggestion 1: Disclose the hidden agenda /109
    Suggestion 2: Listen to understand rather than to praise or refute /109
    Suggestion 3: Tolerate interruptions /109

Possible cause 4: Facilitation methods may backfire /110
    Suggestion 1: Beware extreme statements /110
    Suggestion 2: Beware the devil's advocate role /110
    Suggestion 3: Beware rhetorical questions /111
    Suggestion 4: Don't overuse paraphrasing /111
    Suggestion 5: Beware withholding information, judgments, or opinions /111
    Suggestion 6: Beware motivation through fear /112
    Suggestion 7: Beware the Socratic technique /112
    Suggestion 8: Students reward each other /115
    Suggestion 9: Don't assign grades for participation /115

Suggestion 10: Beware helping students express their ideas /115

Possible cause 5: Domination by default #1: Group is too large /115
  Suggestion 1: Reduce the size of the group /116
  Suggestion 2: Reduce the functional size of the group /116

Possible cause 6: Domination by default #2: Negative attitudes toward the value of small group teaching and learning /117
  Suggestion 1: Review the advantages of active participation /117
  Suggestion 2: Provide practice in listening skills /117

Possible cause 7: Domination by default #3: Students all agree with each other /117
  Suggestion 1: Ask for an explanation of student views /117
  Suggestion 2: Ask for volunteers to take the other side of an issue /118
  Suggestion 3: Engage students by means other than controversy /118

Possible cause 8: Domination by default #4: Inappropriate physical surroundings and resources /118

## Chapter Six: Students Participate Unequally /119

Possible cause 1: Lack of awareness of unequal participation /120
  Suggestion 1: Use a sociogram /120
  Suggestion 2: Talk to students individually /121

Possible cause 2: Group is too large /121
  Suggestion 1: Reduce the size of the group /121
  Suggestion 2: Try pairing learners at the beginning /122

Possible cause 3: Ground rules are lacking or not followed /122
  Suggestion 1: Make ground rules explicit /122

Possible cause 4: Intolerance of silence /122
  Suggestion 1: Explain the positive role of silence /122
  Suggestion 2: Accept silence, both in yourself and others /123
  Suggestion 3: Provide specific training /123

Possible cause 5: Dominant speakers monopolize the discussion /123
  Suggestion 1: Talk to the dominating speaker privately /123
  Suggestion 2: Use specific training /124
  Suggestion 3: Assign a task to the dominant speaker /124

Suggestion 4: Short-circuit dominating speakers by passing the ball to someone else /124
Suggestion 5: Take a turn around the group /126
Suggestion 6: Separate the extroverts from the introverts /126
Suggestion 7: Use feedback on group process /126
Suggestion 8: Deal with students whose personalities include a strong drive to dominate others or to continually seek attention /127

Possible cause 6: Silent students /127
Suggestion 1: Find out why some people are silent and co-operate with them /127
Suggestion 2: Ask questions /128
Suggestion 3: Create an accepting environment /128
Suggestion 4: Get to know the silent student /129
Suggestion 5: Invite silent students into the discussion /129

Possible cause 7: Cliques /130
Suggestion 1: Split them up /130
Suggestion 2: Ask them to share with the group /130
Suggestion 3: Treat the clique as an individual /131
Suggestion 4: Don't get into a personal scrap with them /131

Possible cause 8: Sexism, racism, and other forms of discrimination /131
Suggestion 1: Keep track of contributions of participants /132
Suggestion 2: Use assertiveness training /133
Suggestion 3: Raise awareness gently /133

Possible cause 9: Student presentations /134
Suggestion 1: Restrict the presentation time to 10 to 15 minutes with 10 minutes of question time /134
Suggestion 2: Use student discussants /134
Suggestion 3: Demonstrate and discuss the active role of the audience /134
Suggestion 4: Assign credit for the quality of the discussion or its product, not the presentation /135
Suggestion 5: Remind the presenters to have questions for the audience /135
Suggestion 6: Encourage presenters to focus and simplify /135

Possible cause 10: No interest in speaking /135
Suggestion 1: Talk to the withdrawing students about help-ing others /136
Suggestion 2: Don't fix it if it ain't broke /136

**References for Part Two /136**

# 4/Lack of Interaction

*"They just sit there like lumps."*
*"It's a dead group."*
*"I'm sometimes driven to ask, 'Hello? Is anybody home?' but even that doesn't shake them out of their stupor."*
*"If I'm putting them to sleep, at least it's mutual. They're killing me."*

Ask any group of teachers to describe their worst small group experience and you will hear variations on the "dead class" theme over and over. Teaching, especially in small groups, depends on interaction. Failure to get it is frustrating for everyone.

Students' experience of the problem is slightly different. While the teacher perceives "deadness," the students sense a one-way flow from the teacher. One-way communication leads to apathy, frustration, dependence, hostility, and/or aggression (Bergquist & Phillips, 1975), all of which are as detrimental to learning as they are familiar to teachers and students.

Although it is tempting to blame students for these misunderstandings, it might be more appropriate to blame their previous experiences of learning in small groups. There is nothing we can do about those experiences, but we can do many things to encourage interaction and to supply some of the experience that students are missing. Teachers can also examine whether they are interfering with interaction, perhaps unknowingly.

It is no accident that this is the largest chapter in the book. Lack of interaction is the most common problem in small group teaching.

## Possible Cause 1: Lack of experience with learning in small groups

People who have had little or no experience learning in groups may not have the skills to discuss and interact with one another. As a consequence, they may be unable to maintain productive group interaction even in the best circumstances.

### Suggestion 1: Give students practical exercises

Jean Rudduck describes a systematic program designed to train incoming university students in the skills of small group discussion in *Learning through small group discussion* (1978). The program is designed to provide students with opportunities to eliminate bad habits, familiarize themselves with the workings of small groups, and polish such facets of the art as speaking and responding appropriately.

One of her training sessions is organized in a cumulative manner. It begins with five minutes of free discussion during which an observer (one of the students) records an evaluation of the discussion. During the next five minutes of discussion a time keeper (another student) monitors the speakers and limits each contribution to 15 seconds. During the next five minutes, speakers are limited to 15 second contributions once again, and, in addition, must pause 3 seconds after the previous speaker has finished speaking. During the next five minutes, each contribution is limited to 15 seconds and speakers pause for 3 seconds after previous speakers, and, in addition, speakers must reflect accurately on the contribution of the person immediately preceding them before they speak. Another five minutes of discussion contains all of the above restrictions in addition to a final one, namely that no one may speak a second time until everyone has spoken once. The final five minutes of discussion, which is free of restrictions, is evaluated once again by the same observer. Comparisons between the beginning and the end observation periods would reveal the effects of the training. (Rudduck, 1978, p. 120).

Although this kind of approach needs to be organized by an educational development office, one teacher working alone can help students learn the skills of small group interaction. I know a professor of religion who conducts five-minute practice sessions at the beginning of each class. Within just a few meetings his students overcome some of their most common problems. One of these difficulties is a failure to listen to one another. He sets up a brief exercise in which he asks each student to present an opinion in a sentence or two and then asks the next two students to restate the sentence in their own words. They may ask questions if they wish. In another exercise he asks students to practise disagreeing with an opinion while not attacking the person.

If you want to devise your own exercises of this type, you might skim through this book, familiarizing yourself with the various kinds of symptoms and their causes, and then observe your class's problems and the skills they may be lacking.

## Suggestion 2: Provide handouts on small group skills

The following set of ground rules is an excellent student guide to small group interaction (British Columbia Teacher's Federation, 1970; reprinted in Rudduck, 1978):

**1.** Maintain an attitude of searching for truth, or for a solution. You are seeking the best answer rather than trying to convince other people.

**2.** Try not to let your previous ideas or prejudices interfere with your freedom of thinking.

**3.** Speak whenever you wish (if you are not interrupting someone else who has the floor, of course) even though your idea may seem incomplete. If all the answers were known, there would be no point to a discussion.

**4.** Practise listening by trying to formulate in your own words the point that the previous speaker made before adding your own contribution.

**5.** Avoid disrupting the flow of thought by introducing new issues. Wait until the present topic reaches its natural end. If you wish to introduce a new topic, warn the group that what you are about to say will address a new topic and that you are willing to wait to introduce it after the present topic. There are times when a group is tired of the present topic but hold on to it only because there is nothing to replace it. By introducing a new topic you may be providing a fresh option. On the other hand, if the group prefers to remain with the present topic, there is little danger of your disrupting the group as long as you let them know in advance and give people the option to choose your topic rather than forcing them to attend to it.

**6.** Talk briefly. Saying too much may cause people's minds to wander so that they miss the value of what you wish to express.

**7.** Avoid long stories, anecdotes, or case studies. Listening to one person after another tell long tales of "what happened to me" is boring. However, brief examples are useful to bring abstract ideas and beliefs to the concrete level.

**8.** Be as sympathetic and understanding of other people's views as you can. If you disagree, try to do so without threatening or belittling other people.

### Suggestion 3: Encourage students to provide feedback on the effectiveness of their interactions

Groups, like individuals, need feedback if they are to improve their performance. Students often miss problems of group interaction because they are so preoccupied with their first priority, passing the course. A woman I know, who taught radio and TV communications, tried to encourage students to reflect on the group interaction by arranging regular feedback sessions during the last five minutes of every class meeting. After the first few sessions, she thought of dropping the idea because hardly anyone ever spoke. But she decided to continue, and once the students realized that feedback was going to be a regular feature of her class, the sessions became very lively and the students became more aware of interaction during the class. *A note:* feedback sessions need to be pleasant, and must never become gripe sessions. When someone raises a complaint, the teacher needs to ask the group what they can do about the difficulty.

### Suggestion 4: Get someone to sit in on your class and comment

Outside observers contribute a fresh point of view. Teachers have to teach, students have to learn, but outside observers can devote all their time to observing the teacher-student interaction.

### Suggestion 5: Compare multiple perspectives

In my individual consulting with teachers I have always drawn information from more than one source. Even in workshops, I like to demonstrate the importance of gathering feedback from people with different perspectives. In a typical workshop I ask teachers to prepare a brief small group discussion or seminar on their favorite hobby. For example, participants in one workshop for teachers of young family physicians conducted a small group session on cross country skiing. There were three types of observers: the teacher herself, a group of her peers who volunteered to be the students, and another group of peers who observed from an outer circle.

The participants were amazed at the results. Everyone's views turned out to be very much colored by his or her own perspective, as predicted. The teacher's perspective was that of a ski enthusiast who wanted to share the beauty and joy of skiing with others. Therefore she attempted to encourage new skiers by allaying their concerns about equipment and technique, and she tried to make skiing seem easy by telling stories and not by going into technical details. She was disappointed that the beginners did not seem so interested in skiing at the end of her talk as she hoped they would be.

Learners who had never skied before were confused. They said the level was too sophisticated. They wanted the teacher to demonstrate the skiing moves in detail and they wanted her to draw a side view of the ski on the chalkboard showing the "kick region," because they were confused about this point. The two experienced skiers in the group were unhappy that she did not recognize their expertise in some way. They thought it would have been useful if she had invited them to help explain things to the beginners or if she had devoted part of her talk to advanced techniques.

We observers, on the other hand, who were very conscious of the fact that we were observing a teacher practising small group teaching, noticed that some students did very little talking, and that the teacher did not take advantage of the small size of the group to find how much the students knew instead of assuming that they all knew nothing and pitching the talk to the lowest level. On the other hand, we praised the fact that she had put key words on the board before her presentation. As predicted, we had nothing to say about the content. (Some people argue that information from outside observers is more objective because outsiders have the luxury of being able to focus on the process. I disagree. Their perspective is not objective, merely different. They usually have no way to tell how difficult or inspiring the material is in itself.)

A feedback session which includes several different perspectives takes most of a 50-minute class period. Although you couldn't do this often, it is so effective that it may be worthwhile to do it once. Choose a session about halfway through the course so that you and your students can benefit from the feedback. If you do not have an educational consultant in your institution, invite a colleague or a student from another class or year to participate; it is important that the outside observer not be trying to learn the material.

This method is not difficult to conduct. Simply bring together the observers with various viewpoints and identify the differences and similarities in their perceptions. Then discuss what can be done to improve the learning environment.

## Suggestion 6: Use audio-visual aids

Video- or audiotape can provide yet another perspective on small group interaction. You can observe your body language, speech, and facial expressions, and you can use the image to remind yourself of what you were thinking at the moment so that you can examine your decision making as well as your performance. Examining a videotape can be particularly powerful if done with the help of a student or two, an educational consultant, or both.

Centra and his colleagues (1987) have devised a set of guidelines to help the observers of a videotape. Kindsvatter and Wilen (1977) have a checklist which deals specifically with small group teaching, and Weimer and her colleagues (1988) have produced a checklist called "Self or Colleague Analysis of Videotaped Teacher Sample" which is directed more at large group teaching but can easily be modified to suit small groups.

The addition of other observers and the use of checklists is essential to prevent your falling into the trap that snagged early experimenters with video playback — they believed that the tape revealed objective "truth" uninfluenced by the interpretation of the observer. David Taylor-Way (1987), of Cornell University, has described a method of videotape review in which teachers, students, and educational consultants all watch the videotape at the same time. The tape is stopped whenever someone wants to make a comment. During the pause, people share their perceptions of the episode. I have attended a workshop in which Dr. Taylor-Way demonstrated this method. The outcome was very useful (see also Taylor-Way & Brinko, 1989).

## Suggestion 7: Use checklists to help observe the group

Standardized checklists are useful aids to the observation of group interaction because they can remind you of things that you would not think of on your own. One note of caution: since a standard checklist is, by its nature, not tailored to your group, it can distract you from the most important features of your group by keeping you busy looking at "standard" things.

Almost every book on small group teaching contains an example of a checklist for observation of group interaction. Volume One of Bergquist and Phillips (1975) includes an explanation of the Flanders system for analyzing the interaction of a small group as well as more specialized checklists, including one for the evaluation of the instructor's ability to ask questions and to increase student participation. In Volume Two, there is a checklist for analyzing group leadership functions. Kindsvatter and Wilen

(1977) and Weimar and her colleagues (1988) present checklists specifically designed for small group teaching.

Keep in mind that there are several different categories of things you might wish to observe. First, a number of group activities — setting the agenda, giving information and examples, clarifying, asking questions — are essential to efficient learning. Other activities — supporting, encouraging, expressing, and clarifying feelings — are essential in order for the group to be able to accomplish its task in a humane fashion. And still others are necessary to handle adverse situations or disruptions — restating the agenda, reconciling opposing points of view, confronting.

## Possible Cause 2: Overwhelming authority of the teacher

An overwhleming, inhibiting teacher can create student silence and passivity. A teacher is an authority in several ways: expert in the subject matter, course organizer, leader of the small group, and evaluator. In the face of such authority, students may come to feel that it is the teacher's responsibility to teach them and not take full responsibility for their own learning. They may sit back, prepared to listen, but not to take an active part in thinking about the subject or in formulating questions.

### Suggestion 1: Confirm your perception

The nasty thing about being overwhelming is that you are usually the last to hear about it. Only the students can tell you and they are probably too overwhelmed to do so. You may intimidate your students but be perfectly charming to your peers, your friends, and your children because the intimidation may arise from circumstances that are unqiue to teaching. Therefore, the only reliable judges are the students themselves. So if you think you might be overwhelming them, you need to ask them about it. You may wish to begin with a few quick questions on your next feedback questionnaire:

Please circle a number which indicates an appropriate response to the following questions.

I find Dr. Frankenstein intimidating.

| 1 | 2 | 3 | 4 | 5 |
|---|---|---|---|---|
| never | hardly ever | sometimes | often | very often |

Dr. Frankenstein's authority overwhelms the group.

| 1 | 2 | 3 | 4 | 5 |
|---|---|---|---|---|
| never | hardly ever | sometimes | often | very often |

Even two items on a questionnaire can provide a clue about your students' perceptions of you. If they seem to find you overwhelming you would be wise to follow up the questionnaire with any of a number of feedback methods designed to gather more detailed and more subtle information from students. I personally favor methods based on interviews with students. Because consultants are viewed as neutral, students are usually quite willing to disclose information to them, and they should be skilled in conducting interviews. Chapter 10 discusses how to use an educational consultant.

## Suggestion 2: Talk less

Sound easy? Try it. Teachers are usually not aware of how much we talk in comparison to our students. Also, we are selected for our ability to articulate and explain. Moreover, many of us tend to interpret our role as one of "transmitting" information. This combination of circumstances produces teachers who feel that they have excelled in their work merely by virtue of having explained something well. After we have delivered a splendid monologue, we certainly are not ready to be told that we have talked too much.

Even the simplest measure can provide valuable information about the partition of talk between teacher and student. A colleague of mine, Niall Byrne, has provided me with a striking example, using a very simple code. A social scientist, who had previously described her style as interactive, invited Niall to observe her seminar. As the class began Niall sat beside the teacher, took out a piece of paper, and proceeded to track the amount of teacher talk and student talk in the most rudimentary manner, by drawing a sociogram of lines indicating communication pathways between students and teachers. On the lines he drew arrowheads to indicate the direction of the communication. Each time the teacher directed a comment at the students he drew an arrow pointing away from the teacher. He said nothing. At some point well into the seminar the teacher glanced down at his diagram. What she saw was a series of lines connecting teacher and students, covered with arrow heads pointing away from the teacher. After that point, Niall said, there was a dramatic shift in the pattern of communication. The teacher reduced her talking to a fraction of what it had been and the student talk blossomed.

Another way to calculate frequency of teacher and student talk into questions, answers, and so on. See pages 101 and 102 five seconds you record who is talking. If you want a little more detailed information from this process you can divide the teacher talk into questions, answers, and so on. See pages xxx to xxx for a discussion of interaction analysis for talk measurement.

## Suggestion 3: Point to your own mistakes

Point out your own mistakes and difficulties, especially those you experienced as a student. Students are comforted by hearing that their teacher was once a student with problems similar to theirs.

## Suggestion 4: Beware the Socratic technique

Questioning students in order to draw answers out of them can be effective in keeping their attention and in helping them think through a problem. However, this technique often degenerates into a game of "guess what's on the teacher's mind."

"No one likes to look foolish especially in a situation where mistakes may be pounced upon by a teacher or other students" (McKeachie, 1986, p. 35). Abuse of the Socratic technique kills interaction among students and encourages them to compete with one another for the right answer. It tends to foster a communication pattern shaped like the hub of a wheel, with the teacher at its centre and the students at the end of each spoke. Abuse of this technique leads to a problem of overwhelming authority because the teacher ends up with complete control over the dialogue. A detailed description of this technique and ways to avoid its abuse starts on p. 112.

## Suggestion 5: Avoid argument by authority

Since students cannot represent themselves as authorities in the subject, an argument based on authority disqualifies them from the discussion while it reinforces the power of the teacher. If you question this, I can cite 100 experimental articles to prove my point!

Of course, there are other reasons not to argue from authority. It is in any case not a good model of behavior for someone espousing free academic inquiry.

## Suggestion 6: Refrain from harsh or personal criticism, sarcasm, or punishing remarks

"I get upset with students because I care about the students and the patients." I was told this by a medical teacher who had a reputation for screaming at students in front of other students, nurses, and whoever else happened to be present. I sympathized with his point of view — if teachers don't show emotion when something is really important, students will never learn to distinguish between major issues and less important ones — until I witnessed episodes of screaming, cutting, sarcastic, personal criticism. Even if criticism were justified, this kind of attack makes the environment a dangerous place for the exchange of ideas.

In *Zen and the Art of Motorcycle Maintenance*, Pirsig describes class interaction (or lack of it) under the Professor of Philosophy. He did not yell, but he verbally "beat people up." In the episode in which an innocent student criticized Aristotle, the student began:

"I think there are some very dubious statements here."

That was all he got out.

"Sir, we are not here to *learn* what *you* think!" hissed the Professor of Philosophy. Like acid. "We are here to learn what *Aristotle* thinks!" Straight in the face, "When we wish to learn what you think we will assign a course in the subject!"

Silence. The student is stunned. So is everyone else. . . . Now everyone's face becomes carefully composed in defence against more of this sort of questioning. The innocent student stares down at the table, face red, hands shrouding his eyes. . . . In the next sessions the shamed student is no longer present. No surprise. The class is completely frozen, as is inevitable when an incident like this has taken place. Each session, just one person does all the talking, the Professor of Philosophy, and he talks and talks and talks to faces that have turned into masks. (1974, pp. 356-357)

## Suggestion 7: Avoid evaluation

Particularly when group interaction is flagging it is useful to refrain from evaluating. Listen in order to understand rather than to praise or refute.

## Suggestion 8: Resist premature closure

Resist the temptation to make a summary statement, draw a conclusion, or lay down the principle underlying the discussion before the class is ready for it. Premature closure of this sort undermines the student's sense of accomplishment. Everyone hates the feeling of groping helplessly in the dark until rescued by the teacher's beacon. People like to feel in control of their direction.

### Suggestion 9: Pick up on students' comments

One of the characteristics that makes seminars exciting for students is real interaction spontaneously generated. There is nothing duller for the student than a kind of catechismic ritual of predetermined questions and predictable answers. Unfortunately, the easiest kind of seminar to run is one in which there are no surprises, one in which the teacher does not pursue comments that might lead beyond her or his expertise. But when a teacher has the flexibility and courage to pick up on comments and run with them, classes come alive, exciting things happen, and time passes quickly.

## Possible cause 3: Students unrewarded for participating

Feedback is the primary motivator of students. It provides needed information about the distance learners have travelled toward their goals; without it, students may withdraw their energy from the task. When feedback reveals success, the learner is motivated by a sense of competence and accomplishment. Feedback provides knowledge of success.

The other major source of student motivation is the support and approval that come from co-operative interaction with their peers and their teachers.

### Suggestion 1: Reflect on both content and process of the group

A period should be set aside during which group members reflect on content and process of the small group. Such reflection allows the learners to become more aware of their achievements and to gain perspective. You may want to review the important learnings at the end of a session or discuss the effectiveness of the group or the quality of the interaction.

### Suggestion 2: Encourage students to reward one another

The teacher should not be the official dispenser of rewards. Students know when a peer has done a good job. You might try arranging a special session at the end of the class for constructive peer feedback. This time should follow strict rules so that it does not become bland or destructive. Comments need to consider what can be done to improve the situation, and the person making the suggestion should say how he or she might apply the idea to his or her own performance.

### Suggestion 3: Compare entering tests with final tests

People feel rewarded by a learning experience when they see concrete results. One dramatic way to display those results is to use rhetorical questions. One seminar leader asked, at the beginning of the seminar, "What is Canada's main economic problem?" He did not expect answers from the group at that point, but after some discussion and both questions and answers, he occasionally restated the question. Near the end of the seminar it became obvious to all that they had made considerable progress toward answering the question.

A slightly more formal device is used in problem- or case-based teaching. The teacher sets a case or problem. It appears formidible at the beginning but slowly becomes more tractable as it is clarified and analyzed.

Formal devices, such as quizzes given before and after the session, are more appropriate to large group teaching or tutorials which have mastery of information as their main goal. But a position paper or brief assignment (see page 83) provides an effective demonstration of what students have learned. They might write, for example, a position paper on their reactions to Margaret Laurence's novels. Then, after discussion, they read over their papers and describe briefly how their ideas have been influenced by the discussion. This exercise can be a powerful motivator for a group which initially doubts the value of small group interaction.

### Suggestion 4: Display student comments on a flip chart

It is intrinsically rewarding to see the product of one's work. Unfortunately, the product of intellectual work is rarely visible. A list of the various factions in the Middle East, the causes of jaundice, or the themes of a novel written on a flip chart is a very satisfying way to see what the group has accomplished. It is a good idea for student volunteers to do the writing.

### Suggestion 5: Reward student contributions by using them

Group members feel pride and satisfaction when the group values their contributions. And the group demonstrates the value of an idea or comment by using it or acting on it. Therefore, it is highly advisable to build on student ideas, connect them with themes of the group, compare them with ideas currently in the literature, modify, qualify, elaborate — in some way act on the ideas. I like to use the analogy of weaving a fabric. Each participant likes to see that his or her strand has found a place in the common pattern.

Do not, however, say, "Yes, yes," or, "Good point," ritual-istically after every student comment in an attempt to reinforce contributions. It may backfire. Students know that you can be miles away mentally while you are yessing. The worst mistake is to pass over a student, to ignore a contribution. A student who is often ignored withdraws from interaction. And remember that it is not necessary to agree with students in order to reward them for contributing.

## Suggestion 6: Remember who said what

This suggestion is to be taken literally. *Remember* who said what because you may want to use it later, but do not automatically attribute authorship to every comment or idea that comes up. It is true that students are rewarded by hearing their names, but the group can get pretty tired of being reminded that they have been discussing Robin's point and Beth's point for an hour. Con-tinually attributing group contributions to their authors fosters a competitive, ego-centred atmosphere which is antithetical to the co-operative spirit necessary for group interaction.

An excellent occasion on which to remind the group of the author of a comment is when the author has been passed over. Here is an all too typical example. A woman makes a statement which is not taken up by the group. Twenty minutes later a male makes the very same point. Only this time, it *is* taken up by the group. It is helpful, in such circumstances, to remind the group of the original contributor. Of course, you must do this in a way that does not blame the second speaker, who may be no more than naively sexist. Here is a suggestion: "Thank you Bob. That's the second time this point has been raised. When Julie raised the issue earlier we didn't pick up on it. Perhaps now is the time to address it. Thank you for your patience, Julie."

## Suggestion 7: Let learners arrive at generalizations themselves

A discussion whose outcome the teacher predetermines is less fun than an open-ended one. Some teachers believe that pro-viding a general or abstract statement about the topic or theme helps to orient students in their discussion. Others believe that it is better to let students get caught up in the topic first, then arrive at conclusions for themselves. I'm not sure which is the better method for improving memory. My concern is that put-ting the general statement first will remove the mystery and thereby reduce the reward involved in group interaction.

## Suggestion 8: Allow choice in some aspects of the learning situation

Students take a more positive attitude toward learning or subject matter when they choose the method of learning. George Geis (1976) concluded that dimensions of the learning situation which lend themselves to student choice include pacing, type and management of reinforcers, sequencing, sensory mode (visual or auditory), kind of feedback, content and objectives, and the presentation of the learning material.

Perhaps the wisest move is to conduct your own informal research, that is, to include students in the decision-making process and observe the consequences in terms of achievement, attitude, and opinions. My own classroom research with choice has yielded mixed results: the year I allowed students to choose the readings, the course became rather incoherent, but when students controlled the division of class time among such activities as review of literature, presentations, and discussion, everyone was quite happy.

Despite these mixed results, I believe it essential to effective teaching and learning that students take part in the decision making.

## Suggestion 9: Explain the benefit of learning in small groups

Despite all your efforts to create a rewarding small group experience, some students may see little value in small group learning. A minority treat small group learning as a time to play. Real learning for them is memorizing lectures. In this kind of situation it may be useful to restate the benefits of small group learning:

**1.** Greater, more active involvement, each student gets more speaking time;
**2.** Students and teacher can establish rapport more easily;
**3.** More opportunity to develop skills of personal relationships;
**4.** More opportunity for students to develop the ability to learn from one another;
**5.** More sharing of responsibility; students can be teachers too;
**6.** More commitment to the learning;
**7.** More individualized teaching, more focus on individual student needs;
**8.** More opportunity for immediate feedback to teachers and students;
**9.** Students can more easily gain awareness of their emotional reactions;
**10.** Circumstances conducive to learning to listen, to receive criticism, and to offer it;

**11.** Greater opportunity to learn the process of group problem solving where the pooled resources of the group members are more effective than the sum of individual abilities;

**12.** More opportunity for self-evaluation in comparison with peers;

**13.** More opportunity to learn and practise co-operative behavior;

**14.** Students can more easily develop a sense of responsibility for their own learning.

# Possible Cause 4: Coercing students to participate

The most common ways of trying to coerce students to participate are requiring attendance, assigning a grade for participation, and threatening. These methods might be necessary under extreme circumstances, but consider them a last resort. Remember that students are less likely to become involved if they feel forced; try to attract them.

### Suggestion 1: Encourage intrinsic over extrinsic motivation

It is unreasonable of me to speak against requiring attendance without addressing the question most often asked by teachers: "What if students don't show up?" This is a real fear for some, but it is a fear that grows out of a concept of the teacher as a performer or entertainer. Students should not go to classes to see the show, to comply with institutional rules, or to please the teacher; they should go because it is in their interest to do so or because they want to co-operate with their fellow students.

Try to encourage your students' intrinsic motivation. For example, I introduce my medical ethics small groups by saying, "This is your forum for discussion, your opportunity to clarify questions, test out ideas, find out how other students think about these ethical issues. You will probably never again in your medical careers have an opportunity to share these ideas with your colleagues under such neutral circumstances. If the discussion does not serve your needs, please speak up."

I also ask students to phone if they cannot make it. Then, at the beginning of each class, I announce who phoned. My purpose is to demonstrate that students' primary obligation is to themselves and to one another, not to me, to an institution, or to some set of rules.

### Suggestion 2: If possible, don't assign grades for participation or threaten in order to encourage participation

If students are attending the class for their own benefit or to help their peers, encourage them on the basis of these intrinsic motives only: "Each of you will have experiences and ideas related to this topic. By sharing them you will enrich the discussion, and connecting the material to your own experience will make it more meaningful and easier to learn."

Threat, on the other hand, is an external motivator: "You are graduate students now and you will be expected to participate in class. Twenty per cent of your grade will be based on class participation."

### Suggestion 3: If you must evaluate participation skills, make the objectives very clear

In a small group studying languages, or speech making, or theatre, participation may be not only a means to an end, but one of the objectives of the course. In such cases, when it is essential that students participate, the learning objectives must be made perfectly clear. What exactly is expected of the students? For example, the teacher of social work who requires her students to describe two cases needs to tell them the essentials of a case presentation. A language teacher who wants questions answered in full sentences in German must say so.

### Suggestion 4: Coerced students cannot vote with their feet

Requiring attendance prevents students from expressing their most sincere form of feedback — attending class when it is helpful to them and cutting class when it is not.

## Possible Cause 5: Lack of common background knowledge

A common cause of lack of interaction in a small group is lack of a knowledge base from which to make contributions. Students either literally have nothing to say or believe that they can add little to the topic beyond the teacher's vast knowledge of it.

People are better off talking about the material, asking questions about it, and relating it to their own life experiences and thoughts than they are passively listening to the teacher talk about it. Teachers must therefore prime students with some kind of reading or other experience in preparation for the class, and they must disinhibit students from raising questions if they don't understand something.

## Suggestion 1: Provide a common experience

Almost any common experience can provide the basis for small group teaching: a reading assignment, film, visitor, demonstration, role play, story, game, case study, simulation, or a brief lecture. If all students have had the same experience they can more easily interact with one another. They will be able to support one another in asking questions and in relating the material to their lives.

**Lecture.** The small group discussion can elaborate, illustrate, clarify, or apply the main points of lecture material.

It is a common practice to have a number of small group sessions following a single large group lecture. In this situation the problem of co-ordination of small group sessions arises. If the topic of discussion is set by the lecturer and the exam reflects lecture material only, then students may perceive the small groups as irrelevant or unimportant in the course. It is important that control of both the topic list and the evaluation be shared by the lecturer and the seminar leaders. The small group sessions should divide their time between discussing topics provided by the lecturers and discussing topics emerging from the group. Similarly the exam should be composed of two parts, a part which reflects the content of the lecture and a part which reflects the content of the small group sessions. The students can be required to answer all of the part based on material from the lecture while they choose only one section of the part based on material from their particular group.

**Demonstration.** In the most provoking demonstration I have heard about, a biology professor from Texas put a brocolli plant into a blender in front of a large class, turned it on, blended it into a soup and then drank some of it. The students watched in expectant silence. He then took a frog out of a box, let it hop a few times on the bench, and then put it in the blender. The students shrieked at him not to turn it on. Calmly, he took the frog out of the blender and asked the students why they felt differently about the life of a frog and brocolli. This was his introduction to a discussion of biomedical ethics.

**Problem, puzzle, or question.** A problem or question must be meaningful to the students' experience. If it is too technical or abstract it will not engage them. It should also require thought and knowledge central to the objectives of the course.

In order to illustrate the influence of gravity on pressure in the venous system, Professors Ackermann and Bayliss (1989) in the Department of Physiology at the University of Toronto created a scenario in which a parachutist landed in a tree and hung upside down. The students were asked to comment on the effect of this on brain, lung, and heart functions. The use of these scenarios doubled the time that students spent on cardiovascular physiology. It also doubled the teachers' time since students streamed into their offices all day with questions from their investigation into the scenarios. Students hung themselves upside down to see what was happening to their bodies, and every day the lecture room buzzed with conversations.

**Mini-lecture.** Background material can be provided during the small group session itself, in the form of a mini-lecture, if it is necessary to unstick a discussion. But be sure to signal clearly both the onset and the end of your mini-lecture. If you just slide into lecturing without notice, get up from the table, pick up the chalk, and assume a position at the blackboard, the students will take out their pens and sink into a passive listening mode from which it might be difficult to rouse them when your lecture is over.

## Suggestion 2: Ensure the availability of course material

The assigned readings, tapes, or whatever, must be actually available. Put journals and books on reserve in the library. Order textbooks six months in advance. If you lend books or tapes to students, make sure they are returned each week so that they can be recycled to other people.

## Suggestion 3: Provide both easy and more challenging materials

Students' background knowledge and motivation vary. Since some need more popular or easier readings than others to warm up, annotate the reading list if you possibly can.

## Suggestion 4: Preview the readings

A little advertisement for the reading material can provide a lot of encouragement. Take a few minutes at the end of class to explain the usefulness of the readings scheduled for the next class. You may want to explain why they were chosen, how good they are, or how they support the aims of the course.

## Suggestion 5: Do not review assigned readings in class yourself

If the teacher assigns readings and then reviews those readings in detail, students will feel that they are wasting their time doing the reading. They might as well come to class unprepared and catch the summary from the teacher. Consequently, I recommend not reviewing the readings in class. Some teachers have challenged this recommendation on the grounds that, despite their best efforts, many students do not prepare the readings and the discussion dies. I know this happens. However, I cannot recommend, even as a last resort, that teachers review the readings themselves. My last resort would be to stop teaching and renegotiate the agreement under which the teaching and learning take place. If the students would not fulfill their part of the bargain, I might quit.

## Suggestion 6: Have students review the readings in class

Ask students to present brief summaries of the assigned readings in class. It is also a good idea to ask them to make copies of these summaries to pass around. In this way students help each other learn the material. Although summaries of the readings will serve to provide an understanding of the literature, they will not necessarily stimulate students to think about the material. For that, position papers might be more appropriate.

## Suggestion 7: Assign brief position papers

A position paper is a brief critical or analytical statement of the student's position on some issue or question that arises out of an article. The advantage of position papers is that they require students to go beyond mere understanding of the article to thinking about it. The disadvantage is that the discussion may degenerate into a superficial difference of opinion that misses the real point of the article. Some teachers overcome this disadvantage by requiring students to summarize rather than criticize the main argument.

## Suggestion 8: Use student presentations

Student presentations, which are longer than either position papers or summaries, can be very useful, but they are expensive in scarce class time. Therefore, if this technique is to be effective, its purpose must be made clear. For example, student presentations might provide either the background or the framework for discussion (Rudduck, 1978).

The ground rules for the presentation of the paper need to be agreed upon in advance. Should presenters pause after each major idea for response from the group? Should they hand out an outline or a complete copy of the paper? Should they read the paper or speak from notes?

There are some serious pitfalls in the use of the paper presentation as a means of supplying the knowledge base for discussion. Rudduck (1978) argues that both poor seminar papers and good ones are likely to lose the group. The poor presentation might bore or confuse the group and put pressure on the seminar leader to rescue the group by moving to a didactic mode of teaching. On the other hand, a very good presentation (good in terms of its scholarship) may also lose the group if it introduces ideas beyond the students' grasp. The interaction may then narrow into a dialogue between the group leader and the presenter.

If the paper is too long and rambling, students will forget what they want to say by the time the question period rolls around; if the paper is too closely argued, students may feel too intimidated to ask questions.

One way to overcome the lack of student involvement in peer presentations is to provide the listeners with an active role. Some students could be assigned the role of official respondent to the presentation, with the same task as a respondent in a conference symposium. Other students could be asked to evaluate the presentation.

In summary, (1) presentations should be brief, (2) the ground rules should be agreed upon by the group, (3) there need to be clearly assigned roles for the "audience," and (4) speakers ought to rotate frequently.

## Suggestion 9: Compile a problem list

One way to make sure that students are talking about something that interests them is to generate a list of issues or problems they wish to discuss in the small group. This list can be written on a flip chart just before the class begins or it can be assigned as part of their reading assignment. There is some advantage to the latter in that the list will be generated when the readings are still fresh in people's minds.

## Suggestion 10: Investigate pressure from other sources

It is possible that pressures from other courses, jobs, and/or personal problems are preventing your students from preparing adequately for your course. Job and personal difficulties need individual attention — if it is appropriate for you to do anything.

Ultimately, the solution to this problem requires the cooperation of an entire faculty. They must describe their various demands on students and reconcile them so that the overall workload is realistic. I have never seen this done in all the years I have worked at universities and colleges.

Meanwhile, reducing the workload for your course would reduce the time pressure on your students. For example, you might ask students to prepare for only some of the class meetings or allow groups of two or three students to alternate summarizing readings. But unilateral reduction in your requirements is a poor long-term solution because your course may lose in the competition for students' time.

# Possible Cause 6: Confusion about the topic or about what people have said

Confusion or uncertainty about the subject of conversation can be a discussion killer. Students usually have to track the conversation for a while before they can make a contribution. If the topic continually shifts, some students never get to the point at which they can speak. It's difficult to hit a moving target. Over the years, I have tried to understand the silent student by interviewing students who said little or nothing in class. One of the most common explanations is, "It's not that I didn't have anything to say. Several times I was about to say something but someone else was speaking. Then, by the time it was my turn to talk, the topic had shifted and what I wanted to say was irrelevant." Unfortunately, it is often the most reflective students who end up saying nothing if the topic is continually shifting.

Confusion about what other students have said is a similar inhibitor of discussion. If students can't follow what others have said, they cannot pursue a coherent line of discussion.

## Suggestion 1: Facilitate organized and coherent communication

The group leader needs to summarize progress toward the group objectives and state themes or problems that were left unfinished from the previous session. A flip chart is useful to aid in these tasks since it can provide a permanent record and can visually maintain the continuity during and between sessions. Summaries need not be final statements or conclusions. A statement of the main issues and the current state of the debate is what is needed when students seem confused about where they are going.

Incidentally, there is nothing wrong with a discussion's shifting focus. The problem is that we can only be sure that people want to move on if we ask. What usually happens is that one student changes the subject and everyone else goes along with it because they don't want to be irrelevant, even if they have not said their piece about the previous topic. An important function of the group leader is to give everyone a chance to address a topic before moving on to the next one. Topics that are about to be abandoned may, in fact, just be getting started; many comments may be brewing in students' minds. A teacher responding to a shift in topic might say, "The Hopi represent another interesting culture but one with some distinctly different economic and cultural problems from the Navajo. It might be useful to contrast the two cultures if we have time. Let me write this on the flip chart [writes "Comparison of Hopi and Navajo"]. First, are there any more comments from the article 'The pressure of a changing economy on traditional Navajo life'?"

Similarly, if a conclusion is reached the group leader may have to restate it in order to find out whether it is supported by the group as a whole.

### Suggestion 2: Facilitate effective communication

The group leader ought to assume responsibility for accurate communication between members, restating, paraphrasing, and summarizing when it is useful to do so. See pages 31 to 33 for a discussion of these strategies.

## Possible cause 7: Students don't know one another

It is always difficult to interact with people we don't know. For one thing, it is psychologically risky to reveal one's views or ideas to a group, not knowing how they might receive the ideas. They might be offended or highly critical. Also, the less we know about the background of the listener, the more difficult it is to compose sentences. Our communicating mechanisms include filters and selection devices which choose vocabulary and examples appropriate to the audience. Experiments in which a subject is told to communicate the same message to both a small child and to an adult show dramatic differences between the structure of speech and vocabulary in the two messages. As students get to know one another, their interests, backgrounds, opinions, it becomes easier to talk to one another.

### Suggestion 1: Encourage students to get to know one another by natural conversation

I am not a great fan of games or devices for getting people acquainted. In my experience most of these serve more to alienate people than to bring them together. Information given in a continuous stream without intervening interaction is difficult to absorb, especially when each person is silently rehearsing his or her own introductory speech instead of listening to others. Take, for example, the game that requires each student to interview the person beside him or her and then introduce that person.

In one of the small group discussion sections of an economic geography course, the group leader asked students to form pairs and find out enough information about each other to introduce their partners to the group. One student introduced the young woman to his right as Lily Kathiramalainathan. He added that she lives in a suburban area of the city and that she is majoring in physical education. He said something else too, about her liking cross-country skiing and traveling, but even I, who was taking notes, missed this. What did this interview accomplish? First, few students remembered her name because they were all busy rehearsing their little descriptions so that they would be ready when their turns came up. Moreover, Larry stumbled over the pronounciation of her name thereby ensuring that no one else would dare try it. Second, the method did not serve to select those aspects of Lily's life which are most relevant, and therefore memorable, in the present setting. Why mention the suburbs and physical education? What we really want to know and what we will remember is Lily "What's-her-name's" relation to the subject matter.

I prefer a more natural technique. First, let the conversation proceed a little before introductions, so that enough of the topic unravels to provide a context for the names. Then draw out each student, one at a time, in relation to the subject, with some subject matter in between. The topic of the session mentioned above was "The rapidly changing world." When I talked to Lily, she gave me plenty of relevant information. She told me that she was living in Sri Lanka, where she was born, when it changed its name from Ceylon. I asked her if she could tell us a little about the experience. She said that it had had a more profound effect on her than you might imagine, probably because of the symbolism. She added a little about her life, about her reasons for going into physical education, and about the different conceptions of exercise and body image in Sri Lanka and Canada. She carefully pronounced her name, told me what it meant in Tamil, something like "King of the Mountain," and then gave me an abbreviated version of the name that I could use. Another student, who was listening to our conversation, added that he remembered when the maple leaf became our official flag but that he did not feel it was a very moving event, probably because the change didn't symbolize a change in the country's independence. And during his discussion we found out a little about *his* background.

It wouldn't have been difficult for the small group leader to have introduced all of the members of the group, beginning with Lily and gradually widening the conversation. If the group leader connected Lily's experience in Sri Lanka with the "rapidly changing world" theme, then other students might attempt to recall other relevant experiences.

## Suggestion 2: Use get-acquainted games

Having expressed such strong opinions against games in the previous section, I ought to add that a blanket condemnation of them would be unfair. Below are a few garnered from my friends; you can make up your own mind about them. I think some of them are quite silly. Use at your own risk.

**1.** Stick name tags on everyone.

**2.** Everyone introduces the person on his or her right. (I already maligned this one.)

**3.** Present your own name and everyone's before you. (This becomes an embarrassing but humorous validation of the distinction between short- and long-term memory. At the end of it everyone is able to go through the entire list, and then, after an hour everyone forgets all the names.)

4. Guess each person's occupation, major subject, or some other suitable characteristic.

**5.** Find an adjective that describes you, and rhymes with your name. I chose "Reluctant Richard" since I was reluctant to play useless games.

**6.** People introduce themselves, then answer a set number of questions, say three, from the other students. (I like this one because it is the closest to real dialogue and the questions that students ask are not constrained by the game.)

7. Require each person to relate something about his or her personal life — a favorite sport, TV program, family life, or home town.

**8.** Describe yourself with a metaphor — type of animal, fruit, or car — and explain.

**9.** Write out a famous person's name on a piece of paper and pin it on someone else's back. People find out their names by asking yes or no questions.

## Suggestion 3: Remember students' names and use them

Students will more readily address one another if they can remember people's names. It helps if the teacher remembers the names and uses them from time to time. Use either a seating chart which you sketch quickly on a pad in front of you at the start of each session or one of the memory devices suggested by popular books on memory (see, for example, Lorraine, 1974).

One way to *use* names is to supply the name yourself, as the teacher, when one student addresses another. Another is to ask students to identify themselves before they speak.

## Suggestion 4: Use name cards

Even with all of the suggestions above, people will still forget the names. They need an immediate cue *at the point at which they are about to use the name.* A simple method is to write names on cards in front of each person. These cards must be very large, and preferably not attached to the person. You want them large enough to be recognizable at a glance. It is rude to forget someone's name, so no one wants to get caught looking at it. I use a standard 8 1/2 by 11 inch paper folded lengthwise into threee equal segments, so that the two long ends can be brought together and fastened to form a pyramid. The pyramid stands on one side and on *both* of its other sides the students write their names with a blunt felt tip pen in one inch letters. Writing on both sides is recommended because students sitting beside one another look at the back of the pyramid not the front. If there is no tape available to fasten the edges just make two rips, about a finger width apart and fold over the section between them.

If your group is not seated around a table you will have to fasten the name cards on your clothing. Unfortunately the commercially available stickers for this purpose are very small.

## Suggestion 5: Deal with the title issue

Uncertainty about titles can have the same inhibiting effect on direct interaction as uncertainty about names. In North American higher education this can be a difficult problem because there is no clear set of social norms for teacher-student relationships. Some teachers encourage students to use their first names, others prefer to be called Professor, Dr., Ms, Mrs., or Mr. It doesn't seem to matter much what arrangement is made about titles so long as there is no uncertainty about what title to use or about the meaning of the title.

People hesitate to address someone whose title makes them feel diminished in some way. And they are likely to feel diminished if their use of a title implies that they have less status than others who are using first names. If titles simply signified intimacy there would be less difficulty. It is easy to accept the fact that the teacher knows some students better than others. But the problem is complicated by the fact that titles indicate power as well as social distance.

My worst experience with titles happened in a group discussion about medical ethics attended by both nurses and doctors. The doctors, who were mostly men, called the nurses by their first names, while the nurses, who were mostly women, referred to the doctors as "Dr." I was the moderator of the session. The doctors spoke about five times as frequently as the nurses. Nurses raised their hands to enter the conversation, while doctors just spoke out. I had to use the chair's prerogative to stop the doctors and recognize the nurses. In this case, titles symbolized and reinforced both the hierarchical nature and the sexism of the medical profession.

What can the group leader do about this? In my medical ethics seminar, I referred to the nurses by their surnames: Mrs. Simon, Ms. Brandt, Mr. Williams. In many graduate courses, teachers ask students to call them by their first names, and in some formal seminars teacher and students all address one another by title.

## Possible Cause 8: Low level of trust

Students hesitate to speak in an environment in which their comments may be unfairly attacked or intentionally misinterpreted. There are a number of ways to build trust among students and between the students and the teacher.

### Suggestion 1: Be perceived as someone concerned with students' welfare

For students, one of the most important characteristics of a teacher is her or his concern for them. This characteristic comes up on every survey in which students are asked to name the attributes of a good teacher. But it is important not only to be caring but to be perceived as being caring. The students of an engineering professor I know — a smallish quiet man with a smallish, quiet voice — saw him in the lecture hall not as caring but as dead. That's understandable. Dramatic personalities have a distinct advantage in lectures. But even in his small group sessions, students felt he didn't care about them or about the subject.

I suggested videotaping his sessions. He and I watched the tape together (it would have been better to include some students as well, but he was unwilling) and were able to point out both verbal and non-verbal things that might communicate an uncaring message to students. After our session the atmosphere in his classes improved. Both he and the students felt this, but it is difficult to attribute the improvement to specific changes he made. It may simply be that he became so aware of the problem that he put more energy into his voice.

## Suggestion 2: Be dependable and consistent

The most common issue over which teachers lose their students' trust is the inconsistency between their exams and the material they teach. This discrepancy happens so frequently that, by the time they reach college level, most students have a theory about it. Unfortunately, the most common one is a paranoid belief that the teacher is playing games to catch them out. One first-year medical student said, "They did it again. They killed us on the exam. We thought the course was great until we started hearing from some of my friends in second year that everything we were learning was irrelevant. Then we got very uneasy about the course. Everyone started asking questions about what was on the exam and the teachers got very annoyed because they saw us as grade grubbing. Then they got even on the next exam. It's a vicious circle."

Why are exams so often not aligned with curriculum? Teachers range from dedicated to indifferent, but they are rarely sadistic. And most teachers hate to fail students. My view is that the answer to the puzzle lies in the widespread policy in colleges and universities that grades must fall into a "bell curve."

If a person's teaching is poor, only the brightest or most diligent students can get high grades. The goals are not clearly specified so that the students don't really know where to put their energy, the lectures don't help students organize the material, the readings do not clarify, and so on. But when a teacher is good at helping the students learn the material and recognize the required emphases in a course, even average students will be able to get the important things right on the exam. The result is a high proportion of As and Bs. Many teachers from all over the country have told me that they have been criticized for giving out too many high grades. Their standards were questioned. They were accused by their administrators of getting soft. The administrators argued that since the students cannot be getting smarter year by year, the teachers' standards must be getting lower. (What may really have been happening was that these people's teaching was getting better and better, and both teachers and students were then penalized for that improvement.) Faced with this dilemma, teachers dig into picky points and esoterica for the exam. Obviously these points are not stressed in the course, so lots of students get wiped out. The bell curve is rescued and trust is destroyed.

My suggestion to teachers is to fight for criterion-referenced exams, the only kind of exam that can reflect improvement of teaching. I fantasize about a teacher who would confront an evaluation committee or administrator using as proof of his or her teaching improvement a graph of the rising average student grades over years of teaching.

### Suggestion 3: Be willing to make disclosures and take personal risks

If you expect students to be trusting enough to take personal risks and make disclosures, you have to model this behavior. Admitting that you are wrong or don't know something makes it easier for students to do the same and ask questions. And if you relate a personal anecdote about the research that you are doing, about your teaching, or your family life, it makes it easier for the students to use personal examples in order to make the material meaningful to themselves.

### Suggestion 4: Provide opportunities for students to co-operate and to trust one another

Co-operation helps build a trusting environment. Unfortunately, students often compete with one another. Criterion-referenced exams and co-operative learning activities such as study groups, POPS, or learning cells (see pages 21, 108, 180) help reduce the need for competition.

### Suggestion 5: Involve students in the process of teaching improvement

I have suggested at several points that teachers gather feedback from students in order to understand the learning situation better and to foster co-operation with students. This process should be open to the student. The information gathered should be disclosed and students' active co-operation elicited in making improvements. In fact, we are currently evaluating a model of teaching improvement in which the information gathered from the class — consisting of a list of educational "issues" — is discussed at a round table attended by the teacher, an educational consultant, and a small group of students who volunteer to help the teacher construct useful responses to the issues.

If the students trust you and co-operate with you to improve your teaching, you really can't lose. Conversely, if they are distrustful, you can't win. The truth of these assertions hits me whenever I observe a class recommending one thing and then the subsequent class recommending the opposite while each year the teacher accommodates to the students and each year the class appears to be very happy because of the change. I sometimes think that the process itself (being listened to and so on), and the increased sense of control over their destiny that it gives to students are as important as the particular change.

# Possible Cause 9: Fear of appearing foolish

Students hesitate to contribute to the group if they are afraid of appearing foolish or stupid. I already mentioned the role of teacher authority in intimidating students (see pages 70 to 74). Here the concern is broader than authority and includes fear of the other students as well.

## Suggestion 1: Encourage everyone to speak early

I suggest that you reduce students' fear of speaking by encouraging everyone to say something, anything, as early as possible in the discussion. I have found that the longer someone waits to speak the more difficult it becomes to break the silence. This may be because breaking the silence is dramatic, and the longer the silence the more dramatic it is, and who has something to say that is so earthshaking that it is worthy of breaking a prolonged silence?

The dilemma of the quiet student is too often starkly revealed by a well-meaning teacher who says something like, "Tim has been sitting back there all this time taking everything in and mulling it over. Tell us, Tim, what is your view?" If Tim had anything interesting to say it was either 40 minutes ago before he lost the trend of the discussion and his eyes began to glaze over or it has just fled in Tim's terror in being put on the spot.

My favorite strategy is to ask the simple questions that are part of natural conversation. For example, "Janet, you are at the Western Hospital. Do you see these kinds of cases there?" This kind of question not only gives Janet a chance to talk about something she is familiar with and cannot possibly get wrong, but also identifies her to the rest of the group as from the Western.

If she answers the probing question without any elaboration, say with a simple "yes" or "no" answer, it would be easy for the group leader to follow up with another question, such as: "By the way you said 'no' I gather that you are relieved. Do the social workers see these kinds of patients as a problem?" And so on, until the natural flow of non-threatening dialogue draws her into the discussion.

## Suggestion 2: Protect minority views

Group pressure can lead to ostracism and intimidation of the minority. Since anyone can be in a minority position at some time, everyone in the group becomes apprehensive when the group allows oppression of a minority or of unpopular views. Try to foster a positive attitude in the group toward disagreement. Students presenting dissenting views should be perceived as sources of ideas rather than as trouble makers.

Focus on the argument rather than the person. Refer to a "dissenting view" or "minority view" rather than labeling the person a "dissenter" or a "radical."

## Suggestion 3: Disinhibit students by your own example

Teachers can reduce their students' fear of appearing foolish by showing that they can be a little foolish without worrying about it. You might admit to having trouble with spelling, not feeling well on a particular day, or not being able to understand something.

## Suggestion 4: Respond tactfully to dumb questions

It may be tempting to make a wisecrack or to use sarcasm when a student asks a particularly uninformed question or one that indicates that he or she has not been listening. Resist it. Although the other students may laugh and enjoy your derision, at some level of their consciousness, the fact that your class is not a safe place in which to ask questions will be registered.

## Suggestion 5: Require that all students prepare all topics

Student presentations are generally a good idea because they get the presenters actively involved. However, they foster a "presentation" kind of dialogue in which everyone is conscious of how well she or he does and is sensitive to criticism, rather than an "exploratory" mode in which everyone wants to learn from questions.

One way to draw everyone into student presentations is to assign "respondents" to the presentations whose task it is to react in some way to the presentation. In order to include the rest of the students, ask the presenters to recommend an article which would allow others to understand enough about the topic to ask intelligent questions. The entire group would read this article before the presentation.

### Suggestion 6: Encourage a non-threatening atmosphere

Fear of being wrong is one of the primary ways in which students feel foolish. It is better not to put someone into an embarrassing position by asking questions which require a single fact for an answer. Begin with open questions which require opinions or evaluative judgments. For example, an easy first question for a session devoted to understanding literature might be: "What are some of the themes of this novel? You don't have to mention the same ones that the critics deal with. Let's just make a list of the ideas dealt with in the book."

Another example comes from a law professor who asks whether students are offspring of a lawyer, married to a lawyer, or use the services of a lawyer. This question, aside from giving students a chance to warm up by saying something, allows them to connect the law to themselves personally. Later she draws these students into the discussion with comments such as, "Those of you with connections to the legal professions may know what a tort is."

## Possible Cause 10: Group is too large

The problem of lack of interaction can almost always be solved by reducing the size of the group. There are exceptions, but as a general rule, decreasing the number of students increases the percentage of air time that each can have and makes it much easier for everyone to enter the discussion. The only reason I did not present this cause first is that there is usually little we can do about class size.

### Suggestion 1: Press for smaller classes

Use whatever influence you have to maintain smaller classes. I used to allow five "hardship" cases into my courses over the allotted enrollment, usually students in their final year who "desperately" needed my course. Last year my students expressed so much frustration with the large numbers in the class that I have decided to stop admitting additional students.

As teachers, we have an obligation to take careful note of the relationship between the quality of learning and the number of students in our classes. We need to be prepared to speak up when it is time to make decisions about priorities and budgets.

### Suggestion 2: Divide the class into smaller groups

In Chapter Two, I discussed a number of ways to break the class into smaller groups for short periods of time. At this point it is worth restating an important principle about using these sub-groups: make sure that their task is perfectly clear and highly structured. The organizers of a medical ethics course used groups of eight students each to generate responses to ethical dilemmas. Since the entire class had 250 students, there was not enough class time for all of the small groups to report to the large group, so the course planners randomly selected groups to present their reports. Every group had to be prepared because no one knew when they might be called upon. After a group reported, faculty who had special expertise in the topic of the day responded to the students' ideas. The plan was an excellent way to involve everyone and to bring student ideas to the surface (Byrne & Taylor, 1989).

### Suggestion 3: Divide the class into pairs for intensive interaction preliminary to an exercise

Dividing the class into pairs for discussion or co-operative study takes the dividing principle to the extreme. In this structure, pairs of students talk for three or four minutes each, taking turns, for a given number of turns, say three or four. These sessions can be interspersed with group work and reading. In the paired arrangement, each student is guaranteed 50 per cent of the air time, and is certain not to be interrupted. This frees the speaker to develop his or her ideas without interference or competition and frees the listener to concentrate on what the speaker is saying without having to be thinking of something to say.

## Possible Cause 11: Inappropriate physical conditions

The physical conditions of the group may have a subtle but powerful influence on the relationships between group members and on their interaction.

### Suggestion 1: Arrange the seating so that people can see each other's faces

Most textbooks on small group teaching advise a circle, "C," or "U" shape of seating so that everyone can see everyone else's face. It is much easier to cue others non-verbally that you want to talk if you can look at their faces. It is instructive to observe a small group, taking special note of how participants break into the conversation. Often they wait until they catch the speaker's eye and indicate by such non-verbal means as facial expression or by audibly drawing in air, that they would like to respond to the speaker. The speaker then attends to the incumbent, lowers his or her voice, and makes room for the next speaker. In contrast, a seating arrangement in which all the seats are facing to the front encourages one-way communication.

## Suggestion 2: Use tables

Next in importance, I have found, is the presence or absence of tables. If the chairs are the typical functional straight-backed chairs, I recommend using a table. These chairs do not lend very much support and are often hard to sit on for long periods without frequent readjustment and squirming. Students can lean their arms on the table for support.

The table itself is preferred to an open ring of chairs not only because it provides a surface for papers, books and note taking, but also because it affords some degree of privacy for the wiggling and shifting that often accompany an intense discussion.

## Suggestion 3: Sit at one end of the arc

Rudduck writes:

When chairs are arranged in an arc . . . it is advantageous for the seminar leader to sit at one extreme. If she sits one or two places in, she may cut off the extreme students from the rest of the group. If she sits at the apex, she provides an obvious focal point and can become a telephone exchange for comments — or she may be seen to divide the group so that the two sides act in opposition. At the edge of the arc, the seminar leader seems able to exert procedural control when necessary and yet not get in the way of student-to-student discussion. (1979, p. 59)

## Suggestion 4: Use a flip chart or chalkboard

Flip charts and chalkboards are useful for enhancing student-to-student interaction because they provide both a continuous display of the themes or issues under discussion and a record of the group's accomplishments.

## Suggestion 5: Beware teaching in a lounge or office

My experience with rooms with big stuffed chairs, common rooms, and lounges has not been good, especially if there are no flip charts, notebooks, or chalk boards. Conversation tends to wander. Lounges are made for idle conversation and relaxation. For learning I think we need brighter light, more proximity (to see one another's faces), and the support of a table.

Some people have taken to conducting their classes in their offices. Beware of crowding in the office and of seating arrangements which imply markedly different relationships. In the office there is likely to be one large swivel chair, behind a desk, and several smaller chairs crowded together.

Interaction is facilitated in conditions in which the differences in levels between the participants are not emphasized. Seating should work to reduce the differences not emphasize them.

### Suggestion 6: Know the names of the students

Knowing the names of participants in a group facilitates continuity in the discussion because it enables participants to keep track of the person responsible for each comment. There are a number of strategies in the literature by which teachers can help students learn each other's names. Some of these have difficulties which make their use unadvisable. See pages 88 and 89.

The strategy I favor is the placing of a triangular solid of paper on the desk in front of each student with his or her name in large print on both front and back.

### Suggestion 7: Recognize and attempt to deal with distracting physical conditions

Trying to ignore things like distracting noises or excessive heat or cold compounds students' physical discomfort with the frustration of feeling that the teacher doesn't care enough to address the problem. Make it clear that you are aware of the difficulty and that you care about the students' comfort, and take any possible action. For example:
Teacher: That air vent is making so much noise, it must be difficult for some of you to hear.
Students: It is a bit.
Teacher: Does anyone have any ideas? We could squeeze the tables into an oblong instead of a circle, to put the vent on the side.
Students: Let's try it.
Teacher: [15 minutes into the new arrangement] Is this arrangement any better?
Student 1: I don't think that the table made any difference, but people *are* speaking up.
Student 2: It is a little better.

## Possible Cause 12: Interfering emotions

A number of emotional situations can interfere with class interaction. These are the subject of Part Three.

# 5/Teacher Dominates Interaction

*"He asks us questions and then answers them himself. At the beginning of the course we all waved our hands in the air like fools. No more. We get in there, put on our pleasant masks, and go to sleep."*

The previous chapter dealt with students' reluctance to speak. Of course, when the students don't speak, the teacher usually speaks to relieve the silence; the upshot is that the teacher does all the talking. The situations we are going to consider now are also characterized by excessive domination on the part of the teacher, but the causes are very different: here the teacher monopolizes the show because, for various reasons, that is the way he or she wants it.

These situations are harder to spot because there is a type of interaction — students do talk, offer ideas, ask questions, and so on. What is missing is significant contribution from them. In the language of David Hunt (1987), students are learning from the outside in, not from the inside out. While they may be interacting, they are not taking part in the active thinking: they are not making judgments about the relevance of material, they are not making value judgments, and they are not deciding what learning material is important based on their own experiences. They are playing someone else's game. Learning ought to be their own game.

When the teacher dominates, the pattern of communication is like a spoked wheel. The teacher is the hub, the spokes are the lines of interaction and the students are at the ends of each spoke. Students rarely address one another because the context does not value their interaction. When they do address one another, it is often to criticize or compete. The object of the interaction is external to the students, as if they were little children learning to play a game from an adult. Bit by bit they discern the rules, rewards are dispensed for adherence to the rules rather than for learning, and all rewards are dispensed by the teacher.

## Possible Cause 1: Teacher talks too much

We are dealing here with a situation in which students may be prevented from talking by a teacher who is taking up all the air time. The teacher may not consciously desire this outcome. Some teachers don't understand that interaction is necessary, but think of teaching as a process whereby nuggets of information are consecutively hurled at students. A teacher who embraces this concept of teaching thinks of small group teaching as an excellent opportunity to get closer to the targets of his or her intellectual artillery, to hurl facts with greater force and accuracy.

I encountered the purest example of this pathology in a seminar on management by objectives. Instead of sitting, the professor stood at the table, even though there were only five students, and rained a torrent of loud and passionate definitions at the heads clustered around him. As the words shot out, the heads of the students bent in response like a field of wheat in a violent gust of wind.

Occasionally, the professor stopped and invited discussion. Surprisingly, the students quickly began to discuss the topic. It is probably a function of the high level of articulation and assertiveness of the average management student that they remained uncowed by this experience. Unfortunately, before the discussion could get under way, the teacher stopped it and invited the students to discuss a new topic. I found myself thinking of a story my mother used to tell about my grandfather, who was a wheat farmer on the prairies. Returning home at night, he and my grandmother would climb onto the wagon and the horses would take them home. On rare occasions that my grandfather had fortified himself with home-brewed beer, he would feel the need to commandeer the reins — and the horses would head straight into the ditch.

This professor showed some awareness of the educational values of discussion. But since he was completely insensitive to the conditions that would permit genuine interaction, he killed it before it could ever get off the ground.

## Suggestion 1: Measure your proportion of talk

You cannot change the ratio of teacher talk to student talk if you are unaware of it, and it is difficult, while talking, to measure your own verbosity. The simplest method of keeping track of your talk is through interaction analysis, a systematic method of cataloguing certain features of conversation — how long the teacher talks, how long students talk, who asks questions, who answers them, who rewards contributions, and so on.

The earliest system of interaction analysis, devised by Ned Flanders (Amidon & Flanders, 1967; Flanders, 1970), is still in use and is very simple to use. A coder observes the interaction and, every three seconds, writes down a number corresponding to the verbal behavior taking place at that moment. The following coding chart is a modification of the Flanders code that I took from the first volume of Bergquist and Phillips's (1975, p. 103) *Handbook of Faculty Development*.

## Categories for a Modified Flanders Interaction Analysis
## TEACHER TALK

### Indirect Influence
1. ACCEPTS FEELING OR PRAISES: accepts and clarifies the feelings of students in a non-threatening manner. Feelings may be positive or negative. Praises and gives recognition to the student.
2. ENCOURAGES OR ACCEPTS IDEAS OF STUDENTS: clarifies, builds, or develops ideas suggested by a student. As teacher brings more of his own ideas into play, shift to category 5.
3. ASKS NARROW QUESTIONS: asks questions to which the general nature of the response can be predicted.
4. ASKS BROAD QUESTIONS: asks questions which are thought provoking or which require expression of opinion, attitude, or feeling.

### Direct Influence
5. LECTURING: gives facts or opinions about content or procedures; expresses his own ideas, asks rhetorical questions.

6. CRITICIZING OR GIVING DIRECTIONS: statements intended to change student behavior from a non-acceptable to acceptable pattern; stating why the teacher is doing what he is doing: extreme self-reference; directive statements which serve to show the instructor's superiority.

## STUDENT TALK

7. DIRECT STUDENT RESPONSE: elicited talk by students in response to narrow questions; highly predictable responses; negative responses such as "I don't know"; unison responses.
8. INDIRECT STUDENT RESPONSE: student talk of a broad nature; student opinion or judgement.
9. SPONTANEOUS STUDENT PARTICIPATION: student talk not solicited by the instructor.
10. ADMINISTRATIVE: directed activities, quizzes, distribution of papers, reading of announcements.
11. SILENCE: pauses, short periods of silence.
12. CONFUSION: periods of confusion in which communication can not be understood by the observer.

The chart makes clear what kind of information you would gather from this process and how you might use it. For one thing you can look at the pattern of interaction of your group. A teacher who is having trouble encouraging discussion might gain some insight from an interaction pattern that included much lecturing and criticism (5, 6) and many narrow questions (3) and administrative behaviors (10). The other thing that is fun and often useful is to calculate ratios. The ratio of teacher talk to student talk or of indirect to direct influence have been the subject of much interest in the literature.

You can make your own modifications to the Flanders code or make your own code. All you have to do is carefully describe a particular behavior that you want to observe, and give it a short form name, such as "Y" to signify every time you use the expression "you know," if you are trying to get yourself to stop using that. I invented a code specifically to study the process whereby medical teachers gradually invest authority in their students. The simplest code is just a sheet of paper with a line down the middle, one side headed "Student Talk," and the other headed "Teacher Talk." The observer notes the utterances of teachers and students, either by recording at set intervals, say every 5 seconds, or by recording every sentence uttered.

### Suggestion 2: Break the pattern of alternating between teacher and student

For some teachers, the pattern of responding to each and every student contribution is nothing but habit; others use it more consciously as a style of teaching. In any case, once an alternating pattern is established it is difficult to stop because students wait for the teacher's response before another student will speak. A teacher's failure to respond might be taken as a rebuke..

Wait after a student speaks. Don't feel obliged to comment on or reward each contribution. Wait until several comments are made, then sum up if a summary is useful at that point, and ask for reactions to your summary. If that strategy is too subtle at the beginning, say something like: "Are there any other comments on that?" or "Other reactions, other ideas?" If expectant faces compel you to respond, try looking at other students after one student speaks, to give them the idea that you expect others to address the topic.

If a student asks a question, the teacher can turn the question back to others. This strategy can be overdone and must be used with caution. There are times when the question is directed at the teacher not because of a bad pattern of communication, but because the student would really like to know the teacher's viewpoint.

## Suggestion 3: Resist talking to only one or two students

Exclusive dialogue with one or two students has an effect similar to that of the alternating pattern: it gives the teacher 50 per cent of the air time. The alternating pattern at least allows each student to have a moment in the limelight once in a while; an exclusive dialogue shuts out others and drives them to compete for air time, or, more probably, to give up interacting.

It's very tempting for any teacher to enjoy a discussion with a very bright student or to be provoked into an exclusive dialogue with one. It is necessary to keep your role in mind. One of the services for which we teachers are paid is to subsume our own interests to those of the group.

## Suggestion 4: Wait a few minutes before you intervene

When student discussion gets bogged down or goes off on a tangent, the group leader should at some point intervene. But how soon? I recommend that you wait a few minutes. Literally. If allowed a little time, students often recognize a problem and take steps to correct it. If you note the time when you feel like intervening, and then note either when the students come through or when you cannot stand to keep silent any longer, you will be surprised at how little time has passed. A few minutes spent in neutral may seem like half an hour to the teacher who is holding back but may seem like a few seconds to students who are furiously thinking of what to do next. Remembering this may help to control your anxiety while you are waiting for students to find their way. It is important that you not appear worried to students.

### Suggestion 5: Don't grab the reins

When you *do* intervene, try to do so by restating the agenda, by summarizing the progress made so far, or by some other means which would allow the students to solve the problem. Don't try to "fix it" by telling them what to do.

### Suggestion 6: Remember that listening is teaching too

Some teachers feel obligated to be *active* in their teaching at all times. This misplaced sense of responsibility drives them to fill every gap in discussion and to pounce nervously on every false move. It is useful to remember that one of the tasks for which you get paid as a teacher is to listen to your students.

## Possible cause 2: Teacher's authority is overwhelming

Teachers possess considerable power: they can pass or fail students; they have subject matter authority by virtue of their knowledge of the subject; they have higher institutional status than students. But although the relationship of teachers and students is unequal, the points of view, expectations, and goals of both teachers and students should be respected. This kind of reciprocity is essential to co-operation between teachers and learners, and it is necessary for the full commitment of the teacher and the active involvement of the learners.

In other words, the teacher's authority should not overwhelm or negate the rights of the students as people and as learners. I think of a teacher and students as rowing a boat to a distant shore. The students don't really know where they are going because they have not been there before. The teacher has been there many times so he or she is steering. But the students must row by themselves, and their approach, pauses, and speed are entirely within their control. The teacher's role is to point out the goal, to encourage, even to help with the process. But he or she must not take over the oars.

### Suggestion 1: Negotiate objectives openly

In Chapter One I discussed the manner in which a reciprocal

agreement can be struck between teachers' intentions and students' expectations for a course. I mention it here again because it is important to the students' sense of control over their own learning that the process of arriving at the course objectives be an open one.

## Suggestion 2: Provide the freedom to discover

Learning is more lasting and effective if the learner is in control. Besides, at some point we all have to make our own way to our educational goals, and no teacher can show the best way to get there.

Many small group discussions are too closely orchestrated. They are like games in which the teacher leads the students by the hand through a darkened room to the goal. When they arrive at the goal the light is switched on, and the teacher dramatically announces their success. This is a dramatic ending for a mystery game, but it fosters dependence; students could not find their way a second time.

The fact that students sometimes prefer this kind of blind game to discovery is no reason to use it. One group of students praised their teacher to me by explaining how skillful he was at "bringing out the issues." "We were all over the place at first, and then, out of all that mess, he picks one or two comments to follow up on and we know that these comments will lead to important material. You feel great when you are the one who made one of these comments. Then everyone talks around those areas and again he will ask a question or pick up a point or two which will further narrow down the topic. At the end of the period the major concepts are slowly revealed to us. It's really neat." I don't share the students' enthusiasm. As I listened to them, it occurred to me that they were being deprived of an important aspect of their education — setting goals, determining what is important, making choices and decisions about process and content, exploring.

## Suggestion 3: Have a student lead the class

Teachers cannot relinquish their authority over the subject matter or their responsibility to pass or fail students, but they can share the leadership and it may be wise to do so. In fact, a rotating leadership, in which every student gets a chance to lead the group, is a good idea. As group leaders, students see the educational dialogue from the other side. They begin to ask questions, summarize, and restate goals. They begin to make judgments about the group's progress and think about what the group should do. In short, they begin to take a more active role in their own education. And this active role spills over into their everyday group behavior.

Incidentally, student leadership means that the teacher is free to attend to other things. For example, the teacher can observe the group more accurately undistracted by the decisions of leadership, and therefore make better decisions about how the group process is functioning and how to improve it.

## Suggestion 4: Try leaderless groups

In this context, a leaderless group means that there is no designated leader and the teacher is absent for at least part of the time. Various students will usually take responsibility for the group process and for achieving the goals. Powell's (1974) research on leaderless tutorials (summarized in Rudduck, 1978) produced a list of advantages and disadvantages for leaderless groups. He found that when the tutor was absent, many students doubled their contributions and participation was spread more evenly. Students in the leaderless groups found the atmosphere more relaxed, more stimulating, they spoke more openly and helped each other more, than in groups in which the teacher was present. Moreover, because the teacher is not there, there is more opportunity to practise independent thinking and more likelihood that participants will raise questions of genuine concern to them rather than ones they think the teacher would like to hear.

The big problem with leaderless groups, as Powell pointed out, is that mistakes of content can go uncorrected. Also, in the absence of a trained leader, problems of process go uncorrected. There is more irrelevant talk, fooling around, or domination by individual speakers. One way to overcome this difficulty is to give students training in group leadership. Since there is no better way to train than by example, an excellent way to arrange a leaderless group is to alternate it with a group that is lead by a skilled teacher. People pick up tips about small group leadership much more readily when they know they will be doing it themselves.

## Suggestion 5: Resist answering questions

Refrain from answering questions that students could answer, but be sure everyone knows what you are doing and why. For example, in response to a student question you might say, ''I'm hesitating because I'm thinking of an answer to your question, and at the same time I'm thinking that this process of thinking of an answer is a useful exercise in learning the material. Answering questions is a good way to learn. So let's throw the question open. You think of answers, too. Give it a try. Don't worry if you are right or wrong. The active process of thinking of an answer is helpful."

## Suggestion 6: Provide <u>one</u> answer, not <u>the</u> answer

When students ask the teacher a question, and he or she answers it without qualification, the student will probably assume that that answer is the only one. Answering questions in this way stifles discussion and increases student dependence. Most questions have more than one answer. By simply qualifying an answer as one of several possible answers, the teacher can keep the discussion open. For example, this dialogue followed a question about the pros and cons of general screening for breast cancer:

Teacher: "One answer is in terms of the cost efficiency. Certainly it is not cost effective to screen every person for tumors. But there are other ways to look at the question which might lead to different answers. Does anyone want to take a shot at another?"

Student: "From the viewpoint of an individual who has the tumor, it is a different story. She may be just one person, but it's game over for her if the tumor is not detected."

## Suggestion 7: Avoid the kind of final statements that discourage disagreement or discussion

For example, in a discussion of the ethics of reporting sexually transmitted diseases, the group leader ended a discussion before it began by concluding: "No matter how you look at it, you have to report it."

## Suggestion 8: Never talk just to display your knowledge

I am not making a moral point here about immodesty, although students occasionally are put off or bored by ostentatious displays of knowledge. What I am concerned with here is that information given to puff up the teacher's ego can be irrelevant to or can hinder students' learning.

## Suggestion 9: Establish a friendly, non-threatening atmosphere

Establish an atmosphere in which students do not feel threatened. This means listening, understanding, and responding to them. It means protecting minority points of view. It means refraining from correcting the very first contributions. Criticism, before any rapport or group cohesiveness is established, may push the students into a defensive posture or cause them to court the teacher's approval.

Ask for "safe" contributions at first, contributions in areas in which students may have special knowledge and therefore are unlikely to have difficulty replying. For example, "What struck you about the paintings?" "Which of the readings did you find the most difficult?" "Which did you find most useful?"

### Suggestion 10: Try self-study groups such as POPS, learning cells, and pairing

Self-study groups encourage student-student interaction (see Chapter Two).

## Possible Cause 3: Teacher tries so hard to inculcate certain ideas that there is no real connection with students

A professor, who invited me to observe his small group, primed me for the event by asking me to take particular notice as to how he would "bring out" the essential points from the group. With the look of a proud papa he handed me a sheet of paper listing his "important points." This was not written to be shared with students. This was *his* answer sheet. As students made contributions to the discussion he steered them toward the points that were on the sheet.

The interaction was characterized by lots of questions directed at the teacher but little real dialogue and certainly no dialogue between students. Few students made any contributions of their own; it seemed to me that no independent thinking was going on. Students had caught on to the "game" and were trying to win by discovering the hidden agenda. The teacher was not interested in making contact with them; they had to find out what he was thinking.

There is nothing wrong with propounding a particular point of view. In fact, professors are paid to "profess" their points of view. But the small group provides teachers with a unique opportunity to communicate their points of view in an intimate and compelling manner by drawing out students' experiences with the topic. This is a slow process because students will wander into blind alleys of thought and reach important conclusions by circuitous routes. But in the long run, this appears to produce the most effective learning. The problem is that, in their impatience to guide students, teachers may not respect the students' starting point.

## Suggestion 1: Disclose the hidden agenda

Teaching and learning should be co-operative, not adversarial. If you have a set of ideas that you would like the students to consider, tell them what the ideas are and ask for their co-operation in considering them. (This is pursued further under "Abuse of the Socratic Method," below.)

## Suggestion 2: Listen to understand rather than to praise or refute

The danger of a teaching approach that attempts to "bring out" certain points from the students is that it encourages a kind of impatience on the part of the teacher, who may want to lead students to a predetermined outcome rather than listen in order to understand. This is not advisable. First, the teacher and students may actually be moving toward the same conclusion, but the teacher who is unaware of the students will not recognize that movement, and second, even if students are pursuing a different line of thought, the teacher must understand their thinking in order to connect his or her objectives with theirs

## Suggestion 3: Tolerate interruptions

You may be interrupted while you are attempting to set out some ideas at the start of the class. Don't make a big deal of it. Students will rarely interrupt if the ground rules clearly indicate that discussion will *follow* your comments, but some students take a while to learn the ground rules. If it does come up, don't make a big deal of it.

I know a philosophy teacher whose Jesuit training assists him to develop an argument with the precision and beauty of a forming crystal. The way he used to deal with interruptions, however, hurt his relationship with his students and their respect for both him and his abilities. He would respond to an interruption with a stunned silence followed by a brief restatement of his argument to the point at which the student had asked the question. Students interpreted this response as rebuke for daring to interrupt the flow of pure truth. Indeed, it looked to me like one of the worst examples of arrogance I had ever seen until I discussed it with the teacher later. It turned out that he thought the student had missed a step in the logic, and was helping by providing a brief summary. He thought that doing this also helped the other students to maintain the continuity of the argument.

All that is needed here is the simplest recognition that the stu-

dent has raised a question. This is one way to deal with it:
Teacher: The third argument is that we can be protected from
indoctrination by judicious selection of the content.
Student interrupting: But who chooses the content?
Teacher: Yes. You have raised one of the criticisms leveled
against the argument that I am developing. But let's wait until
I have developed the argument before we take up criticisms,
I don't want to lose the continuity.

# Possible Cause 4: Facilitation methods may backfire

Certain common methods of fostering interaction among
students may instead reduce interaction or simply be ineffective. The ineffective methods can also lead to reduced interaction when teachers' disappointment leads them to blame student apathy for the lack of interaction, and then the relationship deteriorates further in a kind of vicious cycle.

### Suggestion 1: Beware extreme statements

Small group leaders sometimes use extreme or outrageous
statements to provoke discussion. These may require vigorous
defense, or inhibit other people. In either case, the effect is that
the leader does most of the talking (Bligh, 1972).

### Suggestion 2: Beware the devil's advocate role

This device has precisely the same failing as the use of extreme
statements: it encourages polarized dialogue between the teacher
and the one or two students who are courageous enough to
challenge the teacher.

McKeachie (1983) expresses concern that this technique will
be seen as manipulative, that it reduces students' trust of their
instructor, and that it can be used as a screen to prevent students
from winning an argument. The instructor can parry a mortal
attack with, "Well, I just presented that position to see if you
could see its weakness." McKeachie's compromise position, with
which I agree, is to let the students know that you are playing
the devil's advocate. You might say: "If I were to play the devil's
advocate," or "I'm going to defend the opposite position, for
the sake of clarifying the argument." Since the teaching-learning
relationship is most effective when it is co-operative, it is better
for teachers to disclose any games that they play with the
students.

## Suggestion 3: Beware rhetorical questions

The use of rhetorical questions to facilitate small group interactions can dull the response to real questions. Although they are a traditional strategy for stimulating interaction, rhetorical questions can make students feel manipulated, especially if they assume that the audience agree or disagree with the main point of the speaker, as does "You're all with me?" or "I assume that everyone agrees with me up to now?"

This is essentially an embarrassing technique whereby a teacher buries the few dissenters in a false sense of unanymity. The implication is that if you don't agree with me, you either aren't very bright or you haven't been following me very closely, because everything I've said has been too clear or certain to argue about.

My point does not apply to questions to which you really want answers. The problem doesn't arise if you are willing to look at each face and to deal with what people have to say. There are excellent guides to asking real questions in order to stimulate thinking and interaction (see Orme, 1973, and Rassmussen, 1984).

## Suggestion 4: Don't overuse paraphrasing

Paraphrasing is a useful device, but don't overuse it. Restating students' comments when they are unclear helps, but mindless paraphrasing is boring. You will begin to sound like a parrot.

## Suggestion 5: Beware withholding information, judgments, or opinions

It is commonly recommended that teachers withhold information, judgments, and opinions so as not to inhibit students from offering their own thoughts and feelings. I agree that this is useful strategy to prevent teacher domination. But a teacher who holds back can unwittingly create a dramatic and even fearsome tension. To speak or not to speak is a dilemma for the teacher who is trying to encourage interaction.

One strategy that seems to work is to give your opinion in a deliberately understated manner. In theatre they call it "burying the lead." It means not using the most dramatic line at the moment that would create the maximum drama. Here are three answers to the same question, based on classroom talk.

*Intentionally dramatic answer:* The answer to your question is not simple. There are many sides to this issue. But after reviewing the evidence, both from my own research and other sources,

I have come to the conclusion that innoculations are not cost effective.

*Students' reaction:* [Full stop. End of discussion.]

*Drama created by holding back:* Well, I would really like to get your views on the subject first.

*Students' reaction:* [Gasp! He's thought about this issue for 10 years. If I don't have the same view as he I'm going to feel very foolish.]

*Drama reduced by burying the lead:* At this point I would interpret the evidence as opposing innoculations. Of course, there are contrary views in the literature, and there are other factors to consider besides cost. What are your views?

## Suggestion 6: Beware motivation through fear

Fear is a common tactic for motivating students. I remember the introductory remarks of one clinical teacher to a group of students who were about to begin their fourth-year rotation in medicine: "Last week we had to fail a clerk [fourth-year student] because she had no idea of how to handle her patient." Another example is the teacher who told a student, when he was unable to answer a question: "That's a simple question. Don't you know any anatomy? Think! How do you people get here without knowing any anatomy?"

Fear works in the short run. But when the fear-arousing stimulus is withdrawn, motivation dies. The other problem with fear motivation is that it tends to lock students into a survival mentality, one in which they constantly defend themselves instead of taking the risks necessary for learning. And while they are busy defending themselves, they are attending to the potential source of harm, the teacher, not one another or their learning.

Ideally, over time students should move from motivational orientations such as safety and security to higher motivational orientations such as creativity and competency. Students motivated by competency are more likely to shape the direction of their own education, more likely to be self-starters, than students who are motivated by safety and security needs. Fear motivation produces students who react to external pressures.

## Suggestion 7: Beware the Socratic technique

In Chapter Four I described how abuse of the Socratic technique can inhibit student participation. But inhibition of interaction is not the worst consequence of abuse of the Socratic technique. The worst is the distortion of the pattern of interaction so that all communication is directed toward the teacher. The object of the game that the Socratic technique sets up is to find out what is on the teacher's mind. While students are busy trying to second guess the teacher, they are not listening to one another.

I observed a dramatic example of this distortion of communication in a science tutorial. About 15 students were spread around the lab, elbows resting on their lab benches as they sat on tall stools. The teacher stood in front of the chalk board patiently asking one question after another in an effort to draw information out of the class. I was in the back of the room observing. After about five minutes it became clear that one student, who sat directly in front of the teacher, was answering all the questions. The teacher failed in every attempt to broaden the interaction, until he finally gave up and continued the dialogue with this student while the others watched.

I could hardly wait until the tutorial was over, when I had asked for time to speak to the students in the absence of the teacher. Did the other students feel left out? Did they feel cheated because one student was taking up all the teacher's time? What was going on? They looked down and smiled sheepishly, apparently a little ashamed of what they had done. I was completely confused. I probed just a little by saying, "I noticed that one person was answering most of the question." Then one student broke the silence and said, "She was saving us." I asked them what they meant by "saving us?" Another student offered an explanation: "We're not interested in the drill. It's embarrassing and most of us won't play. But somebody has to be the foil to answer all his questions so we can get the stuff."

I was astounded. One student had volunteered to indulge the teacher by playing his embarrasingly silly game so that the others could relax and learn without having to guess what was on his mind. Examples like this in which a dedicated teacher wastes his own and his students' time are on my list of teaching nightmares.

The technique of asking questions to stimulate discussion is also easily abused when the questions require specific and factual answers which are known by the teacher, and when the student is not "in" on the game. The typical response to this kind of questioning is to tune in to the questions for some hint as to what the teacher may have in mind rather than to think through the answer. This puts students on the spot and makes them reluctant to answer at all if they aren't sure that they have the "right" answer.

The activity should not be to play "I bet you aren't smart enough to guess what's on my mind" but to interact in a way that fills in students' gaps in knowledge, builds on the knowlege they do have, and at the same time builds their self-confidence.

Even the socratic technique can be used with happy consequences if we follow a few simply rules:

**1.** Begin with easy questions.

**2.** Begin with open-ended questions which have no single right answer. It might be useful to keep track of the number of closed and open questions you ask.

**3.** Fit questions to the context of the discussion, do not fit the discussion to your own predetermined questions.

**4.** Begin with general questions and move to more specific ones.

**5.** Choose students by some open system, such as moving from left to right or taking volunteers. Students should feel invited to answer rather than targeted.

**6.** Ask higher level questions, ones which require synthesis, analysis, or evaluation rather than just rote memory. ("How would you compare the two plays?" "What do you think are some of the causes?")

**7.** Reassure the students by telling them that this is a learning exercise rather than a drill.

**8.** Assist students who are having difficulty answering. "What I am getting at is an alcohol problem. How would excessive alcohol explain some of the symptoms we have observed?"

**9.** Acknowledge it when your questions aren't working. "I'm taking a circuitous route here because I want you to think about the question rather than just listen to me tell you the answer, but I have got you off on the wrong track."

**10.** Don't ask "yes," "no," or "fill in the blank" types of questions, but design questions that allow students to develop ideas and full thoughts in answer.

**11.** If one student persistently fails to answer questions, do not give in to the temptation to embarrass the student. You need to provide opportunities for students to answer, you must never brow beat them.

**12.** Be sure students understand that the questioning technique is for their benefit, not an indulgence of your own.

**13.** Do not discourage students from discussing the answers among themselves.

**14.** Do not dwell on a wrong answer. Acknowledge the error quickly and move on.

**15.** If a student fails to answer a question, rephrase the question or approach the issue from another direction.

**16.** Don't evaluate every answer by approval or disapproval. I don't deny the importance of encouraging contributions, especially from students who rarely talk, but I am arguing that it is rewarding enough to students if their comments are taken seriously. If you judge every answer, then you are stuck when it comes to the shy student whom you would like to encourage but whose answer is a little vague or irrelevant. When an answer is vague, probe for a more specific one, from either that student or another. Eventually the full story will come out and the shy student will have contributed to it.

**17.** Remember that there are other ways to stimulate discussion, many of which are discussed in this book.

### Suggestion 8: Students reward each other

If the teacher is the only one who rewards student participation, he or she might come to be seen as the official dispensor of rewards, and dialogue will change into a wheel shape with the teacher at its hub.

Although inexperienced group learners rarely have the skills to reward one another, a teacher or group leader can help them to acquire these skills by occasionally pointing out a student's recognition of the contributions of another student.

### Suggestion 9: Don't assign grades for participation

Here is one student's description of the atmosphere created by a policy of grading for participation: "Everyone is trying like mad to impress the teacher for the almighty grade. It's impossible to ask a real question. If you don't know something you keep quiet about it so that the teacher doesn't find out that you don't know it. You only ask questions when you know the answer, to score brownie points."

### Suggestion 10: Beware helping students express their ideas

Drawing out half-formed ideas by helping students to state them is a good idea, but don't put words into students' mouths. Jean Rudduck put it so well: the student "rarely comes back to complain that what the seminar leader said is not what he meant to say!" (1978, p. 33).

## Possible Cause 5: Domination by default #1: Group is too large

Group size is a very important factor in student-student interaction. The smaller the number of students and the more familiar they are with one another the more easily they can interact. The smaller the group, the easier it is for participants to get to know one another. If interaction among all members of the group is desirable for the goals of the group, the numbers should be small enough to allow comfortable face-to-face seating around a table, say 8 to 12 students. If face-to-face interaction by everyone is not essential, up to 20 students might be allowable: if vicarious interaction will suffice, even more students may comprise the group.

**Suggestion 1: Reduce the size of the group**

Although it is not always possible, the simplest thing to do is to reduce the size of the group.

You can split the group into two. You can alternate between groups. There might be some benefit in your occasional absence from each group as you shift from one to the other (see pages 95 and 121). There is a rule of thumb, among my colleagues in faculty development, that a teacher can effectively monitor up to three such groups. Two is better than three.

Another way to reduce the size of the group is to arrange a "fishbowl" configuration in which an inner ring of students interact as a discussion group while an outer ring observe the interaction. After a while, the students change places. Students in the outer ring tend to get bored if they are there too long, an interesting measure of the superior power of the small group in holding attention.

A third way to reduce group size is to organize a debate between subgroups.

**Suggestion 2: Reduce the <u>functional</u> size of the group**

As I mentioned in the introduction, a small group does not automatically function as a small group just because it has only 10 or 12 students. Several characteristics, in addition to the number of members, enable students to interact easily. Even a group of 20 or 30 can function as a small group if:

**1.** The group leader is skilled;

**2.** The participants are homogeneous with respect to important characteristics such as their relationship to the subject matter, their preparation, and background information;

**3.** The group continues interacting *regularly* and for many sessions; and

**4.** The group functions as a social group outside of the class.

# Possible Cause 6: Domination by default #2: Negative attitudes toward the value of small group teaching and learning

Many students bring negative attitudes toward interaction with their peers with them from primary and secondary school. They are accustomed to a classroom in which teachers supply all of the significant comments while students commit the irrelevant distractions. One student answered when I asked him why his group never addressed comments or questions to each other: "It's just sharing ignorance."

### Suggestion 1: Review the advantages of active participation

Set aside a period of time for discussion of student attitudes toward the value of interaction. There is a good case for the conclusion that everything is more easily or better learned in small groups although it may be more time-consuming.

### Suggestion 2: Provide practice in listening skills

These include such skills as paraphrasing, summarizing, rewarding others, and learning to tolerate pauses after someone speaks (see pages 31 to 33 and 122 to 123).


# Possible Cause 7: Domination by default #3: Students all agree with each other

Since discrepancies in viewpoints are often necessary to fuel a discussion, complete agreement among participants about a topic can kill their interest in discussing it among themselves. They will become more interested in directing comments at the teacher who either has a different point of view or is able to adopt one. Student agreement, therefore, can produce the same effect on group interaction as the teacher who takes an extreme view.

### Suggestion 1: Ask for an explanation of student views

Ask students to explain their positions on an issue in detail. Differences will emerge in their views as they become more explicit, and these differences will often be important ones even though they are based on fine distinctions.

### Suggestion 2: Ask for volunteers to take the other side of an issue

When students debate an issue they are usually surprised to find out that their viewpoint can be challenged. Even if the debate does not change anyone's position, it can stimulate a more exact appreciation of the finer points of the issue.

### Suggestion 3: Engage students by means other than controversy

Difference of opinion among students is not the only basis of active involvement among students. If there are no differences, then use some other means such as applying the group ideas to real problems, or changing the conditions of the issue and starting over. For example, a psychology class discussing reinforcement theory may have no controversy about the rat experiments until applications of those experiments are made for humans. Any conclusion may seem acceptable in the abstract until it is applied to your life, country, body, or whatever.

## Possible Cause 8: Domination by default #4: Inappropriate physical surroundings and resources

The room, its ownership and location, seating arrangements, and availability of some recording surface visible to all (a flip chart, a chalk board) are important to fostering student-student interaction. See pages 96 to 98 for suggestions.

# 6/Students Participate Unequally

*"Some of them talk constantly, others never say anything. I can't figure it out."*
*"If I don't talk, nobody ever says anything. I feel like I'm babysitting the class and the teacher."*
*"I never get a chance to say anything. Sometimes that's okay; sometimes it makes me really mad."*

Chapter 4 included teaching and learning situations in which too little student involvement and interaction inhibit effective learning. Chapter 5 dealt with situations in which interaction is ineffective because it is dominated by the teacher. Here I address those teaching and learning situations characterized by grossly unequal speaking time among participants. There is interaction, but not everyone takes part in it. Some students are asking and answering all the questions.

This bothers some teachers; others simply say, "What's wrong with not talking?" They tell me about students who never say a word and then turn in A papers. They feel that one shouldn't force everyone to be alike. Their view is summarized by one teacher who said, "Some people don't talk as much as others. Why should we force everyone to conform to the conversational levels of a minority?"

Their point is well taken. People have many learning styles and preferences. It would be silly to force every student to learn in the same way. I have spoken with some excellent students who preferred watching a discussion to joining one. They said they learned more from watching and listening because then their thoughts were uninterrupted. On the other hand, the majority view among educators is that *active* student involvement aids the learning process and active involvement is often aided by speaking. So how should the teacher respond, if at all, when faced with grossly unequal speaking time?

I believe that in most cases the opportunity to speak helps a student to learn. I do not believe that every student must be compelled to talk. But before a teacher allows a student to be silent in peace, he or she should make sure that the student really wants to remain silent for a good reason and is not, rather, being prevented from speaking by one or another of the difficulties I am about to discuss. The teacher must also make sure that the student's silence is not compromising other students.

There are a number of ways to reveal and correct problems of unequal participation, but first the teacher needs to know that there is a problem.

## Possible Cause 1: Lack of awareness of unequal participation

You have to know about the problem before you can take steps to correct it. Be careful not to place too much reliance on student feedback from questionnaires. The issue of unequal participation is subtle and students may not be aware of the problem even if you ask them. I have often found that students who are shy about speaking up in groups are also reluctant to admit their shyness.

One of the first steps you might consider taking is to measure just how unequal the student participation really is.

### Suggestion 1: Use a sociogram

A sociogram is a useful tool for examining the distribution of participation. In its simplest form it is a diagram in which interaction is depicted by lines drawn between circles that represent persons in the group. An arrowhead on the end of the line indicates the direction of the message. I suggest that you not try to keep a sociogram while you are trying to lead the group; ask a student, teaching assistant, or colleague to do it. Fifteen minutes at two different times during the class period will be sufficient. The sociogram will reveal to you at a glance who is doing most of the talking.

Incidentally, don't try to hide what you are doing from the students. If you discuss the data with them, you are more likely to get their co-operation in any remedy you suggest. Indeed, after a discussion it may not be necessary to devise a remedy since the discussion often turns out to be a remedy in itself.

### Suggestion 2: Talk to students individually

If you have the occasion to speak to students individually, especially students who have not contributed much to the class, ask them how they feel about it and, if it is a problem, what they can do about it. Teachers are often reluctant to do this for fear of embarassing the student. I have done it consistently over the years and have yet to find a student who is unwilling to talk. In fact, they always seem quite relieved that I have raised the subject and interested to pursue the topic even though I always give plenty of opportunities to change the subject.

# Possible Cause 2: Group is too large

Obviously, the larger the group the less time there is for each person to speak. Group size is a problem for interaction in general because as the group becomes larger most students are increasingly reluctant to speak up. But group size offers a special problem for sharing among speakers. This fact is intuitively obvious if you consider the smallest possible group, the dyad, or two person group. Even the most inveterate monopolizers of conversation have to pause for a breath now and then, providing an opportunity for the listener to enter. Failing that, the listener can stop listening, turn away, grimace, or do whatever is needed to stem the tide of words. Those strategies are weakened if one other person joins the conversation. The speaker might simply turn to the remaining listener and continue. And they are further weakened in a group of 20. Smaller groups allow the less assertive students more room to enter a discussion.

### Suggestion 1: Reduce the size of the group

See page 95.

### Suggestion 2: Try pairing learners at the beginning

See page 96.

## Possible Cause 3: Ground rules are lacking or not followed

A lack of ground rules for group process can lead to unequal participation.

### Suggestion 1: Make ground rules explicit

Every group has ground rules for interaction, but they are not always explicit and they are not always helpful to the learning process. The ground rules regulate matters such as how the air time is to be shared, how long each speaker may hold the floor, whether and how speakers can be interrupted, and so on. It is useful to arrive at an agreement about these ground rules early in the development of the group, and to make them explicit.

Another way to create ground rules is to discuss them with students, as one teacher did here: "I find that the small groups go much more smoothly if students are in agreement with a set of ground rules for small group process. I think it will be worth our while to take 15 or 20 minutes to discuss the following questions: how do we let the less assertive (or more polite) students get into the conversation? How do we interrupt someone? How long should each person hold the floor?"

Rather than leave the ground rules open for discussion, you may wish to lay down rules you have found to be conducive to good process. Whatever you do, be sure to summarize the agreement and restate it for the next several meetings until the set of norms has been established.

## Possible Cause 4: Intolerance of silence

The universal physical principle embodied in the saying "Nature abhors a vacuum" manifests itself in the small group where it becomes "Groups abhor silence." Someone will always jump in to fill any space and they will often be the same persons every time, the ones whose tolerance for silence is lowest.

### Suggestion 1: Explain the positive role of silence

Discuss the positive role that silence can play in group process in signaling everyone that the group has patience and will wait for contributors who need to think before they can speak. You may need to do this several times before group members begin to see that it works, but this will be a valuable learning experience for everyone.

### Suggestion 2: Accept silence, both in yourself and others

Be a model of accepting silence. Don't appear uncomfortable during a silence, or rush to fill it. People's worst fear of silence is that it will freeze everyone with panic. Indicate that silence is a period of thinking. If you decide to break a silence, do so in a manner which reveals that the silent time has been well spent: "What I was thinking just now is that our approach may have been limited because of some facts that were missing."

### Suggestion 3: Provide specific training

Again, I will refer to a specific training programme such as that developed by Jean Rudduck (see pages 66 to 68). The pertinent exercise, for the problem of silence, is asking students to wait three seconds after the previous person has spoken before speaking themselves. If students can learn to pause for a few seconds after the previous speaker has finished, there will be enough time for less assertive speakers to enter the discussion.

## Possible Cause 5: Dominant speakers monopolize the discussion

Teachers often react to dominating speakers with anger and hostility, probably because domination violates their cherished values of fairness and politeness, their sense of control in the classroom, or leads them to blame themselves for being too weak to confront aggression. But the dominant speaker is rarely an aggressive bully. Usually he is someone who simply doesn't think that people are listening and says it again. The best strategy is to find out what is going on and act accordingly.

### Suggestion 1: Talk to the dominating speaker privately

The first thing to do is to find out why the student is talking so much and whether he or she is aware of doing it. The typical student, in my experience, is not aware of dominating the discussion, but talks too much or too assertively because he or she is an outgoing person by nature, thinks that people have not heard or fully appreciated the point, or feels a need to compete with other assertive speakers. Talking to this person privately accomplishes at least two things: first, it serves as a reminder of your mutual responsibility to provide an opportunity for all of the students to take part in the conversation. Second, and possibly more important, it serves to let the person know that you noticed him or her. In some cases this kind of recognition is enough to reduce the student's need to dominate the conversation. When the need to dominate is more persistent, other measures may be required (see Chapter 9).

### Suggestion 2: Use specific training

Specific training in sharing speaking time may be useful. Jean Rudduck (1978) gets students to take part in discussion exercises in which each speaker is limited to 15 seconds per contribution. A timekeeper is appointed to signal the intervals. After several training sessions of this kind, students have a better idea of what 15 seconds feels like and they have experienced the pleasure of a fast-moving discussion. It doesn't take the group long to develop the habit of 15-second bursts, once they begin to appreciate that everyone can speak and that ideas flow more quickly when people speak for short periods of time.

### Suggestion 3: Assign a task to the dominant speaker

The dominant speaker may become more sensitive to differences in speaking time and the importance of sharing time if he or she is assigned to keep track of the pattern of conversation. This person, for example, could be the timekeeper in the exercise above.

### Suggestion 4: Short-circuit dominating speakers by passing the ball to someone else

Sometimes the group leader has to take action right away, during the class, to control dominant speakers. I once led an ethics seminar attended by people from all positions in the health care hierarchy. Sadly, the predictable thing happened. The chief of a powerful medical department began to dominate the conversation. He spoke without raising his hand while others had their hands up waiting to be recognized. I tried the advice I have been giving faculty for years. I cut him off, but in a friendly but unequivocal way: "I have to cut you off Dr. Blank because there was a hand up before you. [point to the hand] Yes?" The fact that I still have my job attests to the success of this method. The idea is to make the move impersonally, in the course of fulfilling your role as group leader.

It is more difficult to cut off the dominant speaker when no one else's hand is raised and when everyone else is about to fall asleep. Here you run the risk of drawing attention to the dominant speaker and of embarrassing him or her, thus creating a climate in which all students might hesitate to speak lest you embarrass them too. My solution to this problem is to cut off the speaker but pass the ball to someone else. It is difficult to explain this but easy to illustrate. Do not say:

**1.** "John, I think we should give someone else a chance."
**2.** "I have to remind you about the ground rules . . ." Also, do not:
**3.** Look at your watch and frown, or
**4.** look impatient and uneasy, fidget, and look away from the speaker to discourage him or her.

In my experience all of the above will either exacerbate the problem or frighten the group. Instead, you might try one of the following:

**1.** [Talking over John's voice] "John . . . before . . . before you go on to another point I'd like to get some reaction to what you have already said and to hear other ideas that your comments and others have provoked. Marcie, you viewed this issue in a little different way, if I heard you correctly, or Tim. Can we hear from one of you?"
**2.** [Again, talking over John's voice] "You have . . . you have given us a lot to think about. I saw several others giving me signals that they would like to jump in at this point."
**3.** [Interrupting] John has raised an interesting point which everyone wants to address, so let's be brief so that there is time for everyone to speak."
**4.** "I'd like to offer the suggestion that you've taken this issue as far as you can, you see both sides and this is good. But you may get more value out of turning now to . . . ."
**5.** [To show the student whom you had to cut off several times that you really bore no hard feelings toward him or her, said with a friendly smile.] "That's three times you were trying to get in on me and I didn't let you."

In my experience, some variation of the above will be easier for the dominant speaker to take and less frightening to the group. Your emphasis has not been on the transgression but on the need to continue the interaction. The spirit that you try to establish is that you are not ignoring John or unhappy with him. You are just performing your job as seminar leader. You are delighted with his energy and enthusiasm, but you will continue to exercise your obligation as group leader.

## Suggestion 5: Take a turn around the group

This is a frequently used method of forcing dominant speakers to share their time with everyone else. This strategy shares the drawback of so-called icebreakers: the natural flow of conversation is broken by an artificial device. The tenth speaker may be bursting to answer the first speaker but has to wait her turn. Meanwhile, the first nine speakers may not even be interested in the topic, but they would be if they heard the controversial issue that the tenth speaker would have said if we had let her jump the queue. Another problem with the fixed turn-around-the-table strategy is that students tend not to listen while they are scraping the barrel for something to say. It is better to wait until they have something to say.

I would rather not interfere with group motivation by a strategy that requires students to speak in some rigid order unrelated to their desire to speak. A better way would be simply to wait until several had addressed the issue and then ask, "Are there others who would like to address this issue? Who has not yet had a chance to address this issue?"

On the other hand, if you have had success with this strategy, then stick with it for a few sessions. Don't get discouraged if at first it produces only embarrassed "Why me?" responses. The first time serves notice to everyone that a turn around the table is a possibility in your classes. From that time on students will listen more carefully and actively — they will not be caught with nothing to say the second time.

## Suggestion 6: Separate the extroverts from the introverts

Extroverts are likely to dominate introverts in a discussion if the two personality types are mixed in one group. Dayton Roberts of Texas Tech told me about dramatic improvements in a discussion after he used the Myers-Briggs Type Indicator to split his class into two groups, the extroverts in one, the introverts in the other (1987).

## Suggestion 7: Use feedback on group process

In the previous suggestion, I pointed out that a greater awareness of the group's pattern of communication might help the dominant speaker understand and curb excessive speaking. This kind of awareness is probably valuable to all members of the group, since the responsibility for group interaction rests more with the entire group than with any one individual. One way to reveal the pattern of communication to a group is to audiotape or videotape their discussion and play it back to them.

To prevent students from becoming so nervous about videotaping that it disrupts the learning process, I would recommend the following:

**1.** Assure students that the tapes will be wiped out as soon as they are discussed and that no permanent record will be kept.

**2.** Tape only a small portion of the dialogue, say 10 minutes.

**3.** Replay it immediately and discuss it.

**4.** Elicit the students' comments and suggestions.

**5.** Tape a second time and replay it again.

**6.** Admit your own shortcomings, mistakes, as group leader. Say what you would do to improve.

**Suggestion 8: Deal with students whose personalities include a strong drive to dominate others or to continually seek attention**

Part Three is devoted to difficult students and personality difficulties such as compulsive talking.

# Possible Cause 6: Silent students

Most people are occasionally inhibited from speaking in a group for some reason or another — aggressive or competitive classmates, a difficult topic, unsympathetic listeners, or our own lack of energy. It is usually possible to draw occasionally silent students into the discussion by means of the common techniques for encouraging interaction. However, the students I am speaking of in this section are those who rarely speak in class even under ideal conditions. Special effort must be taken to understand and help these students.

**Suggestion 1: Find out why some people are silent and co-operate with them**

The first step is to try to understand the silent student. I have found that there is no single "type" of silent student. Students may be silent for a number of reasons.

Students have different speaking frequencies with which they feel comfortable. Some have quiet personalities. They do not regard themselves as silent, they do not feel shut out of the conversation, and they are actively participating while speaking only rarely or using very few words when they do speak. They don't talk any more outside than they do in class. The actual frequency of speaking is probably less important than the opportunity to speak when one wants to. As long as students are not being short changed, we should recognize their individual speech patterns and not pester them.

Cultural reasons cause some students to be more quiet than others in class. One student, who was from a Caribbean country, told me that her early schooling had not encouraged her to talk. A Chinese student said the same. These two were very talkative outside class, but had almost nothing to say in class. Both suggested that they would appreciate help in making it easier for them to enter the conversation, because they felt that the other students were having more fun and it would be easier to maintain attention, they thought, if they talked occasionally.

There are students who are silent because of shyness, feelings of inferiority, or other conditions they would like to overcome. I have talked with a number of these students about things each of us could do in class to help them overcome their inhibition about speaking. For example, I told one student about my use of questions to draw her out. She looked terrified, as if I was intending to embarrass her in front of the class. So I tried it out on her right there after class in the one-to-one situation. I asked her about her career choice.

The next week in class I asked her a question. She knew what was coming and that I was trying to help her, and she did not panic. After a few tries it became easier for her to talk in class.

All of these strategies, whether aimed at an individual student or at the group as a whole, are much more effective if they have the co-operation of the person you are intending to help.

## Suggestion 2: Ask questions

This topic is addressed on pages 31 to 34, but at this point I would like to reiterate a few of the ideas that are of most help to the silent student:

**1.** Ask questions which are easy to answer.

**2.** Follow up on your questions with the silent student. Don't just drop Jane after the first "yes" or "no" answer. Make sure she is well connected with the topic before you go on. For example, "I see, you're arguing against the idea. For similar reasons as Carlo, or did you have another reason?"

**3.** Use open-ended questions so that the person can say a little more than just yes or no: "What do you think?"

**4.** Beware not to push too hard with your line of questioning or you might make the student feel defensive.

## Suggestion 3: Create an accepting environment

We all create accepting environments in our day-to-day life by smiling, making eye contact, humour, and so on. But if we try to analyze expressions such as smiling, for example, we find that their role in human communication is very complicated and subtle. Dr. Janice Porteous, a post-doctoral fellow in the Department of Philosophy at the University of Toronto, who has studied the origin of smiling in primates, has concluded that the smile originated in a fear response or a submissive response (1989). It is a sign of vulnerability and non-hostility, which lets other members of the species know that the smiler will not attack. But before we interpret smiling as a universal sign of friendship, consider Jack Nicholson, in the film "The Shining." He does a lot of smiling and making eye contact in this film but is terrifying! Actors know that a smile can mean almost anything depending on the context.

The key to understanding the impact of your expressions and of the atmosphere you create in your classroom is in the eyes of the beholders. Find out how your students perceive the psychological environment of the class, particularly the degree of threat, severity, criticism, or acceptance. It is difficult to extract this kind of subtle information by the use of a questionnaire. I recommend interviews with the class in the teacher's absence.

## Suggestion 4: Get to know the silent student

In order to connect the topic to the students' interests or abilities, you need to know what they are. McKeachie (1983) suggested that the first assignment be a brief life history including the students' interests and experiences. He uses these autobiographies to glean enough information about individual students to select examples that are relevant to their life experiences and to discover what special knowledge each one may have. He recommends asking non-participants to contribute in a problem area in which they have special knowledge. Although I prefer what I call the conversational introduction, McKeachie's suggestion is an excellent supplement. The more knowledge you have about your students the better. But I would not like to see a kind of "Big Brother" situation in which I held all the information and everyone else knew nothing about one another, or about me.

## Suggestion 5: Invite silent students into the discussion

Many non-participants would like to join the discussion but are not assertive enough to make it on their own. They give the usual cues that they would like to say something, for example, taking a breath audibly as if preparing to speak, making eye contact with the speaker, raising their heads or eyebrows, or even beginning to speak. You can make sure that someone like this gets the floor. It's not a good idea to wait until there is a silence. By then the point that the silent student wanted to make would surely have been made by someone else. I would interrupt, especially if a few students have been dominating the conversation. I wouldn't worry about losing continuity. Discussions have a certain logical direction of their own, and if one person is delayed in making the next point it will usually be made by someone else. Besides, we must remember that the real goal is to ensure that the students learn, not that they conduct a perfect conversation.

Breaking into a discussion can be done very simply with a smile to indicate that you are enjoying the discussion but are asking for a brief pause: "Hold it for a minute. There are a few people who have been trying to say something. If they wait too long their points won't be relevant anymore."

# Possible Cause 7: Cliques

A small group can take on a dominant or silent role just as an individual can, and by their force of number can be much more dominant and more difficult to deal with than an individual. A dominant clique can ignore the rest of the group, and a withdrawing clique can enjoy its own snide remarks, "in jokes," and side comments. The members of the clique may feel quite superior to the rest of the group and see no need to change their intentionally disruptive behavior. I shall discuss how to deal with this in Part Three. For the purpose of this chapter, let's assume that the clique is merely a bit insensitive rather than ill-intentioned. What can we do?

### Suggestion 1: Split them up

The standard high school solution is to split up the clique. I guess it's a solution of sorts. But by splitting up the clique you label it as bad and dissipate its energy instead of harnessing it to help the group achieve a lively and co-operative spirit. I would rather enjoy the clique than destroy it.

### Suggestion 2: Ask them to share with the group

Since we are talking here about a well-meaning group, not a goon squad, a direct approach might work. I have never tried this myself but it sounds reasonable. If anyone who reads this tries it, please let me know how you made out. I would indicate to the clique that I was enjoying their humor, friendship, and comaraderie. The spirit of my comments would be "too bad we all can't share your group spirit." This approach would have been appropriate in a math class I once observed where a clique of engineers were making it clear to everyone that they were something special. The teacher handled the schism badly by taking sides with the arts and science students against the engineers. He practically called them goons, which they found vastly flattering. He might have done better to have tried something like the following:

*Teacher* [Smiling and looking a bit reflective]: You know, one of the goals of a small group is to achieve a kind of ease and humor with one another that comes from trust and friendship. We have a good example of it here in the engineering group [pointing vaguely to where they are seated and turning to them]. I hope that as we get on into the year some of your spirit will infuse into the rest of the group.

*Engineering student:* Yeah. We need more engineers!

*Teacher:* I hope it's not that. One of the values of small group learning is that it allows students from various programs to get to know each other better; I'd like to think that we can all get to know and enjoy one another. I'm asking the engineering group especially to make an effort to include others.

### Suggestion 3: Treat the clique as an individual

The suggestions in this chapter for individuals apply equally well to a clique: finding out why they are dominating or withdrawn, getting to know them individually, questioning, videotaping and discussing the tape, and so on. If they *are* acting silly, a videotape is usually embarrassing for them.

### Suggestion 4: Don't get into a personal scrap with them

Whatever you do, don't take on a clique. Some primitive instinct causes an in-group to solidify under pressure from an outsider. Some of the ugliest behavior I have ever seen in a classroom was caused by students saving face in front of their peers. They might say things that they would regret having said and you would regret driving them to say it. Unless, of course, the group is already pretty ugly. Then turn to Part Three.

## Possible Cause 8: Sexism, racism, and other forms of discrimination

Unfortunately, unequal participation is sometimes caused by the exclusion of students because of their sex or ethnicity. In countries like Canada and the United States, widespread sentiment against discrimination based on sex, race, or religion allows people to believe that discrimination of this kind does not exist. But it does; it is often subtle, and it deprives students of quality education.

Susan is a shy person with a very soft voice. She made a comment in class that went unacknowledged. About 20 minutes later, when Ralph made a similar comment, there were many responses. For the rest of the period the teacher referred to the comment as "Ralph's point," without recognizing the fact that Susan had said it first. Susan withdrew from the conversation in anger and frustration. She told me this story, adding that she wanted to tell everyone that it was her point, but that would have sounded petty and competitive. What difference did it make who had the idea first? On the other hand, she just couldn't bring herself to enter a debate about "Ralph's point" when Ralph got the idea from her. She did not dramatize the point because she doesn't think very much of her ideas because no one ever recognizes them. If I recall, Susan had put the idea in the form of a question, something like, "Why don't we try. . . ?" whereas Ralph had grabbed everyone's attention before he even introduced the idea. He started something like this: "I've got it! We should. . . ."

My interpretation of this situation is that no one in the group, not even the teacher or Ralph himself, was aware of who had planted the seed for the idea into the group. They were not being malicious. They were simply acting out one kind of discrimination that still exists against women.

Dieter, who was born in West Germany and retains a slight German accent, remained silent throughout a discussion which dealt with a part of history in which Germany played an important role. He told me later that he didn't enter the discussion because he is tired of other students characterizing him as a Nazi and making fun of him no matter what he says. "What am I supposed to say, that Germany deserved the bombing of Dresden because of the atrocities? Dresden was an atrocity itself. My parents died there."

What can the teacher do in these situations?

## Suggestion 1: Keep track of contributions of participants

Make a diagram of the class with a small circle for each participant. During the class you can annotate the diagram with abbreviated notes indicating who said what. At the appropriate moment you can recall Susan's authorship of the point.

## Suggestion 2: Use assertiveness training

This suggestion is aimed specifically at discrimination against the unassertive speaker who is being passed over in class. The unassertive speaker is often a woman, because women are socialized to be more polite than men, and politeness is mistaken for weakness.

I don't expect the average teacher to conduct assertiveness training classes, but any teacher can address the specific problems of assertiveness that arise in small group teaching. Unassertive speakers, for example, tend to end sentences with a rising inflection as if they were asking a question, or to tack a question on the end. In answer to a question asking for an explanation for a fungus epidemic in the northern forests, one student said: "The amount of rainfall? Isn't the amount of rainfall important too?" Unassertive speakers include more qualifiers and built-in apologies in their speech: "I think it's probably a question of rainfall too, although I really am not sure." And unassertive speakers wait until others have spoken and use less emphatic language when they do speak.

These characteristics of unassertive speech could be raised for discussion and class members could suggest ways to overcome the problem. If you have observed and noted examples from your class, use them to illustrate the points. Nothing is more powerful than examples people have experienced first hand.

## Suggestion 3: Raise awareness gently

People may not be aware of or may not recognize discrimination when it occurs. When the teacher feels the need to point it out, therefore, it can be more productive to do so gently. For example, in the case of Dieter:

Teacher: "I get the impression from some of the comments that Dieter was the Vice Chancellor of Germany of the last war. Funny Dieter, you don't look old enough. How old were you in 1944?"
Dieter: "Three."
Teacher: "What are your memories of Germany and the war?"
Dieter: "All I know is what my uncle and aunt told me — that my father was a printer, my mother was an editor, and that they both were killed in Dresden during the bombing."

# Possible Cause 9: Student presentations

This option was mentioned before on page 83. Student presentations are useful learning strategies because they get the presenters actively involved and provide information on which to base the discussion, but unless you make plans to prevent it, there is a danger that the presenters will do all the talking.

## Suggestion 1: Restrict the presentation time to 10 to 15 minutes with 10 minutes of question time

See to it that presentations are brief. Additional material can be handed out to students in the form of selected articles or point form summaries. We all must learn to condense information in these times of information explosion.

## Suggestion 2: Use student discussants

Give as many students as possible an active part to play. Appoint student discussants to respond to the presentation and give them clear guidelines for what they have to do. These guidelines should note the need to read assigned material, the fact that the function of a discussant is to address no more than one or two of the presenter's points, indicating agreement, disagreement, or omissions, and that, above all, the discussant's comments should be brief.

## Suggestion 3: Demonstrate and discuss the active role of the audience

If you do not want to appoint specific students as discussants, you can secure widespread participation by making it clear that anyone in the class is welcome to respond to a presentation. Students may hesitate to ask questions bcause they don't want to appear critical of their fellow students. Part of your job is to identify and deal with these inhibitions.

I would begin by explaining to students that it is natural to feel inhibited about responding to your classmates' presentations, especially critically, but that it is important for presenters to receive honest feedback in order to improve. Then I might try an exercise aimed at disinhibition, such as requiring each student, in turn, to make one criticism and one comment in praise of the presentation. If the class is really timid, it might be useful to begin by gathering comments about your own presentation, so that they can see that even teachers' presentations can be criticized. If you have the time, an excellent method of ensuring that the interchange between presenters and audience is constructive and positive is to allow the speaker to repeat the presentation after making changes based on the feedback. Students' recognition of the improvement from first to second try — often a striking improvement — is encouraging for presenters and stimulates more comments from the audience in subsequent sessions.

### Suggestion 4: Assign credit for the quality of the discussion or its product, not for the presentation

Presentations should not turn into a contest between the presenters or between presenters and the audience. The purpose of presentations is to foster co-operative learning. The audience has an active role in this co-operation, and the reward structure should reflect this role. The listeners help to make the learning valuable by their questions and discussion. The presenters should try to engage discussion.

### Suggestion 5: Remind the presenters to have questions for the audience

An excellent scholarly presentation begins with a problem, presents the researchers' solutions, and ends by inviting the audience to tackle problems that remain unsolved. This is not only an excellent research technique, it gives the audience something to bite into, and it increases active participation. Suggest to the presenters in your class that they raise some unsolved problems or unanswered questions.

### Suggestion 6: Encourage presenters to focus and simplify

Presenters need to narrow their topics. They should be able to talk about something specific and concrete. The audience can then enter more easily. If the topic is by nature complex, encourage students to begin with a case or example so that listeners will have something to attach their thoughts to.

## Possible Cause 10: No interest in speaking

Until this point I have assumed that non-participating students would like to participate more. This is not always so. Some students don't feel like participating. One student told me it takes too much effort; he had a graduate degree in biochemistry before he came to medical school and he really doesn't think it fair that he has to teach others. Another said that she learns more when she listens than when she talks. She argued that it's her education and she doesn't feel obliged to participate if it doesn't help her learn.

I had mixed feelings after listening to these people. First, I was relieved because they were not suffering and did not present me with a problem. But I was also uneasy, because I think of small group teaching and learning as more co-operative than they seemed to. Many courses, my own course on educational development included, would be severely diminished if it weren't for the generous contributions of many talented and experienced students. I believe that those who refuse to participate may short change other students.

### Suggestion 1: Talk to the withdrawing students about helping others

You may believe that knowledgeable but withdrawing students could be very helpful to the learning of everyone else. Talk to them about it. Whenever I have done this, the students have been flattered and delighted to share the teaching role. Although one of them became rather obnoxious, the others have made enriching contributions.

### Suggestion 2: Don't fix it if it ain't broke

On the other hand, if some of the more experienced students hold back, they leave more air time for others who may need it. As a teacher, you can be happy that an atmosphere has been established in which students don't feel obliged to show off their knowledge and monopolize the conversation. If the situation works, leave things alone.

## References

Ackerman, V., & Bayliss, C. (1989). Personal communication.

Amidon, E.J., & Flanders, N.A. (1967). *The role of the teacher in the classroom*. Minneapolis: Association for Productive Teaching.

Bergquist, W.H., & Phillips, S.R. (Eds.). (1975). *A handbook for faculty development*. Washington, DC: The Council for the Advancement of Small Colleges.

Bergquist, W.H., & Phillips, S.R. (Eds.). (1977). *A handbook for faculty development, Vol. 2*. Washington, DC: The Council for the Advancement of Small Colleges.

Bligh, D.A. (1972). *What's the use of lectures?* (3rd ed.). Hertfordshire, England: Penguin.

British Columbia Teachers' Federation. (1970). *The use of discussion groups for exploration purposes* (off-set litho pamphlet).

Byrne, N. (1989). Personal communication.

Byrne, P.N. & Taylor, I. (1989).  Personal communication.

Flanders, N.A. (1970). *Analyzing teaching behavior.* Reading, MA: Addison-Wesley.

Geis, G.L. (1976). Student participation in instruction: Student choice. *Journal of Higher Education, 47*(3), 249–273.

Hunt, D.E. (1987). *Beginning with ourselves: In practice, theory and human affairs.* Cambridge, MA: Brookline.

Kindsvatter, R., & Wilen, W.W. (1977). Improving classroom instruction: A self- and shared-analysis approach. In S.C. School & S.C. Inglis (Eds.), *Teaching in higher education: Readings for faculty.* Columbus: Ohio Board of Regents, pp. 307–331.

Lorraine, H. (1974). *How to develop a super power memory.* New York: Signet.

McKeachie, W. (1986). *Teaching tips: A guidebook for the beginning college teacher* (8th ed.). Toronto: D.C. Heath.

Orme, M.E.J. (1973). *Teaching strategies kit.* Toronto: The Ontario Institute for Studies in Education.

Pfeiffer, J.W., & Jones, J.E. (1985). *Reference guide to handbooks and annuals.* San Diego, CA: University Associates.

Pirsig, R.M. (1974). *Zen and the art of motorcycle maintenance.* New York: Bantam.

Porteus, J. (1989). Personal communication.

Powell, J.P. (1974). Small group teaching methods in higher education. *Educational research, 16*(3), 163–171.

Rasmussen, R. (1984). Practical discussion techniques for educators. *The Journal of the Alberta Association for Continuing Education, 12*(2), 38–47.

Roberts, D. (1987). Personalizing the learning climate. A workshop given at the 12th Annual Meeting of the Professional and Organizational Developers Network in Higher Education, Kerville, Texas, October 12–15.

Rudduck, J. (1978). *Learning through small group discussion.* Surrey, Guildford, England: University of Surrey.

Taylor-Way, D. G. & Brinko, K. T. (1989). Using video recall for improving professional competency in instructional consultation. In S. Kahn et al. (Eds.) *To improve the Academy, Volume 8.* Stillwater, Oklahoma: New Forums Press.

Taylor-Way, D.G., & Holmes, S. (1987). Using videotape in faculty consultation. Workshop presented at the 12th Annual Conference of the Professional and Organizational Development Network in Higher Education, Kerrville, Texas, October 12–15.

Weimer, M., Parrett, J. L., & Kerns, M. M. (1988). *How am I teaching? Forms and activities for acquiring instructional input.* Madison, WI: Magna Publications.

# Part Three/ Group Motivation and Emotion

## Troubleshooting Guide

### Chapter Seven: Students Are Tuned Out /144

Possible cause 1: Little interest in the subject /145
    Suggestion 1: Explore students' personal motivation to study the subject matter /145
    Suggestion 2: Address students' professional motivation: make sure the course is relevant /145
    Suggestion 3: Tap into students' values /146
    Suggestion 4: Tap into students' experiences /147
    Suggestion 5: Don't just *tell* students that a topic is relevant or interesting; present evidence /147
    Suggestion 6: Deal with fear of failure: make sure students know what to do in order to pass the course /147
    Suggestion 7: Emphasize the beauty of the subject /148
    Suggestion 8: Engage students in problem solving /148

Suggestion 9: Allow time for students to give personal meaning to ideas or concepts /148
Suggestion 10: Make it fun /148

Possible cause 2: Lack of diversity of opinion /149

Possible cause 3: Disparities in student ability level /149
Suggestion 1: Divide the students by ability level /149
Suggestion 2: Divide the curriculum into parts requiring different ability levels /150
Suggestion 3: Encourage the more able students to help the less able /150

Possible cause 4: Relevance of the group process is unclear /150

Possible cause 5: Ground rules are unclear /151
Suggestion 1: Discuss the specific ground rules /151
Suggestion 2: Don't hesitate to change the ground rules if they are not working /152

Possible cause 6: Poor time management /152

Possible cause 7: Too long without a break /152
Suggestion 1: When attention fades, suggest a break /152
Suggestion 2: Include breaks in the ground rules /152

Possible cause 8: Media and handouts distract instead of contributing /153
Suggestion 1: Hand the stuff out right away /153
Suggestion 2: Use visual aids as conversation starters /153

Possible cause 9: Students are unrewarded for participating /154

Possible cause 10: Student preoccupation with the exam /154
Suggestion 1: Address the exam agenda #1: Deal with worry about the exam /154
Suggestion 2: Address the exam agenda #2: Define the small group activity as useful for the exam /154
Suggestion 3: Address the exam agenda #3: Remind students that there is more to the course than can be evaluated on exams /155

**Chapter Eight: Teacher Is Tuned Out /156**

Possible cause 1: Lack of institutional support for teaching /157
Suggestion 1: Support teaching too /157
Suggestion 2: Create a spectrum of career arrangements to match various staff talents /158
Suggestion 3: Relate promotion and tenure decisions to talent /158

Suggestion 4: Document teaching activities /158
Suggestion 5: Reward excellence in teaching /159

Possible cause 2: Disruptive or unco-operative students
demoralize you /159
Suggestion 1: Consider co-operative interaction as a
metaphor for teaching and learning /160
Suggestion 2: Team teaching can solve the problem of a
narrow conception of teaching /161

Possible cause 3: Lack of feedback from students /161
Suggestion 1: Learn about feedback techniques /162
Suggestion 2: Broaden your concept of feedback /162

Possible cause 4: Constraints on teacher's freedom /163
Suggestion 1: Plan tutorial sections on exams /163
Suggestion 2: Do not allow team efforts to stifle individual
initiative /163
Suggestion 3: There is more to the course than can be
evaluated /164

Possible cause 5: Lack of stimulation /164
Suggestion 1: Maintain a support group /165
Suggestion 2: Join professional associations and attend their
conferences /165
Suggestion 3: Read /166
Suggestion 4: Take a break from teaching /166
Suggestion 5: Separate the major goals in your life /166

Possible cause 6: Teacher penalized for increased
productivity /167
Suggestion 1: Replace rigid course schedules with incentives
for efficiency /167
Suggestion 2: Replace norm-reference exams with criterion-
referenced exams /168

Possible cause 7: Negative attitude toward students /169
Suggestion 1: Get to know some of your students informally
/170
Suggestion 2: Try role reversal /70

**Chapter Nine: Students Do Not Co-operate /171**

Possible cause 1: Students do not accept the assumptions of the
course /172
Suggestion 1: Rethink the assumptions of the discipline /172
Suggestion 2: Don't let discussion of the presuppositions
replace the content /172

Possible cause 2: Students challenge the teacher's authority /173
  Suggestion 1: Have a constructive response ready /174
  Suggestion 2: If the challenge is constructive, give the students control /174
  Suggestion 3: If the challenge is destructive, do not give them control /175

Possible cause 3: Heated disagreements among students: Strong feelings or interpersonal hostility /175
  Suggestion 1: Prevent disagreement from degenerating into polemic /175
  Suggestion 2: Keep the disagreement impersonal by using perception checks /176
  Suggestion 3: Don't try to resolve a personal argument or take sides /177
  Suggestion 4: Use the tools of your discipline to deal with the disagreement /177
  Suggestion 5: Resist settling arguments by authority /177
  Suggestion 6: Use disagreement to teach negotiation skills /178

Possible cause 4: Excessive competitiveness among students /179
  Suggestion 1: Expose competitive behavior /179
  Suggestion 2: Expose some of the common power moves /179
  Suggestion 3: Arrange for co-operative learning /180
  Suggestion 4: Set up co-operative evaluations /181
  Suggestion 5: Do not reward competition in the group /182
  Suggestion 6: Split the group into pairs /182

Possible cause 5: Disruptive behavior: Power or attention seeking, deceit, evasions /182
  Suggestion 1: Discuss the disruption privately with the student /183
  Suggestion 2: Help the student become aware of disruptive behavior by describing it /183
  Suggestion 3: Help the student become aware of disruptive behavior by on-the-spot cueing /184
  Suggestion 4: Assign an observer role to the disturbing student /184
  Suggestion 5: Ask students to take different roles /184
  Suggestion 6: Confront the student /185
  Suggestion 7: Intervene tactfully without previous agreement with the student /186
  Suggestion 8: The last resort /187

Possible cause 6: Students' insensitivity to the feelings of other students /188
    Suggestion 1: Respond to emotional messages too /188
    Suggestion 2: Inquire into the nature of students' feelings /189

Possible cause 7: Students unaware of variations in conversational styles /189
    Suggestion 1: Don't assume that the offensive speakers have bad intentions /190
    Suggestion 2: Enlist the help of the offensive speakers /191
    Suggestion 3: Refer to suggestions about controlling dominant speakers in Chapter Six /191

Possible cause 8: Interfering emotional messages from the teacher /191
    Suggestion 1: Find out how your emotions are interpreted /192
    Suggestion 2: Explain the emotional side of your message too /192

**References for Part Three /193**

# 7/Students Are Tuned Out

*"They're bored. Their attention drifts. They fall asleep. They mumble apathetically. Many stay away and more leave early. You don't need training in human motivation to see that these people have lost interest. Why?"*

If the teacher doesn't want to teach or the students don't want to learn, not much learning will go on. Motivational problems are among the most difficult with which an educator has to deal. By inquiring into the reasons for students' lack of interest, you can sometimes discover ways to motivate them. After all, they have actually enrolled in the course — they must have had a good reason for doing so, and they have a stake in the course's going well.

In the following chapter, I discuss how you can explore students' motivation and your own and how such an analysis can lead to improvement in the climate of learning.

Because lack of motivation can be caused by the kinds of technical problems considered earlier, the contents of Part Three necessarily overlap, from time to time, with material discussed in previous chapters. I hope you will forgive me and not be too disconcerted when I refer you to previous sections.

# Possible Cause 1: Little interest in the subject

Students are frequently required to take courses they have not chosen. A psychology major who likes social psychology may loath the statistics course required to complete the program. An engineering student may hate a writing course. A history major may almost fail economics. The list is endless — and familiar to us all.

### Suggestion 1: Explore students' personal motivation to study the subject matter

Students often have more than one reason to study or not to study a subject. They may be afraid to fail or eager to excel. They may want to master the subject for its own sake or because it is relevant to practical needs. Some may be studying just for the fun of it.

I recommend that you first try to find out how your students feel about the subject matter. This information will not be easy to obtain because they will sense that you have a heavy personal investment in the course and may therefore be reluctant to talk frankly. For this reason, I suggest that you use a method of gathering feedback that guarantees confidentiality. For example, ask students to write their expectations for the course on 3x5 cards. Collect the cards and quickly read them aloud to the class. With that information, you are in a good position to address the discrepancies between your goals and the expectations of your students.

It is difficult to gather this sort of information in a face-to-face discussion since students may be reluctant to admit that they have chosen the wrong course. I was reminded of this reluctance two years ago in my course on improving teaching and learning. The course is not aimed at teaching teachers how to teach. But some of the students attend believing that they are going to get teaching tips. One of these people admitted: "You know, I lost all interest in your course on the first day when you said that we should not be here if we had come to learn how to teach. I felt like getting up and leaving the room, only I was too embarrassed. But during the course of the session you introduced material that caught my interest and I decided to give it a try. By the end of the second session I was hooked, so I stayed."

### Suggestion 2: Address students' professional motivation: make sure the course is relevant

For many students, passing the course is simply one of a number of tickets to professional credentials of some kind. This is particularly true of professional, technical, and trades people who may be pursuing a career goal from very early in their education and tend to become impatient with learning anything that appears unrelated to their careers. The central problem is that what you need to know to be *allowed* to practise your chosen profession is not necessarily identical with what you need to know to be *able* to practise it. It is important to point out to these people the connection between your subject matter and their careers.

Relevance is an important issue for medical students. Departments which have found ways to connect their subject matter with clinical practice can motivate their students, and the problem of relevance disappears entirely when the students begin to see real patients. It is informative to see how departments have changed. When pathology was an unpopular course, students perceived it as the study of dead organs in bottles. The redefinition of pathology as the study of the disease process relates it directly to the ultimate goal of caring for sick people. Histologists refer to their subject as the study of the building blocks of the body; linguistics teachers make a similar case to students of speech pathology.

There are those who argue that courses whose relevance is not easily demonstrable, such as writing in the schools of applied arts, should be dropped. Others say that they are important because of their contribution to a liberal education. An examination of the arguments for and against a liberal education is beyond the scope of this book.

## Suggestion 3: Tap into students' values

Although we may not know cearly what they are, we all have a set of legislative beliefs called "values." One of the most fruitful hours I have ever spent with a class was in a discussion of their values. I began by asking what the students wanted in life. Most answered, "A good job." For many of them, a good job meant money. "But what is the money for?" I asked. "You don't collect it, like a stamp collector." It turned out that money meant different things to different people. For some it meant the security to continue their work. For many it meant freedom from work so that they could play more, go sailing, enjoy good restaurants, and travel. But why is work, travel, eating, or sailing worthwhile? The group admitted that there was a point in the chain of justification beyond which they could give no further explanations. At the end of the chain they found a set of assumptions about what is worthwhile, beautiful, or fun. Many of them found that clarifying their values helped them see the connections between what they wanted and the goals of the course.

## Suggestion 4: Tap into students' experiences

Connect the course with the students' life experiences by suggesting possible examples from their own experience, by asking them to develop examples, and by using experiential learning, learning that is grounded in the actual experiences of the students rather than in abstract concepts. One of the advantages of a small group is that you can enlist the help of the students in personalizing the material by illustrating with examples from their everyday lives. For example, in a small group on the psychology of emotions, one teacher asked students to describe the situation when they last felt a particular emotion.

## Suggestion 5: Don't just tell students that a topic is relevant or interesting; present evidence

Relevance, importance, or interest are qualities that the listener can attribute to the topic. These are conclusions that the listener makes after hearing the evidence. By calling the material "relevant" you are usurping the students' right to make their own judgment. Don't say, "This is a very important idea in her work. . ." without adding, "Critics consider this one of the most important ideas in her work. . . " or, "I think it is one of her most important ideas. . ." or, "This idea has contributed significantly to the revolution in our thought about. . ." or, "This idea has often been cited by critics of. . . ."

## Suggestion 6: Deal with fear of failure: make sure students know what to do in order to pass the course

When students are afraid of failing a course, the only thing that they can think of is mere survival. Even students who start out with a keen interest in the subject matter can lose that interest if they become obsessed with passing. One student expressed the dilemma this way: "In high school I used to love math. I was the kind of student the other kids hated. I did all the extra problems at the end of the chapter. Then I came to university, failed the term test, and panicked. Now I'm just trying to survive. It's the same math but I have to force myself to study it."

This sort of shift in motivation can be explained by Maslow's (1970) theory of needs. Maslow maintains that our needs are arranged in a hierarchy, from such basic physiological needs as food, sleep, and security to higher needs like friendship, competence, and creativity. When a lower order need is not satisfied, we become stuck at that level and cannot move to a higher motivational level. Students who are afraid are stuck at the survival level and, like any animals who are threatened, they have little interest in creativity, play, or the beauty of the subject matter.

Your first approach, therefore, ought to be to assure students that they can pass and tell them exactly what they have to do to pass. If the course is math or statistics, pass out example problem sheets throughout the year and let them know that the exam will be made up of questions like those on the problem sheets. In arts courses you could give examples from previous exams. No surprises. If the students can handle the examples, they can pass the exam, and people who have trouble with the examples can have extra help.

## Suggestion 7: Emphasize the beauty of the subject

In *The Gentle Vengeance* (1981), Charles LeBaron wrote of his first year as a Harvard medical student. He presents a moving case for inspiring medical students by disclosing the beauty of the subject matter.

A colleague, Dolores Gold, who is a research psychologist, told me about a lecture on Calligula she had attended as a graduate student. She admitted that she had had no interest in the topic whatsoever and had attended simply because it was part of the colloquium series sponsored by her department. Yet the lecturer managed to make the subject so fascinating that he kindled in her a life-long curiosity for Roman history.

## Suggestion 8: Engage students in problem solving

This approach provides a real, relevant problem to focus on. For example, in a seminar on law, the teacher began: "If you were up in your summer cottage and passed a drowning swimmer, would you have an obligation to save him?" Put the cases so that the students are obliged to make a decision.

## Suggestion 9: Allow time for students to give personal meaning to ideas or concepts

It takes time to relate material to one's own experience or life. The small group is the ideal place to take this time. Encourage students to raise personal examples, to relate the ideas to their own experience, to apply the ideas and new information to problems in their own lives, and to phrase the ideas in their own language.

### Suggestion 10: Make it fun

Students overwhelmingly prefer small groups to large lectures — they are more fun. Primarily, "fun" means achieving a sense of accomplishment, feeling that they have learned something, and co-operating and sharing with each other (Byrne & Taylor, 1989). Many of the suggestions in this book are things that a small group leader can do to assure that students achieve a sense of accomplishment or a feeling of classroom co-operation.

Start by providing opportunities for students to interact. For example, they can break into study groups (see pages 95 and 96) or they can respond to each other's papers. One way to accomplish the latter is to ask each student to write a paragraph or two stating his or her position or response to an article or problem. Then ask pairs of students to exchange position papers, to read each other's papers, and write comments in the margins; finally, the pairs discuss their comments.

# Possible Cause 2: Lack of diversity of opinion

The members of the group may bore one another because they all think alike. This issue was discussed on pages 117 and 188.

# Possible Cause 3: Disparities in student ability levels

Weaker students may become discouraged or dependent on stronger students while stronger students may be bored or slowed down by weaker ones. Disparity in ability levels can be frustrating for everyone.

### Suggestion 1: Divide the students by ability level

Most college and university curricula are already organized into some form of hierarchy. Typical course descriptions include "beginning," "intermediate," or "advanced" language courses, "History 101" and "Graduate Seminars in History," "Introductory Math" and "Advanced Calculus," and so on. Moreoever, the system of prerequisite courses is designed to ensure similar academic background among students. Despite such efforts, however, even a small group of students will probably include wide variations in speed and style of learning. Should we further homogenize our groups? Should we, for example, offer special "accelerated" courses or "cram" courses for the fast learners so that we don't hold them back? And should we designate courses as "experiential" or "abstract" to accomodate different learning styles?

Bruno Bettelheim believes that we should not separate children by ability level. He argues that it is more important for children to learn co-operative skills and helping skills than for them to achieve the fastest possible intellectual progress. I think this argument holds for college level in the early undergraduate years when students need to learn about their ability and interest by comparison with those of others. I think that one of the most important pieces of information students can get from general courses is whether they have an extraordinary ability or interest in that particular area. People who learn in isolation, be it physical or intellectual, do not have the chance to make this discovery, as Bertrand Rusell, for example, who was educated by a nanny and tutors, noted in his autobiography.

### Suggestion 2: Divide the curriculum into parts requiring different ability levels

A less radical solution is to split up the curriculum into several parts, each requiring a different level of ability. For example, a tutorial could easily concentrate on basic concepts and examples for the first half and then more subtle applications for the second half.

### Suggestion 3: Encourage the more able students to help the less able

In the competitive atmosphere of our higher educational system there appears to be little motivation for the able student to help the less able. Although many of us believe that our lives would be improved if our society were more co-operative, we tend to be reluctant to take the first step for fear of being put at a disadvantage. But helping benefits both members of the interaction, and students need to be aware of that. Teaching something, for example, is an effective way to learn it, and communication skills and relationship skills involved in helping others may be as valuable to a person as mastery of a subject.

## Possible Cause 4: Relevance of the group process is unclear

Students can withdraw their energy from the group because they think that the group process is not useful. This is discussed in Chapter Three.

# Possible Cause 5: Ground rules are unclear

Students will withdraw from the game if they don't know how to play. The analogy with games is not a bad one. Twenty-two players fight over a soccer ball for an hour and a half when all of them could afford to buy soccer balls of their very own. In the heat of a fiercely contested game we don't realize how much co-operation underlies the play. Similarly, small group interaction is guided by a set of implicit or explicit rules: the roles of the teacher and the students, speaking times, interruptions, toleration of silence, and so on. If these rules are unknown or violated, the group cannot continue.

## Suggestion 1: Discuss the specific ground rules

Take 15 minutes to half an hour of the first class to reach an agreement with respect to the ground rules for group interaction. Begin by thinking carefully about an ideal set of ground rules for the objectives of your small group, based on your experience with past groups. To save class time, I would write up and hand out a set of ground rule issues along with your class plan on the first day. Invite students to add any additional issues and then discuss them one at a time.

Decisions about ground rules should always be influenced by the purpose of the group. For example, if one of the objectives of the group is to give everyone practice in talking about the issues, you might have a rule ensuring that everyone has an equal chance to speak. Summarize the decisions and make copies of them for the next meeting of the class.

Your discussion could go like this: The first question is, What are the functions of the small group leader? Which of the following functions do we want your group leader to perform?
**1.** Recognizing speakers by a show of hands (or should people speak whenever they want to?);
**2.** Keeping the group on topic, by summarizing, redirecting;
**3.** Ensuring that everyone has a chance to address a topic;
**4.** Facilitating clear communication by paraphrasing;
**5.** Connecting contributions from various students to the topic and to comments made by one another.

The second item is the selection of the small group leader. Who shall it be — the teacher, or students, perhaps on a rotating basis? The advantage of myself as group leader is that I can summarize and redirect the discussion when it gets off topic because I know what the major issues are. On the other hand, if students lead the group they will benefit by practising the skills of small group leadership while I would be freed of that duty to pay more attention to the content. Let's discuss this. . . .

Third, what are the rights and responsibilities of the participants? Let's discuss the following list:

**1.** Should we speak when there is an opening, or only when a raised hand is recognized by the chair?

**2.** Should we interrupt one another, or wait until someone is finished?

**3.** If we should interrupt, how should we?

**4.** About how long should each person speak at one time?

**5.** Should we reward one another for jobs well done?

### Suggestion 2: Don't hesitate to change the ground rules if they are not working

For example, after you have been leading the group for a few sessions, students may feel more confident about leading themselves. Don't hesitate to renegotiate the ground rules.

# Possible Cause 6: Poor time management

Time should be planned wisely, notice should be given in advance of how time will be spent, and then the schedule should be adhered to. See pages 29 and 30.

# Possible Cause 7: Too long without a break

There is no ideal time span between breaks in small group learning. Studies have showed that in a lecture situation attention wanes after the first five minutes and keeps declining until near the end of the period. The general wisdom about lecturing is to lecture for no more than 20 minutes at a stretch. But small groups are different. Participants are continually starting over again — reorganizing, redirecting the conversation, resetting the agenda — so the 20-minute rule doesn't apply. Besides, the stimulation of interacting with others keeps everyone awake. To demonstrate to yourself the arousing power of speaking, raise your hand to ask a question during a boring lecture. You will feel yourself wake up and your pulse quicken.

### Suggestion 1: When attention fades, suggest a break

Keep an eye out for failing attention. If attention appears to fade, ask students if they need a break.

### Suggestion 2: Include breaks in the ground rules

There is some benefit to including formal breaks in the ground rules, even if students decide not to take them when the time comes. Since group members tend to pace themselves, the expectation of a break has the effect of concentrating the group energy. Everyone works hard because they know the break is coming. Moreoever, there are times when people do not think of stopping but need to because their energy is down and they need a change.

## Possible Cause 8: Media and handouts distract instead of contributing

The most exciting event in a room is the lively exchange between the people. Handouts or slide shows should be used to stimulate conversation, not to replace it. A professor of social work brought a small pile of excellent pamphlets, brochures, and information sheets describing various community services and then proceeded to discuss with the students the very material that was contained in the brochures. The students told me later that it was maddening. They knew that the "answers" were face down on the table. They felt as though they were being treated like children and answered questions grudgingly. "Why can't he just give us the stuff?"

### Suggestion 1: Hand the stuff out right away

I recommend handing out anything that you have to hand out right at the beginning of the small group session. Some of my colleagues would argue that detailed, complex handouts may stifle the spontaneity of the group. Students will spend their time reading and trying to understand the material rather than taking part in the discussion. The answer is either to precirculate the material or to distribute it at the class and refer to it briefly so that students are not preoccupied with it. For example, you might say: "What you have in front of you is a chart of the major theories of human development. I will briefly summarize the theories in these articles and point out where they fit into the chart. As other theories come up, I'll point out how they fit into the chart. So don't be fussed by the chart just now. It will be useful to help you to recall and organize the theories we deal with today."

### Suggestion 2: Use visual aids as conversation starters

Use these aids to stimulate discussion, not to replace it. A plant pathologist uses a large number of slides of diseased trees in his lecture. The slides form a coherent pictorial essay, the first one of the outside of the tree, and the second revealing the inside so that the entry point and depth of penetration of the disease could be seen, and so on. The sequence is excellent for a lecture, but it would be inappropriate for a small group session because it leaves students in the dark, watching a performance. Instead, the tutorial might serve to answer questions about the mechanism of the disease or discuss methods of control. The teacher might show one or two in order to illustrate a point that is raised in the group and remind the group about the sequence.

## Possible Cause 9: Students are unrewarded for participating

Students will withdraw their energy from the group if there is nothing in it for them. See Chapter 3.

## Possible Cause 10: Student preoccupation with the exam

The effect of the exam is especially deadening in groups which are student initiated such as discussion sessions or question and answer periods because, if student motivation is dominated by the exam, there is no point listening to other students. The secret to passing the exam is to get the teacher to talk because only he or she knows what is important — meaning what is on the exam.

### Suggestion 1: Address the exam agenda #1: Deal with worry about the exam

One of the principles of effective communication is to address the other person's agenda before pursuing your own. People don't attend very well when they have to go to the washroom. The washroom agenda is an easy one to deal with, but the exam question isn't. If your course is organized so that students know exactly what they need to know in order to pass the exam, then they will be more able to control their anxiety and distraction from the exam.

### Suggestion 2: Address the exam agenda #2: Define the small group activity as useful for the exam

The purpose of some small groups is to review problem sets or to clarify difficult concepts which will be on the exam, goals which are entirely compatible with exam-oriented students. You may need to point this fact out if students do not realize it.

A more difficult situation occurs when lecture material is examined but tutorial material is not. To please the exam-oriented students, such tutorials have to be slavishly tied to the lecture, elaborating and clarifying points made in the lecture. Students who are not obsessed with the exam may find this deadly boring. One solution is to reserve a small section of the final exam for tutorial work. Tutorial leaders would contribute questions to that section related to the work of their tutorials. Students would answer only those questions relating to their own tutorials.

### Suggestion 3: Address the exam agenda #3: Remind students that there is more to the course than what can be evaluated on exams

Much of what is valuable about small group learning cannot be tested on an exam. The stimulation, the understanding of others' points of view, the practice thinking, the learning to interact and co-operate with others do not translate into essay exams or multiple choice exams. Sometimes students need to be reminded of these benefits of the small group. See Chapter 7.

# 8/Teacher is Tuned Out

*"It's no wonder I can't keep them awake. I can hardly keep myself awake."*

Every job has its hazards. I used to tell people I was a psychologist until I got tired of hearing about the personality problems of their children. Now I tell them I am a teaching improvement consultant and researcher. Their reactions are revealing.

Those who have had no experience with the university say they are glad to hear of its concern about teaching. Those who have had experience look at me, puzzled, and ask who pays my salary and why do the teachers use my services: do they volunteer for improvement programs or does the university require them to go? Colleagues in community colleges often ask why university professors would put themselves through the psychological risks and considerable effort of improving their teaching when it doesn't count. In the community colleges it is different. Teachers there are expected to teach, and their teaching performance is valued and evaluated. These colleagues believe, as do many other people, including undergraduates, that the university is not set up for teaching, that its priorities are reflected in an institutional reward system which punishes teaching.

Although lack of institutional reward is a major reason that teachers withdraw their energy from teaching, there are other killers of teacher motivation which affect universities, community colleges, and schools alike. The most frequent reason that any teachers request help with their teaching has nothing to do with promotion or achievement or a sense of ability; it is the fact that they have stopped enjoying teaching.

The difficulty that I am concerned with here manifests itself in teacher boredom and burnout: drifting attention, little interest or enthusiasm for subject or students, arriving late to class and leaving as soon as it is over.

## Possible Cause 1: Lack of institutional support for teaching

The support given to teaching varies greatly in institutions of higher learning. Community colleges and some small liberal arts colleges have a commitment to students that is unknown in many large research-oriented universities. The focus on students has been found to be one of the major factors in high faculty morale (Rice & Austin, 1988). Lack of support for teaching is costly for faculty and students alike.

### Suggestion 1: Support teaching too

This suggestion is directed more to departmental chairs, deans, and presidents than to individual teachers. I entitled the suggestion as I did because I intentionally want to avoid framing the issue as one of teaching *versus* research or teaching versus university and community service. Teaching will always lose when the question is black or white, teaching or research; no one wants to sacrifice university research. And it isn't necessary to do so. Good researchers are also often good teachers. The question that ought to be posed is whether teaching can be recognized and rewarded in addition to the other priorities of the institution. The problem is that universities and colleges too often rigidly require everyone to fit the same teacher-scholar mould and they reward research and pay lip service to teaching. A teacher once put the problem to me this way: "You teach at your peril. Every minute spent preparing a lecture or talking to a student is a minute taken from your career growth."

Administrators and planners must begin to recognize that we can maximize our productivity only if we take advantage of the differences in talents among professors. A few professors should primarily do research and teach only a few graduate courses closely related to their specialties. Others, whose scholarly fields are broader, or who have talent for connecting their material to the broader issues, should teach small undergraduate courses. Still others, who are naturally dramatic and skilled at organizing material for the undergraduate, can handle the large undergraduate classes. As a teaching consultant, I am constantly asked to make actors out of highly introverted bench scientists while a steady stream of excellent undergraduate teachers leave the university because they do not publish enough to survive. The problem can be resolved by having different tracks to career growth within the university.

## Suggestion 2: Create a spectrum of career arrangements to match various staff talents

Creating different tracks to career growth does not mean creating a group of second-class, part-time contract people to teach undergraduates, who get paid a fraction of the salary of a regular professor and who have no opportunities for self-renewal through sabbatical or scholarship. These migrant laborers of academe, or marginal academics, as they are called, are often subjected to dismal conditions of work and brutal exploitation (Clark, 1988).

Creating different tracks means specifying *clear role descriptions* for all faculty, even though they do different things, with promotion and merit tied to excellence and achievement.

## Suggestion 3: Relate promotion and tenure decisions to talent

For all faculty who teach, promotion and tenure should reflect the quality of their teaching in proportion to the amount of teaching that they do relative to other tasks. And there must be clear criteria and standards for evaluating teaching.

## Suggestion 4: Document teaching activities

Faculty should be encouraged to document their teaching activities. Professor John Centra and others (1987) have recently published a handbook that details a method of systematically measuring teaching for promotion and tenure. Some departments have gone further, they have instituted standard forms to help faculty collect information for their dossiers and have invited guest speakers to address their faculty on how to organize a dossier. For published work on this subject see the book by Knapper and his colleagues (1977), *If teaching is important . . . : The evaluation of instruction in higher education;* Centra's (1979) book, *Determining faculty effectiveness,* or Braskamp and colleagues (1984), *Evaluating teaching effectiveness: A practical guide,* and Murray's (1980) short monograph *Evaluating university teaching: A review of research.* All of these books provide guidance to the uses and limitations of various methods of evaluating teaching.

It is important to follow the evaluation with faculty development activities such as workshops, individualized consulting, and funding for educational conferences. It is useless to point out deficiencies in faculty teaching performance unless you are ready to help remedy them.

### Suggestion 5: Reward excellence in teaching

Set up awards for excellence in teaching. Arguments against awards have been made on the grounds that awards affect only a few teachers. However, my experience with awards is that their development and promotion are useful because they prompt discussion of the criteria for good teaching.

Award excellence in teaching by providing research assistance. Most departments do not have the funds to do this. Universities have become dependent on the ability of researchers to get outside funding. On the other hand, universities are increasingly hiring short-term contract teachers to do the undergraduate teaching. My suggestion here is that some of that money might be better spent on small grants to pay for summer research assistants for senior tenured faculty in return for their teaching of undergraduates.

## Possible Cause 2: Disruptive or unco-operative students demoralize you

Poor student performance, either academic or behavioral, can discourage teachers. If teaching is a process of helping students, and if teachers are motivated to help learners, they may become frustrated if their helping is thwarted or if the students fail to achieve.

According to Professors Carole and Russell Ames (1984), who have studied teacher motivation, there are two different kinds of "helping" teachers. The first are guided primarily by moral responsibility and feel good about their work when they can help a student to overcome a problem or to feel better about something. Disruptive, uncommitted, or unco-operative students are seen as needing help — these are teacher problems for which the teacher takes responsibility, not student problems. With enough ability and effort on the part of the teacher, the problem can be overcome. Teachers guided primarily by moral responsibility see these problems as opportunities to achieve psychological or social goals.

The problem with this position, as Ames and Ames point out, is that it can lead to extremes in which teachers focus on strategies which reduce their guilt rather than help students' mastery of the material. Also, it can lead to burnout when the teacher becomes exhausted from giving.

The second type of teacher whose motivational system is based on helping, according to Ames and Ames, includes those who are concerned primarily with helping students accomplish *mastery*. They focus on devising strategies to increase student learning and accomplishment rather than on appearing responsible or able. Such teachers feel good about their work when they can help students achieve. With the right strategies, such teachers believe, they can help students achieve their tasks despite any difficulties. The fact that they do not always succeed is a source of frustration for them.

But not all teachers are motivated to help students. Some teachers are motivated, instead, by a need to express their own competence and ability. These teachers will be dispirited by failure, for example, by poor evaluations of their teaching by students. Teachers guided by this third motivational system tend to be concerned primarily with maintaining a sense of their own ability to perform as teachers. They are focussed on defending their ability and tend to evaluate disruptive, uncommitted or unco-operative students as a threat to their self-esteem. They are likely to blame the students and to use punishments or demands for student behavior change (Ames & Ames, 1984).

### Suggestion 1: Consider co-operative interaction as a metaphor for teaching and learning

It seems to me that all three of these motivational orientations assume that teachers are more powerful than they actually are. If teaching is a co-operative interaction to help the learner, then the teacher's role is important in this interaction and student co-operation is essential. You can't push on a string. There has to be a dialogue, some kind of tension between the two parts of the interaction, before the effort of the teacher will have any effect.

Examine your own reaction to students who present you with problems in a context of teaching and learning as a shared activity rather than in one in which you are the sole performer or helper. Without students' willing participation, teaching and learning cannot happen — the dedicated helper creates dependencies and resentments, and the superb performer ends up saying, "I told it perfectly but they didn't listen."

Does this mean that there are situations in which a teacher

cannot succeed? Yes. You can't do it all. There are situations under which your teaching ability or helping posture or strategies for achievement will not achieve what you expect. Don't take all the credit if you succeed and don't take all the blame if you fail as a teacher.

**Suggestion 2: Team teaching can solve the problem of a narrow conception of teaching**

If you believe that your teaching strength lies in your ability to give memorable performances, then get a director who can judge the audience, interpret the script, and keep the theme of the play in mind. I have observed several successful teaching events that were orchestrated by a kind of teaching director. The individual performers were panelists or discussants who did not have to be concerned about the goals of the course or about whether the question they addressed related to the students' experience.

If a course is taught by a team, one or two can orchestrate the course while a number of performers give the lectures, conduct the small group sessions, and mark the papers.

# Possible Cause 3: Lack of feedback from students

Enjoyment of teaching is usually tied to feedback from students. I recently had this conversation with an arts professor: "I'm a tenured professor and my evaluations are okay. No one is on my back about my teaching so you might wonder why I'm calling you. I'm just not getting anything out of it anymore."

"What do you mean? Teaching no longer stimulates your thinking?"

"Not really. I never really expected much stimulation from undergraduate teaching. It's the dead faces, the lack of enthusiasm."

"What do you mean by lack of enthusiasm?"

"Oh, lack of anything that lets me know minds are working out there — questions, arguments, comments. If the ball doesn't bounce back into my court I can't hit it again."

I like the analogy with racket games because of the assumption of reciprocity. A similar situation arose in our small group clinical teaching. This is as close to a direct quote as I can remember: "You know, Richard, I don't want to hurt your feelings, but I think that your teaching improvement program really doesn't make any difference. When I have a good clinic group I'm brilliant. But when I have a dead group then I'm dead myself. That's all there is to it. It's not a matter of my teaching ability."

"What is a good clinic group?"

"Oh, one that shows interest, asks question. You know, a bright group."

In both of these examples it was the feedback to the teachers which rejuvenated them. Many teachers have told me that they teach to see that spark go on in the students. And when they see it, they are rewarded.

## Suggestion 1: Learn about feedback techniques

This is not the place for an exhaustive review of feedback techniques for the improvement of teaching. Fortunately, two recent publications provide detailed instructions for the use of methods of gathering feedback to improve teaching, *Classroom assessment techniques: A handbook for faculty* by Cross and Angelo (1988) and *How am I teaching? Forms and activities for acquiring instructional input* by Weimer, Parrett, and Kerns (1988).

## Suggestion 2: Broaden your concept of feedback

When we think of feedback we think mainly of what Norbert Wiener (1980) called negative feedback, or corrective feedback, the kind of information that is fed back into a system to tell it when it has gone off course or that tells a person where she or he has gone wrong. It's no fun.

But feedback doesn't have to be corrective (Menges, 1987). Wiener also developed a concept of positive feedback, the kind of feedback that amplifies a signal instead of correcting it. This is the feedback that is responsible for the resonance that makes a microphone blare. The signal gets bigger when it feeds back into the mike and it keeps getting bigger. Applied to education, the concept of positive feedback fits the explanation that the two teachers gave me in the examples I just quoted. You get encouraged by hearing from your students and the encouragement makes you a better teacher with more enthusiasm, and then students give you more feedback and show their appreciation for your effort and you get even more encouraged.

An interesting fact about this upward spiral of encouragement is that it doesn't appear to depend on students' praising the teacher. We have found (e.g., Tiberius, Sackin, & Cappe, 1987; Tiberius, Sackin, Slingerland, Jubas, Bell & Matlow, 1989) that detailed feedback — whether it be praise or criticism — communicates a belief that the students see the teacher as important to their learning, and this belief in itself is very rewarding.

# Possible Cause 4: Constraints on teacher's freedom

Too many constraints on a teacher's freedom to teach what and how she or he likes is another cause of loss of enthusiam for teaching. The professor who strolled into a classroom clutching the bowl of a pipe and not knowing what he was going to teach until he lit up, is a dying phenomenon. Not only is the room probably now a non-smoking area, a number of changes constrain the professor's traditional freedom. Undergraduate courses of hundreds or even more than a thousand students require close co-operation of several lecturers or one lecturer and several tutorial leaders; distance education programs require a team effort to design and deliver a vast curriculum; and the accountability movement has pressured professors to write objectives for their courses and to evaluate in strict conformity with those objectives.

Co-operation, teamwork, and curriculum alignment are all important, but we shouldn't kill the teacher's creative outlet in the process. The organization of teaching ought to leave room for spontaneity. There is something wrong when a teacher says, "Everything has become so legalistic that there is no joy in teaching anymore. I have to give students a detailed course outline and they treat it as a legal document. If I mention something that is not on the outline they treat it as a breach of contract. I'm wasting their time if I teach something that isn't going to be on the exam. And I can't put anything on the exam that isn't strictly on the outline."

## Suggestion 1: Plan tutorial sections on exams

To solve the problem of the large class with multiple sections, the exam can be designed so that a percentage of it is reserved for questions based on the individual discussion sessions. Students answer a common set of questions taken from the core material and, in addition, those questions relating to their own discussion groups.

## Suggestion 2: Do not allow team efforts to stifle individual initiative

Individual teachers, curriculum planners, media technicians, and others who develop courses as a team need to combine individual responsibility and creativity with group interaction and co-operation. Committees, for example, are not very effective vehicles for writing coherent material. Whether the goal is the development of a lecture, a curriculum, a media tool, or an evaluation, I would suggest this process:

**1.** An idea session in which the group contribute ideas to the person responsible for a particular task, say, for writing a syllabus plan or lecture;

**2.** People work individually to develop first drafts;

**3.** The drafts are circulated to the group for comments;

**4.** The comments are returned to the authors;

**5.** The authors write second drafts;

**6.** The group meets to reconcile inconsistencies between views of the various participants.

### Suggestion 3: There is more to the course than can be evaluated

Passing a course is students' first priority. I've said that before in this manual. The point I would like to make now is that passing isn't their only priority and the material that can be evaluated is not the only worthy learning goal. Unpredictable and individual learning is exciting for students to experience and for teachers to see and participate in. It is one of the magical elements of teaching and one of the things that make it worth doing. And it needs to be included in the implicit agreement that teachers make with their students at the beginning of the course.

"Now that I have explained the course outline and the evaluation, I would like to say a few words about something I have begun to call the 'unpredictable curriculum.' By this term I mean the knowledge and skills that you will learn which are not on the outline and which I cannot evaluate. I have found that these spontaneous learnings are sometimes the most exciting aspects of the course for me. If you take a narrow view of this course and open your minds only wide enough to take in the material on the course outline, you will miss some of these unexpected things. That would be a pity. I should add that my interest in the unexpected is partially selfish. It is these spontaneous events which furnish much of my enthusiasm for the course. So for my sake, if not for your own, be prepared to explore, take risks, and enjoy this course beyond the narrow set of concepts and ideas that we can put on the exam."

# Possible Cause 5: Lack of stimulation

Intellectual stimulation is a powerful motivator for teachers, a fact clearly revealed by the common perception that undergraduates drain a professor's energy while graduate students recharge it. Graduate students presumably have sufficient knowledge and experience to be able to sustain discussions which are stimulating and helpful to the teacher whereas undergraduates are typically passive consumers. High-ranking professors commonly enjoy the privilege of teaching only graduate courses, leaving the large masses of undergraduates to those lower in the hierarchy. Of course, this isn't always so. One senior professor of physics, for example, preferred to teach undergraduates because, "Undergraduates ask the naive questions which cause me to rethink the topic from the ground up. They force me to challenge some of the presuppositions my graduate students and I would no longer challenge. Besides, I like the mental exercise of explaining the material in a simplified way. It forces me to take a new perspective on it."

Of course graduate classes can be depleting too, if students lack the interest or ability to contribute. How can a teacher get enough stimulation?

## Suggestion 1: Maintain a support group

Teachers who cannot rely on their students for intellectual stimulation should maintain some kind of regular intellectual support group, possibly a discussion group consisting of peers with similar interests.

My own situation is a good example. Although I have the privilege of working with some of the most brilliant and exciting biomedical researchers and dedicated clinicians to be found anywhere, when it comes to teaching and learning, they are consumers and they make no apologies about it. They are sophisticated consumers who ask provoking questions, but their interest is in the specific educational problems they are trying to solve rather than in finding general contributions to educational practice or theory. I share their interest in solving specific problems, but I have further needs that it would not be legitimate to ask them to meet.

My interest group is a free discussion group which meets every other week. There are about 15 more or less permanent members of whom 8 or 10 show up at any one time, and the topic of the day ranges across areas such as faculty development, improvement of teaching, and helping skills. This group is extremely valuable to me in maintaining my enthusiasm for my work and teaching.

## Suggestion 2: Join professional associations and attend their conferences

The best association I have ever attended, for the encouragement of my teaching, without question, is the Professional and Organizational Development Network in Higher Education (called POD for short). The members are talented and experienced and the workshops are practical, helpful, and conducted in an interactive manner — there are no passive observers.

Professional organizations specifically related to your field will give you access to others who share your problems and concerns. Many of these conduct educational and practical sessions.

Finally, I recommend professional educational associations such as the American Educational Research Association or the Society for Higher Education.

## Suggestion 3: Read

New material which either relates to your course or stimulates you as a teacher may or may not be more stimulating or better for the students than the old material, but if it keeps *you* from stagnating, everyone will benefit.

## Suggestion 4: Take a break from teaching

When teachers teach the same material over and over again to small groups of students throughout the entire year, it comes as no surprise when students complain of lack of enthusiasm. One way to ameliorate this kind of situation is to do some of the more didactic teaching in larger groups and through self-study, so that the teachers are able to have an occasional break from their teaching.

## Suggestion 5: Separate the major goals in your life

A little booklet called *How to manage your time more effectively with a Day-Timer* by Charles R. Hobbs (1987) that came with my Day-Timer appointment book makes such a sensible point about a general strategy to prevent burnout that I would like to add it as a last suggestion. The recommendation is to set out the major goals of your life and then to work on each one of them a little bit. It is when you become obsessed with one to the exclusion of the others that you are on the road to burnout. As a faculty member you may have teaching goals, scholarly goals, and professional goals; from your personal life you may add other goals to this list such as social and family goals, spiritual goals, financial goals, political goals, cultural goals, athletic goals. Make sure that you spend some of your week on each of your major goals.

Trade off within a category but never between categories. This means that you should not exclude everything else from your life because you are preparing for a course or writing an article. Such obsessional behavior saps both motivation and efficiency.

# Possible Cause 6: Teacher penalized for increased productivity

In most jobs, workers are rewarded for increased productivity. Teaching is the one exception that I know to this principle. There are two reasons for this: rigid course schedules and norm-referenced exams.

**Suggestion 1: Replace rigid course schedules with incentives for efficiency**

Over lunch a colleague told me about a professor who decided to do something about the creeping boredom of teaching the same course year after year. He designed a series of interactive computer disks by which students could learn the material by themselves. The disks freed his time so that he was more available for individual consultations with students, which he thoroughly enjoyed. He put an enormous amount of time into this effort and the result was of the highest quality. Students praised the program and tests showed that the material was learned to an even higher level and with less class time. In his annual meeting about merit, courses, and so on, the department chair praised the computerized course, then asked: "So what are you going to teach next year?" The professor got no reward for increasing his productivity. He had invested his time and expertise — "capital" for a professor — in developing a computer-assisted program so that he could teach two courses in the time it ordinarily takes to teach one. But he was not allowed to keep any of the profit — time saved — of his investment. Had he been allowed to keep that time, he might have been motivated to design another computer-assisted course. As it is he regrets having designed the course. He feels cheated.

Our conversation then turned to the consequences of an increase in productivity of *learning* at universities and colleges. We entertained ourselves with the imaginary scenario of a teacher reporting to his chair that he had just halved the time needed to learn the material for an introductory course. The scene is a humorous one for us because, having spent our entire careers in higher education, we know that the concept of reducing the time for the learner is unheard of. In contrast, below the lunchroom where we sat runs a subway tunnel whose walls advertise commercial courses on everything from language to computers, and these posters invariably include, in large print, the expected time to mastery of the skills: "Learn Spanish in just six weeks"; "Learn basic computer programming in seven evenings." Efficiency is a very important selling point to the consumer.

In these times of the rise of consumerism universities might consider one of the most precious commodities of the student: time.

I'll admit that it might not be appropriate to advertise the time it takes to reach mastery in a philosophy course since each student will no doubt learn something different in the course, depending on his or her background, ability, and interest. But we might consider the average time it takes the class to reach certain criteria as a measure of the effectiveness of the teacher.

### Suggestion 2: Replace norm-referenced exams with criterion-referenced exams

Norm-referenced exams, those designed to produce grades which are distributed in a bell shaped curve, put everyone in a no-win situation. This means that no matter how much you work to improve your teaching, your students will never do better on the exam and you will never have any evidence of improved performance. But that's not the worst of it. The worst part is that your exam will gradually drift toward trivia, driven by the requirement to find increasingly more esoteric and picky little points with which to stump the students so that you can maintain the bell curve. And what the students study will follow the exam as the night follows the day. As one teacher admitted: "We don't ask them anything that is important anymore. All the really important points they know by heart. If we asked these they would all get 100 per cent and that would destroy the bell curve." A typical student from the same course commented, "You can't study the important material if you want to pass. You have to go for the little picky details, the kinds of things you will forget as soon as the exam is over. That's what they ask us."

Imagine the production manager in a ball bearing factory. The quality control officer rejects about 20 per cent of the bearings because they are not within the specified tolerance. So the production manager increases the quality on the next production run. Quality control in turn raises the standards in order to again reject 20 per cent of the bearings. Again, the production manager modifies the machinery. This continues for several production runs until the criteria for the bearings are completely out of line with their purpose. It sounds crazy, but it is no different from what happens when teachers are required to norm reference their exams.

If the purpose of teaching is to help the learner, then the most valid measure of teaching excellence is the teacher's ability to get as many students as possible to learn the core material in the least amount of time or with the least effort. Yet if university professors turn in A grades, their "standards" are questioned

— their teachings skills are never praised. If the system prevents teachers from ever demonstrating improved performance, they will lose the incentive to improve.

## Possible Cause 7: Negative attitude toward students

Nothing is more important than teacher attitude toward students. If the students perceive the teacher as caring for them, they will view almost anything she or he does in a favorable light. If students see the teacher as uncaring, they will interpret the most innocent moves and strategies negatively.

Student comments about a teacher they perceive as caring:

Student comment about a teacher they perceive as uncaring:

1. She has vast experience and knows so many people. It's exciting to get the inside story on people who are just names in textbooks to us.

1. She's a name-dropper.

2. He's a very humble, confident person. He's not afraid to admit when he doesn't know something. It makes me feel better to know that the prof has weaknesses, too.

2. He doesn't know what he's talking about.

3. He is so gentle with the class. If someone asks a stupid question he will never embarrass the person. You feel safe to speak out in his class.

3. He's afraid of us.

4. She follows a set of notes so that if you get lost or something for a minute you can find your way again.

4. She'd be lost without her notes.

5. He's not bothered by petty little things like someone coming in late or leaving early or a little talking.

5. He can't control the class.

6. She really controls the rowdies in the class. It's the first class where I have been able to hear every word of what the teacher is saying.

6. The iron lady? She's okay if you like to learn in a prison.

## Suggestion 1: Get to know some of your students informally

Try to understand the culture of the students, their motivations and interests as well as their worries, pressures, and fears. This kind of understanding usually prompts a more sympathetic attitude toward students.

## Suggestion 2: Try role reversal

You can't be a student in your own class, but you can do the closest thing to it. You can sit in on a colleague's class or some group that puts you in a position similar to that of your students.

Joyce and I recently took pre-natal classes. She was reluctant to go with me because I get so restless when teaching is bad. She didn't want me to make a scene. The teacher confirmed my worst expectations and I confirmed Joyce's. We dropped out after a few sessions. The silver lining for me is that I have a vivid, if painful, reminder of the effects of poor teaching strategies, and I will never either recommend or use those strategies.

Observe your responses and feelings carefully whenever you are put in a situation similar to that of your students. It is very instructive.

# 9/Students Do Not Co-operate

*"They're hostile and negative, they grab for power, they interrupt each other and me, they work one little idea to death in some struggle for attention. They're driving me crazy."*

Although blatant antagonistic behavior is not common in higher education, it is very distressing when it does occur, possibly because we are seldom prepared to deal with it. It is helpful to know some ways to respond to the more common causes of antagonisms.

Many teachers' first response to behavior of this kind is anger. Unfortunately, this is usually the worst response. Anger narrows your focus and reduces your ability to assess and constructively deal with the situation. An angry teacher is also predisposed to blame students who may be innocent. In fact, in my experience, the two main causes of hostile situations are innocent misunderstandings between group participants and obsessions over which participants have little control.

The first four causes below deal with misunderstandings and the next five deal with obsessions and compulsions. The last cause deals with intentionally disruptive behavior. I ordered the causes in this way, with intentionally disruptive behavior last, in an attempt to counter the common tendency toward blaming students for any disruption.

# Possible Cause 1: Students do not accept the assumptions of the course

Every human activity is based on some assumptions. If students will not accept the presuppositions of the course, there can be no group discussion. In my colleague's course on psychiatric techniques, one student said: "I don't believe in mental illness. This whole discussion is useless." Such statements may provoke useful examination of the basic assumptions underlying a course; but the inquiry should not be allowed to usurp the objectives of the course.

### Suggestion 1: Rethink the assumptions of the discipline

I taught an introductory educational psychology course at the University of Pennsylvania in the late 60s, when U.S. male students could get deferred from the draft (and Vietnam) if they were pursuing an educational occupation. Because of the deferment, there were more radical thinkers in the course than ever before. When I assigned the usual paper, the students challenged me on the ground that the assignment limited them to a rational approach. They argued that there were other routes to truth and cited everyone from Tim Leary to Lao Tzu to prove it.

I would have had a small revolution on my hands if I had simply laid down my terms on a take-it-or-leave-it basis. Besides, an authoritarian view would be unacceptable at a university dedicated to objective inquiry. So we discussed the presuppositions of our course and the role of the university in society. We talked about the nature of the social contract between myself and them and between them and the university and society which supports the university. We discussed the implications of abandoning the material which is accepted as useful to the preparation of teachers.

It seemed to me that those students, because of their radical challenge to every assumption underlying the course, acquired a far deeper understanding of the course material than students who accept the assumptions and simply memorize the material.

### Suggestion 2: Don't let discussion of the presuppositions replace the content

Students who challenge the presuppositions of a course are usual-

172

ly in the minority. The majority of the students in my educational psychology course were trying to qualify for a teaching certificate and were keen to learn the material. A prolonged discussion of the presuppositions would usurp the rights of the majority to engage in the education for which they enrolled. (I include myself in this minority who would enjoy the philosophic issues more than the facts.)

I know now that one of the best things to do — which I did not do — is to make a decision about the amount of time to be set aside for consideration of the presuppositions, and to make this decision with the agreement of the students. Also, it is important to explain to those who are not interested in presuppositions that the issue is, nevertheless, an important one to the course. Otherwise, they may feel bullied by a minority into wasting time on something they had not bargained for.

If this happens again I'm going to be more ready. I will say something like this: "Some of the students have challenged the presuppositions of this course. Specifically, they have argued that they should not be forced to write a paper for the course because this requirement forces them to respond in a rational manner, depriving them of non-rational options. I am delighted that this kind of issue has surfaced because an examination of the presuppositions is one of the most important activities of higher level scholarship. Next week I would like to devote an entire class period to this topic. In preparation, please read the following article and come prepared with whatever non-rational sources you would like. Unfortunately, we will have to leave the topic after next week, whether we have resolved it to our satisfaction or not, unless we would like to radically change the nature of this course, that is, make it an introductory course into the philosophy of education.

"There is another possibility I would be willing to pursue. Some of you may be interested in meeting separately whenever we can spare time and a room, to pursue the assumptions underlying rational discourse. Please see me after class next week if you would like to do that."

## Possible Cause 2: Students challenge the teacher's authority

One of the most common fears teachers have disclosed to me over the years is the fear of losing their authority. Of course, it's no fun to teach students who are ridiculing or heckling you. (I discuss destructive behavior in Cause 5). But, short of that kind of rudeness from students, my view is that we should welcome any attempt from students to take over the authority and responsibility for the course. After all, learning is the purpose of the entire effort. We teachers are helpers. The more teaching that students take over, the easier our job and, often, the better the learning becomes. Imagine the sheer joy of teaching a course in which the students work up a reading list, precirculate the materials, make brief presentations to the group, lead the group sessions, and grade one another's papers. What would we do? We would assist students to find appropriate literature and coach them in making presentations and in leading the small group. We would make comments on the process and ensure that the goals were being met.

We teachers usually control every aspect of the course: we decide the curriculum, set up the evaluation, and even determine the methods of teaching, although we would be wise to accommodate our teaching methods to the needs of the learners. If we were able to share some of this responsibility, students would be more motivated and would learn important skills such as leading small groups, evaluating, library research, and presentation.

## Suggestion 1: Have a constructive response ready

No matter how devoted we are to helping students learn, most teachers also get some satisfaction from our authority — we have some ego involvement in leading, making decisions, evaluating, and so on. It isn't surprising, then, that we react defensively when a student challenges our right to control a certain aspect of the course. But defensiveness rarely does any good, and it destroys the trust between teacher and student. Students need to feel that the teachers are there to help them, not to get our jollies on an authority trip. I would like to suggest that you respond by finding ways to share the responsibility for the course.

## Suggestion 2: If the challenge is constructive, give the students control

If the students' challenge to your authority is constructive, and they want to take responsibility for their learning, then everyone will be better off if you help them do it. Besides, evidence indicates (for example, Geis, 1976) that learning is enhanced by giving students control over their learning.

Here are some of the ways that students can be helped to take more responsibility for their learning:

**1.** Rotate leadership of the small group, give feedback to the

174

small group leader (students and yourself), and hand out a set of guidelines for the small group leader.

**2.** Set aside time for students to reflect on their own activities and accomplishments so that they can learn how to work more effectively in groups and teams.

**3.** Encourage students to contribute to the decisions regarding clarification of the learning problem and selection of the necessary resources.

**4.** Include in your evaluation plan an opportunity for students to self-evaluate and to evaluate one another.

### Suggestion 3: If the challenge is destructive, do not give them control

There are some students who are driven to seek power. Often their agenda competes with their ability to learn and interferes with others students' learning as well. When you give them the opportunity for genuine sharing of power, they do not take it. See Cause 5 below.

## Possible Cause 3: Heated disagreements among students: strong feelings or interpersonal hostility

Heated disagreement can be a good thing in the small group. The emotion and excitement attending a debate can enhance the meaningfulness of the subject for the students and can help them to remember it. However, disagreement can be destructive as well if a group polarizes into two extreme positions or if the discussion degenerates into interpersonal hostility.

### Suggestion 1: Prevent disagreement from degenerating into polemic

The "summary" is an excellent device for preventing disagreements from degenerating into one-dimensional polemics. Issues are rarely just two sided. A summary enables the group to see the limitations of their statements and to see other dimensions of the argument.

One of the most heated debates I have witnessed was over animal experimentation. Some students were categorically opposed and others were just as rigidly in favor. The commentary had become characterized by slurs and innuendo such as "Nazi mentality" and "anarchists." At this point, the teacher, a small, soft-spoken woman, simply restated the two positions. When the students against animal experimentation heard the sweeping boldness of their statement played back to them they began to make some qualifications about type of animal. "We are not that concerned with cockroaches and bacteria," they said. "What we mean by animals is animals with feelings." (How we know whether cockroaches and bacteria have feelings is another question.) The group in favor of experimentation began to qualify what they meant by a "worthwhile" experiment. The debate got unstuck as it ran off in two directions, defining which animals have feelings and what is a worthwhile trade-off between experimental value and suffering.

## Suggestion 2: Keep the disagreement impersonal by using perception checks

Direct criticisms at ideas rather than at persons. A group usually discourages obvious hostility. But personal hostility is often disguised as legitimate emotion about a topic, and it is therefore important for the small group leader to help separate anger and harsh criticism directed at persons from anger expressed at an issue. The former is unacceptable; the latter needs to be identified so that it is not confused with the former. The perception check is a way to find out what another person really means in order to avoid acting on false assumptions and incorrect interpretations.

Ned and Donald disliked each other. Ned saw Donald as a slippery little weasel who was playing a con game with the group, and he took it upon himself to expose Donald's ploy. Donald saw Ned as someone who was always picking on him because Ned was jealous of his ability. The teacher's intervention probably did little to change the way these two saw one another. But interpersonal therapy was not the goal in this case, restoring effective group process was. The teacher attempted to cut through Ned and Donald's evaluations of one another to find out how each understood the issue and how each perceived the other.

*Donald:* "You're trying to make me look like an idiot!"
*Ned:* "Why are you so angry? I'm just telling you how I feel."
*Teacher:* "Can we rephrase those statements a bit to separate your personal evaluations of one another from your perceptions? Donald, what is it about Ned's *statement* that made you feel idiotic?" [Do not ask Ned why he thinks Donald is an idiot.]
*Donald:* "Well, he said that the idea I presented has been in the literature for 20 years."
*Teacher:* "There were some brilliant theorists in the field 20 years ago, as there are today. Just because you thought of an idea which had already been thought of does not make it any less

creative for *you* to think of it. Ned, are you saying that the idea is invalid today because it's 20 years old?"

*Ned:* "No. It's still a good idea. It's a great idea, but it's not Donald's. He made it sound like it was his idea."

*Teacher:* "Are you're saying that you would like credit to be given to the original author?"

*Ned:* "Definitely."

Incidentally, experts in communication tell us that it is probably not a good idea to try to soften the message when you are clarifying emotional messages. I would use the word "idiot" if that is what the student used. You may want to substitute a more descriptive word, but don't use a euphemism. You could say: "What is it about Ned's statement that made you feel stupid (or foolish)?" But don't say, "What is it about Ned's statement that made you feel uncomfortable?"

### Suggestion 3: Don't try to resolve a personal argument or take sides

Antagonists may have a long history behind their hostility. Getting drawn into their interpersonal problem will take so much class time that the rest of the students will not receive the education they deserve. And don't take sides. There may be more to the issue than you observe. It's difficult enough to teach without playing judge with few facts. Besides, a classroom is not a therapy room.

### Suggestion 4: Use the tools of your discipline to deal with the disagreement

Disagreements present an opportunity for emotionally charged debate.

If science students are involved in a heated disagreement, invite them to think of published experiments, or to design experiments of their own which would resolve the debate. Or discuss the statistical analysis or the interpretation of data of the experiments.

If history students are involved in a heated disagreement, examine the historical validity of their sources and the methods available for interpretation of text. You may even get into a discussion of the theory of textual interpretation, and of the presuppositions and values underlying your interpretation.

### Suggestion 5: Resist settling arguments by authority

Our most important goal in higher education is to teach people how to think. To help students think effectively we introduce them to the approaches to truth that are inherent in the disciplines. But we undermine efforts toward this most important goal whenever we fall back on authority to settle a disagreement.

It is easier to resist an appeal to authority when students disagree with one another than when they disagree with us. It is easy to lose patience with their lack of respect for our years of study. It is tempting to short-cut the discussion by saying, "Take it from me, I've been in the field for years and I know that this is the answer." We must remember that we teach by example more than by what we say. We don't want our students arguing from authority.


## Suggestion 6: Use disagreement to teach negotiation skills

One of the benefits of small group learning is that it provides an opportunity for students to learn interpersonal skills while they are learning the subject matter. Opportunities to practise such interaction skills as communication and co-operation arise daily, but to practise the skills of negotiation the teacher has to wait for a real argument to arise. I am suggesting that one response to an argument is to use it as an opportunity to practise negotiation skills.

R. Fisher and W. Ury (1981) offer a delightful introduction to the art of negotiation in their book *Getting to Yes: Negotiating agreement without giving in.* It is a brief, very readable book and contains many examples. I recommend it for teachers, particularly teachers of small groups. The authors criticize what they call "position bargaining," the standard way by which people argue, in which each side takes a position and attempts to convince the other of its merits. Instead, they advocate "principled negotiation," in which the participants see themselves as problem solvers rather than adversaries. The problem that needs solving is to clarify the *interests* of each party, rather than their positions, to invent a set of options for mutual gain, and then to agree on a set of criteria by which to choose from these options.

Fisher and Ury believe that position bargaining, which pitted each party against the other in a contest of wills, only succeeded in hardening positions or causing one to knuckle under. Their method rests on the assumption that people can, in fact, invent options for mutual gain and can agree on a set of objective criteria by which to evaluate these options. Their methods for generating options and reaching criteria include brainstorming, role playing, and discussion.

# Possible Cause 4: Excessive competitiveness among students

One of the most surprising books I have ever read is *No contest: The case against competition* (1986) in which Alfie Kohn presents evidence to show that competition is basically a destructive motivation in most human activities. A large part of the book deals with demonstrating that students learn more efficiently and reach more creative potential under co-operative than competitive conditions.

Competitive students in small groups spend so much of their time deflating and up-staging others on the one hand and bragging and defending themselves on the other, that they have little energy left to engage in the subject. Moreover, they engage in a host of destructive devices designed to get them credit for what others have said and to make them appear more knowledgeable and more able than others. A few very competitive students set up win-lose interactions in the classroom into which other students can be drawn.

### Suggestion 1: Expose competitive behavior

We live in such a competitive culture that we may be unaware of destructive competition when it occurs in our small group. The group can do something about competition only if they are aware of it. Describing specific competitive behavior makes it evident to everyone. Stick to the behavior, do not accuse people of being competitive. For example, you might say to two students who are monopolizing conversation, "I can see that you two are really into this issue, but there may be others who would like to get in. You have been volleying back and forth so quickly that others may be prevented from getting in." Do not say, "You two are so competitive that you are being insensitive to others in the group." (This statement assumes that they are aware of their competitiveness and insensitivity. They may not be. Raising their awareness to their behavior may be all that is necessary.) Or say, "That's the third time that you have said, 'I totally disagree,' when Eva made a point." Do not say, "Why are you always trying to put Eva down?"

### Suggestion 2: Expose some of the common power moves

In addition to describing competitive behavior that actually appears in the classroom, it may be useful to describe some common competitive or power moves even before they appear. This is like inoculating the group with a vaccine instead of waiting until it has the disease and having to use rather powerful methods. The students learn to recognize power moves and can curb their own behavior or take steps to prevent others from usurping power. Besides, before anyone has engaged in the disruptive behavior, everyone can have a good laugh at the thought of using such strategies.

There are several common strategies. Here are some that I have seen in classes I have observed.

**1.** Continually responding to every comment made by anyone in the group, verbally or non-verbally (wrinkle brow, raised eyebrows, joke, shrug, or whatever, to show some reaction to every comment). While these responses may be charming in the one-to-one situation, a group has more than two people in it and these kinds of responses take much more than one person's share of the air time.

**2.** Attacking or confronting other students in extreme terms to gain attention rather than out of interest in the topic. For example, continually saying,"I totally disagree," is a very effective attention-getting and group-controlling device.

**3.** Defending prestige of image. Excessive self-reference and self-congratulatory statements (name dropping, anecdotes, examples) whose only purpose is to boost the image of the speaker. For a more thorough discussion of verbal abuse, see Suzette Haden Elgin (1987), *The Last Word on the Gentle Art of Verbal Self-Defence*.

### Suggestion 3: Arrange for co-operative learning

Co-operative learning arrangements such as POPS, learning cells, and learning pairs (see pages 20 to 23) can help to overcome destructive competition. There is a growing enthusiasm recently for co-operative learning. For example, a recent issue of *Educational Leadership* is devoted entirely to co-operative learning arrangements, collegial learning, as they call it. What are people saying about it?

First, co-operative arrangements lead to higher achievement, satisfaction (fun), involvement, and responsibility and to lower tension and frustration. What is particularly exciting is that long-term retention, critical thinking, and a deeper understanding seem to be associated with co-operative learning. However, the second major recent finding is that teachers apparently cannot bring about effective co-operation simply by removing the competitive arrangements and allowing students to co-operate. Co-operation, like any other human activity, requires skills, and students rarely have those skills because our competitive society does not encourage them. People have to be taught how to co-operate.

David and Roger Johnson (now revised with a third author, Edythe Johnson Holubec, 1986), present some of the ways in which students can be taught to co-operate. They say that five basic elements are necessary for co-operative learning to work: positive dependence (students have to believe that they sink or swim together); a lot of face-to-face verbal interaction; individual accountability (no one can sit back and let others do the work); leadership, communication, trust-building and conflict-resolution skills; and finally what I would call feedback but the Johnsons call group process, that is, how the group is working and how its work might be improved (Brandt, 1987).

What does a co-operative arrangement look like that incorporates all of these characteristics? Roy Smith (1987) asked students to form their own groups of four to research aspects of medieval life and present their findings in the form of a newspaper that could have been written in the Middle Ages. Each student in the group was to contribute one major piece of writing to the newspaper, which included news stories, feature stories, editorials, weather, cartoons, and advertisements. They researched independently but during class time they shared their information, edited, proofread, and designed the pages.

The arrangement worked well and Smith and his students were highly satisfied in terms of both class goals and their own satisfaction.

## Suggestion 4: Set up co-operative evaluations

Assigning a single grade to everyone for work on a group project can encourage co-operation. When all members of the group pull their weight, working with others can be an exciting and valuable experience. But people feel burned when some do all the work while the others go along for the ride.

I have heard some remedies for this defect in group work assignments from both teachers and students who where unwilling to forfeit the benefits of group projects because of a potential for unfairness. In one rather elaborate system, students were asked to estimate the percentage contributed by each member to the group. The teacher then discussed the estimates with each student. It is not surprising that this method led to uncomfortable hassles with students.

The best way to prevent unfairness is to arrange group work but separate evaluations. That is, to evaluate individual learning resulting from the group work rather than a group product. For example, in the POPS system, although students study together, they are tested individually. Or a paper can be written by two students who are then evaluated separately if each has the responsibility for a specific part of the paper. For example one reviews the literature and the other designs an experiment.

### Suggestion 5: Do not reward competition in the group

In attempting to encourage interaction by complementing students for contributions, teachers may unwittingly encourage competition. A particularly blatant example of competition occurs in medical clinics when young medical students compete with one another for the senior physician's attention. After one clinic, I overheard a student say to another student, obviously impressed with his ability to get noticed by the senior attending staff: "You really scored with Dr. Becker today. He went nuts over your diagnosis. You've got a residency in the bag."

Such competition isn't all bad. It stimulates attention. But it also encourages students to cover up rather than disclose any ignorance so that it can be corrected. Students can slip through the system without knowing simple procedures because they are afraid to ask and appear stupid.

### Suggestion 6: Split the group into pairs

Groups bring out the competitive behavior in people who have that tendency. In a one-to-one situation a student is less likely to be interrupted, will have more opportunity to speak, and will receive more understanding because the other person can take the time to ask questions and clarify.

## Possible Cause 5: Disruptive behavior: power or attention seeking, deceit, evasions

From time to time students will engage in disruptive behavior which appears to be caused by some kind of individual psychological need, such as an excessive need for power or attention, rather than by the group process. Although occurrences are infrequent, this behavior is so disruptive that the question of how to handle it has become one of the most frequently asked questions by teachers.

The reasons for students' disruptiveness are extremely varied: when someone asks me what to do about the disruptive student I respond with a spectrum of strategies to try in order of severity. If the mildest one doesn't work, go on to a less mild one and so on. I used to try to figure out whether the disruptive student was just mouthing off a little or needed psychotherapy. But I have virtually given up trying to diagnose the severity of disruption from teachers' descriptions. What one teacher describes as a slightly extroverted personality, another will describe as a raving maniac.

The three most common types of disruptive students, in my experience, are those who are unaware of the behavior, those who are aware of the behavior but cannot control it, and those who either do not care or do not want to control it. Typical behaviors include egocentrism (telling irrelevant personal anecdotes, speaking to a favorite point long after the group has left it, general insensitivity to where the group is at the moment), abusiveness (insensitivity to the feelings of others, picking on others, making fun of people, using sarcasm), eliciting sympathy (the poor me syndrome), and rigid dogmatism (taking an inflexible position and advancing it aggressively without listening to other arguments).

### Suggestion 1: Discuss the disruption privately with the student

The first approach should be to talk to the disruptive student individually and privately. Embarrassing students publicly is unnecessarily punitive and may make the atmosphere tense for everyone. Begin by describing the behavior, not by labelling or evaluating the person. You might say: "I kept track of the communication pattern at our last class and I noticed that you spoke about five times more than any other student." Don't say: "Why are you trying to dominate the discussion?" Try to find out what causes the disruptions. You might ask the student at first if he or she can explain the frequency of talking. Don't ask what causes the compulsive talking. Finally, disclose to him the consequences of the behavior that have prompted your talk. If you are personally troubled, say why. But also say precisely what you think is happening in the group. Use specific language. For example, you might say that several people have not spoken at all in the last two sessions, and that when you talked to them about their silence they mentioned not being able to get a word in edgewise.

### Suggestion 2: Help the student become aware of disruptive behavior by describing it

It is always surprising to me how students can be unaware of even extreme disruptive behavior. Offer to help disruptive students become more aware by describing specifically what they do and what consequences it appears to have in the group. Help them to observe themselves.

## Suggestion 3: Help the student become aware of disruptive behavior by on-the-spot cueing

One compulsive talker asked me if I would remind him when he was talking for too long. One way to do this without drawing the group's attention to the student is to agree on a signal, such as raising your hand to your cheek, to let the student know that he is rambling on and on. I have found this a little too subtle. What I have done instead is to agree with the student privately on some action that I would take if his or her behavior became disruptive. Our exchange at the point at which we reached the agreement sounded like this:

*A compulsive talker:* "I would rather that you say something. It's easier for me if you cut me off than if I just keep talking until I hang myself."

*Teacher:* "Okay, if you agree that I should intervene, I will. Just to let you know what I'll say as I interrupt you, it will probably be something like this: 'Before you go on to something else I'd like to get some reaction to your point about blank. Or maybe someone else would like to address the issue from another perspective.' In other words, I'll try to open it up, to get some reaction from others to the point you made or just to get someone else to contribute."

You may need to talk to the student privately after each class to reinforce his or her perception.

## Suggestion 4: Assign an observer role to the disturbing student

If lack of awareness is the student's problem, he or she may be able to develop that awareness by stepping out of the student role into an observer role. We are always much better at diagnosing other people's problems than our own. The compulsive talker could be assigned the task of keeping track of communication patterns with a score sheet or sociogram (see pages 120 and 121).

He or she could enter a tick mark under people's initials every time they speak, or, better still, keep track of the times people tried to talk but couldn't get into the conversation, or note the person to whom the comment was addressed. Later, the data and conclusions could be shared with the class. Observation of this kind not only helps the student become aware of the problem, it provides a model for behavior which might help to overcome it.

## Suggestion 5: Ask students to take different roles

A rigidly dogmatic student, for example, may be asked to assume the opposite point of view for a few minutes in order to become aware of the arguments in favor of the other side.

## Suggestion 6: Confront the student

Confrontation is a useful tool in the helping professions (see, for example, Egan, 1982, pp. 186–198). In my view teaching is a helping profession too and confrontation has a place in teaching. I would confront the disruptive student privately rather than in the group. A confrontation in front of the group might look to the disruptive student like a put-down. The confrontation must be seen as an attempt to help the student. In the following example the teacher is trying to understand the student: "If I understand you correctly, you feel that no one really wants to hear what you are saying. So when you make a point, you feel that they have not heard you or have not appreciated the point, you repeat the point in different words. You might do this two or three times. Of course, what happens is that your listeners eventually do get bored of hearing things repeated and they tune you out whenever you speak. And that seems to reinforce your tendency to repeat. Is this the way you see it?"

This example may not seem very confrontational. But the teacher is confronting the student by forcing an awareness of the mechanism underlying his problem by presenting that mechanism in a clear and descriptive manner.

Another feature of this confrontation is the suggestive and tentative nature of the suggestion that not being listened to *seems* to reinforce the student's tendency to repeat, and the request for confirmation. This is certainly more productive than a yelled accusation like, "You know what your problem is? You talk too much. Not only that, you repeat yourself until you bore everyone."

Another characteristic of effective confrontation is the gradual introduction of the elements of the student's disruptive behavior or the gradual introduction to the remedies, a method Egan calls the method of successive approximation. Contrast: "How about if you practice, during the next class, saying something in the shortest possible number of words, and saying it only once," with, "If you had more self-esteem you wouldn't think that people are tuning you out and you wouldn't have to repeat yourself. You have to try to think more highly of yourself."

Gaining self-esteem is a worthy goal but one which many of us work on for a lifetime. It isn't something a person can just "do." However, there are small, specific steps students can take in the class which might help to break the habit of repeating.

And breaking the habit might contribute to the build-up of self-esteem.

### Suggestion 7: Intervene tactfully without previous agreement with the student

Suggestion 3 above described a strategy for intervening during the class with the student's agreement. This kind of co-operation is ideal, but it is not always possible. How can you intervene without permission of the student, in order to save the group from a disruptive speaker?

I was once put in this position by a colleague, Robert Cohen, with whom I have had the pleasure of working for many years. Robert is a very talented educator who is not in the least afraid of taking risks. Robert and I were conducting a session on the subject of small group learning. At one point he asked me if I would leave the room for a few minutes because he wanted to talk to the group. I thought that he was going to get some feedback from the group about me and discuss it with me when I returned. Instead, he set me up. He cooked up a plan with the students in which one student would attempt to take over the agenda, ignoring the agenda that the group had set. This student would suggest his own agenda and then proceed as if his agenda had been accepted by the group. Part of the plan was that the other students would act as if they were too timid to protest.

Then Robert called me back into the room and told me to pick up where I had left off. Within a minute the student assigned as the "heavy" introduced his agenda and began to address it. I sprang up from the table with a pleased expression on my face, happy to accept the student's contribution. I wrote it on the flip chart, repeated it to make sure that I had it correct, and asked the rest of the group, one at a time, if they had any contributions to the agenda before we voted on which ones we should take up first. After a few students gave me a competing agenda, Robert stepped in to stop the session. He told me about their game and then asked the student who played the dominator what he thought about my response. The student said it was amazing. He felt so good about having his agenda listened to and put on the chart that he really didn't feel like arguing against a voting procedure. Besides, he said he would have been embarrassed to argue against something so fundamental as voting. He said: "What was I going to say, 'No. I don't want to vote — I want my agenda to be the only one'? Everyone in the group would have laughed at me."

If the strategy you use incurs social disapproval, intervene in

186

a manner in which you, rather than the student, bear the brunt of it. I don't recommend stopping the group discussion or any other method which draws attention to the disruptive person. Remember, if one student is embarrassed, the atmosphere becomes more dangerous for all the students. You may want to cut off a speaker by interrupting him or her, talking over his or her talk in a loud voice, and aiming your comments specifically: "'Before you go on to another point, let's get some other reaction to that.'" Or, when someone is being repetitious, you might say: "You have made the point clear [quick summary of the point]. Now let's give someone a chance to respond to it or to tackle the issue from a different point of view."

## Suggestion 8: The last resort

All of the above suggestions are based on the assumption that disruptive students are basically well intentioned. However, occasionally a student is intentionally disruptive because of some agenda at variance with that of the group or some emotional problem or personality disorder. Most teachers do not have the training in psychotherapy to know when to refer a student for counselling. Besides, unless a student asks for it, we have no moral right to advocate counselling. Also for moral reasons, I reject negotiating with administrators to have a disruptive student removed from a course. The teacher's position is simple: a student is causing a problem which is hindering the group and the student is unwilling to co-operate toward a resolution.

What we are faced with in such cases is a challenge to the unwritten contracts between the teacher and the students and the written contract between the teacher and the university or college. In a sense it is not a personal problem between the teacher and the disruptive student. Even if the teacher were willing to allow the student to take over the class, the teacher would not be allowed to continue by the institution and the students would not attend the classes.

The final resort is to return to the original contract between the students and the institution. This must be done openly, after informing the disruptive student. Some of my colleagues are quick to take issues to the group. I reserve it as a last resort. It is too easy for the teacher to manipulate the group to force a student with a minority view to toe the line. But when it becomes very clear that the student is unwilling or unable to co-operate, I have reached the end of my line as a teacher. I am not a psychotherapist. This is a serious decision point, and I feel morally bound to inform the student of my decision to consult the class and others: "John, what I am saying in a sentence is that our group is no longer a good learning environment and that this is partly because of the disruptive behavior you are determined to continue. I will not continue to teach the class under these circumstances. My next step is to take this issue to the class and ask them what they suggest. After all, it is *their* education too. Then I will take that information to the chair of our department and discuss it with her. I'm telling you this now not as a threat, but to inform you of what I plan to do. I do not want to do anything behind your back."

The hope is that, even if this extreme situation ends with the disruptive student's removal from the class, this approach will have enabled you to retain your co-operative relationship with the class. You are not a police officer.

## Possible Cause 6: Students' insensitivity to the feelings of other students

College and university students are eager to learn the rules of their new environment, to engage in rational discourse, argue logically, and solve problems objectively. In this environment expressions of emotion and feelings can be embarrassing reminders of a more naive period of their lives. The result is sometimes a rebound to the other extreme where students become insensitive to the feelings of other students.

Understanding feelings is important for effective small group interaction. For one thing, a lot of what people want to communicate is emotional. For another, understanding what someone is saying requires understanding the emotional context of the message. Finally, one of the causes of negativism and hostility in a small group is the frustration that grows out of feeling that one's emotions are not being understood.

### Suggestion 1: Respond to emotional messages too

Pay attention to the emotional content of a message as well as the thought or idea. In the following example the teacher paraphrases in order to clarify a student's statement, but she also shows sensitivity by inquiring about the not so hidden message.
Gord: The Luddites were a bunch of idiots.
Teacher: Do you mean they did not know what they were doing?
Gord: Sure they did, but you can't stop progress.
Teacher: [to the group] Let's talk about what we mean by progress. But first, Gord, your statement seems to communicate an

emotional message as well. You did use the word "idiots." Do you feel very strongly about the Luddites?

Gord: If we think like that we are all going to end up with diseases and animal skins on our back. I hate to think of the kind of world it would be.

Teacher: Yes. So one of the things that you would call progress is cures for diseases. Would anyone else like to define progress?

## Suggestion 2: Inquire into the nature of students' feelings

Although I am experienced at interpreting expression of emotions, either verbal or non-verbal, I am frequently wrong. Once when one of the more talkative students in my seminar suddenly became silent, I interpreted his silence as confusion about the point I was raising, I explained the point in simpler language and in greater detail, followed by asking him whether he had understood me. "Yes, I follow you," he said dripping with sarcasm. He turned pink and completely clammed up. I was very bothered by this. Later I found out from another student that he often got angry at the elementary level of my explanations. I had embarrassed and angered him into silence by talking down to him. Because of my misinterpretation of his feelings, I was treating him with an even more elementary explanation and he assumed that I was being deliberately condescending.

Fortunately, I don't trust my judgment anymore. I have learned to check out my interpretations of people's feelings either privately after class or even publicly during class. Surprisingly, it rarely causes embarrassment. Usually, students are relieved to be able to recognize and deal with emotions.

# Possible Cause 7: Students unaware of variations in conversational styles

If one student is treating the class with the verbal equivalent of a blowtorch, even those holding brightly burning candles can feel overwhelmed. Some students naturally talk rapidly and vociferously and interrupt frequently, while others speak more slowly and wait a few seconds after someone else has spoken before speaking. These differences can be due to cultural, family, or individual traits. We see the cultural clashes frequently in Toronto because we have many recent emigrees in our classes. Teachers have appealed to me with this problem, which they find particularly troublesome because of the suggestion of racial prejudice involved in restraining any one group.

The problem can destroy the atmosphere in the class because students with less assertive conversational styles infer that the assertive speakers dominate the class intentionally. They become angry and resentful, often becoming even more quiet and withdrawn and even not attending class. Let me illustrate this phenomenon with a very recent example from my own course, not because this example is particularly glaring, but for the opposite reason, that it represents a very subtle illustration of the phenomenon. By choosing this example, I mean to emphasize that the phenomenon is an everyday occurrence rather than something that depends on rare conditions.

About one third of my graduate course on educational development are staff from the medical school who are enrolled in the Master of Education with a Specialization in the Health Sciences program. The rest are teachers from other universities or from colleges of applied arts and technology, and graduate. students. The students from the medical school are more talkative and contribute more quickly to the discussion, probably because they all already know one another. The result was that for the first week or two the medical people talked almost exclusively and the material therefore became grounded in the medical rather than in other contexts.

Complaints reached the departmental chair, who then raised the issue with me. I noted with interest that the unassertive students had chosen to complain to the chair about the problem rather than to approach me directly. Here are some of the suggestions that I followed. They turned out to be very successful.

### Suggestion 1: Don't assume that the offensive speakers have bad intentions

I believe that a clash of conversational styles is at the root of many problems of so-called domination, rather than a pernicious desire to rule. Fortunately, I was able to take advantage of a separate meeting with the medical people to answer their questions about the new master's program. At the meeting I raised the question of the sharing of speaking time. I asked them what they thought caused it and what could be done about it. These are the kinds of comments I received.

"I'm glad you brought this up. I enrolled in this program so that I could have a break from medicine and we talk about the medical situation all the time. "Yes. I would very much like to know how the others feel about these topics."

"What can we do if they don't speak? Maybe you should go around the class taking one person at a time. But that tends to kill the spontaneity."

"Maybe it's because we know one another and each of them is alone so he doesn't dare speak until he feels more at ease with the class."

"Why don't we just ask them some questions about their situation? If we leave it all to Richard, it is going to look obvious."

"I agree. The onus is on us to change the balance."

In the next class the medical people asked questions of the others and the discussion was never one-sided after that.

### Suggestion 2: Enlist the help of the offensive speakers

The medical people in my class corrected the balance in the conversation by sharing the group leader's responsibilities. It is more difficult to use this method when one or two students are involved rather than a group of five or six. The lone student, by asking questions of other students, may appear to be usurping the role of the group leader and thereby incur even more resentment. Other students may see that person as attempting to take over the leader's role as well as dominate the class. The answer, of course, is to facilitate the atmosphere in the class which encourages students to ask questions of one another rather than have the teacher asking all the questions.

### Suggestion 3: Refer to suggestions about controlling dominant speakers in Chapter 6

I used differences in speaker assertiveness to illustrate clashes between conversational styles, but the two suggestions given above can be equally well applied to clashes arising out of differences in speed of speech, interruptions, excitability, or loudness. The specific problem of the dominant speaker is addressed in Chapter 6.

## Possible Cause 8: Interfering emotional messages from the teacher

Teachers may cause student hostility and negativism by sending emotional messages to students that indicate anger or rejection, messages that teachers might not know they are sending. Most teachers have learned how to communicate their thoughts but few have any idea about how to communicate emotional messages. This means that we sometimes send the students an emotional message that interferes with our cognitive message. Experiments on the interpretation of emotions by facial expressions indicate that people's judgments are not very accurate.

In the last five years I have become acutely aware of my own blindness to my non-verbal messages, unfortunately by means of my father's becoming sight impaired. I had no idea that I told jokes which could be perceived as jokes only because of certain facial expressions. In the last few years Dad has become unable to discern my facial expressions when I sit across the room from him. I have found that increasingly he will take me seriously, missing the joke, unless I am close enough so that he can see my expression.

We send emotional messages by sound too, in the tone of our voice. Last year at a conference I sat with a group of non-hearing students. Those in the group who could not hear at all were alternatively reading the lips of the guest speaker and watching the signer. As a person whose career is improvement of teaching I was fascinated with this process. Later I asked the translator how she communicated the jokes that the speaker was telling, especially the puns and the jokes which required the audience to hear the tone of voice or accent. She said that the kinds of jokes I mentioned are indeed very difficult to translate to the non-hearing. She said that at times, the best she can do is to describe everything the speaker has said, explain the pun or the voice intonation and why it is supposed to be funny, and then, quickly, as the punch line is being told, add: "Hearing joke, laugh now!" so that they can laugh in the right place.

## Suggestion 1: Find out how your emotions are interpreted

Our tones of voice, rates of speech, hand gestures, and facial expression all communicate emotional messages. It is useful to know what emotional messages you are sending so that you can make them more compatible with your cognitive message. But even video tape does not reveal our emotional communications to us, because, as we watch ourselves on tape, we are reminded of the intended emotional context of our message and we interpret the video accordingly.

The only way to learn the emotional message that you are sending is to ask your students. I would use the discussion method described in Chapter 4 because it is specifically designed to disclose this kind of subtle information.

## Suggestion 2: Explain the emotional side of your message too

Certain emotions — such as sadness at a personal disappointment — may provoke expressions and a voice your students might misinterpret as lack of interest in the subject or even as rejection. If you are aware of your emotions it is a good idea, in order to avoid misunderstanding, to interpret your emotional state before students do: "Do I sound uninterested today? I am just as interested as I was last week, but I was up all night with my own new baby. I tell you what. If I lift up my eyebrows, interpret that as near hysterical enthusiasm." Or: "Let me take a few deep breaths and slow down. I have been running around since eight this morning so I'm all geared up. If my speech starts to speed up and I appear nervous, remind me and we'll take a stretch break."

# References

Ames, C., & Ames, R. (1984). Systems of student and teacher motivation: Toward a qualitative definition. *Journal of Educational Psychology, 76*(4), 535–556.

Brandt, R. (1987). On cooperation in schools: A conversation with David and Roger Johnson. *Educational Leadership, 45*(3), 14–19.

Braskamp, L.A., Brandenburg, D.C., & Ory, J.C. (1984). *Evaluating teaching effectiveness: A practical guide.* Beverly Hills: Sage.

Byrne, P.N., & Taylor, I. (1989), Personal communications.

Centra, J. A. (1979). *Determining faculty effectiveness.* San Francisco: Jossey-Bass.

Centra, J.A., Froh, R.C., Gray, P.J., and Lambert, L.M. (1987). *A guide to evaluating teaching for tenure and promotion.* Syracuse: Syracuse University.

Clark, B.R. (1988). The absorbing errand. *AAHE Bulletin, 40*(7), 8–11.

Cross, K.P., & Angelo, T.A. (1988). *Classroom assessment techniques: A handbook for faculty.* Ann Arbor: The National Center for Research to Improve Postsecondary Teaching and Learning.

*Educational Leadership.* (1987). *45*(3). (The entire issue is devoted to collegial learning.)

Egan, G. (1982). *The skilled helper.* Monterey, CA: Brooks/College.

Elgin, S.H. (1987). *The last word on the gentle art of verbal self-defense.* New York: Prentice-Hall.

Fisher, R., & Ury, W. (1981). *Getting to yes: Negotiating agreement without giving in.* New York: Penguin.

Geis, G.L. (1976). Student participation in instruction: Student choice. *Journal of Higher Education, 47*(3), 249–273.

Gold D., (1988). Personal communication.

Hobbs, C.R. (1987). *Time power.* New York: Harper & Row.

Johnson, D.W., Johnson, R., & Holubec, E.J. (1986). *Circles of learning.* Edina, MN: Interaction Book Company.

Kohn, A. (1986). *No contest: The case against competition.* Boston: Houghton Mifflin.

Knapper, C.K., Geis, G.L., Pascal, C.E., & Shore, B.M. (1977). *If teaching is important. . . : The evaluation of instruction in higher education.* Toronto: Clarke, Irwin.

LeBaron, C. (1981). *Gentle vengeance: An account of the first year at Harvard Medical School.* New York: Richard Marek.

Maslow, A.H. (1970). *Motivation and personality.* (2nd ed.). New York: Harper & Row.

Menges, R. J. (1987, April). *Concepts from cybernetics and control theory applied to instructional consultation.* Paper presented at the meeting of the American Educational Research Association, Washington, D.C.

Murray, H.G. (1980). *Evaluating university teaching: A review of research.* Toronto: Ontario Confederation of University Faculty Associations.

Rice, R.E., & Astin, A.E. (1988). High faculty morale: What exemplary colleges do right. *Change, 20*(2), 51–58.

Smith, R.A. (1987). A teacher's views on cooperative learning. *Phi Delta Kappan,* 663–666.

Tiberius, R.G., Sackin, H.D., & Cappe, L. (1987). A comparison of two methods for evaluating teaching. *Studies in Higher Education, 12*(3), 287–297.

Tiberius, R.G., Sackin, H.D., Slingerland, J.M., Jubas, K., Bell, M., & Matlow, A. (1989). The influence of student evaluative feedback on the improvement of clinical teaching. *Journal of Higher Education, 60*(6), 665–681.

Weimer, M., Parrett, J.L., & Kerns, M-M. (1988). *How am I teaching? Forms and activities for acquiring instructional input.* Madison, WI: Magna Publications.

Wiener, N. (1950). *The human use of human beings: Cybernetics and society.* Boston: Houghton Mifflin.

# Beyond Trouble-shooting

# 10/Using Outside Help

*"Help!"*

A trouble-shooting manual deals with common problems and likely remedies. It obviously cannot include every problem that could occur nor can it provide all the remedies that may address each problem. The trouble-shooting section of your electric appliance manual usually contains no more than a few simple suggestions such as "Check to make sure it is plugged in." After these, the manufacturer typically provides a list of service representatives to call. Similarly, in using this manual to improve your small group teaching, you will at some point confront a problem for which the manual offers little help. When this happens, I recommend that you seek the services of an educational consultant. There is a large and growing group of professionals who specialize in improving the teaching and learning process. They are not always called educational consultants, but, whatever they are called, their help can be invaluable for situations whose remedies are beyond your resources or this one.

In this final chapter I would like to discuss who these educational consultants are, when to consult one, what you can expect from them, and how to make the best use of them. For those of you who would like more detailed answers to these questions, I recommend *Consultation in higher education: A handbook for practitioners and clients* by Pilon and Bergquist (1979), *Face-to-face: A sourcebook of individual consultation techniques for faculty/instructional developers* by Lewis (1988), and *Educational development through consultancy* by Boud and McDonald (1981). And for those of you who have no access to an educational consultant, I end the chapter with some suggestions that may help you to be your own consultant.

## Who are educational consultants and what do they do?

Educational consultants are resource persons who can be called upon to help you with your teaching. Many colleges and universities have highly trained professional consultants, and an even larger number of colleges and universities have "peer teachers," people with little special education in teaching methods, who help by observing your teaching and raising comments from the point of view of a fellow teacher.

Educational consultants are growing in number in higher education despite tight budgets. According to Professor Glenn Erickson's (1986) survey of over 600 colleges and universities across North America, over 60 per cent of all institutions have available to faculty some sort of classroom observation by peers. Moreover, 60 per cent of universities, 54 per cent of professional schools, and 44 per cent of 4-year colleges provide consultation services about teaching from *trained* colleagues or other instructional resource people.

What do educational consultants do? Pilon and Bergquist (1979) describe 10 different roles that consultants take in higher education. One conclusion from their study of these roles is that teachers most frequently expect the consultant to function as "expert advisor." Perhaps this expectation is formed by everyday experience with the people who install our storm doors and repair our appliances. Our relationship with these workers does not require a long-term commitment on our part and no more than minimal interaction. We prefer to leave the job to them. The expert advisor role is helpful for improving teaching as well, provided that the problems are simple enough for the consultant either to fix or to tell you how to fix. But such expert advice can be obtained more efficiently by reading a manual like this or one of the many books on the principles of effective teaching. I recommend the latest edition of McKeachie's book, *Teaching tips: A guidebook for the beginning college teacher* (1986), the second edition of Eble's *The craft of teaching* (1988), *Mastering the techniques of teaching* by Lowman (1984), *The art and craft of teaching* edited by Gullette (1984), and, for clinical teachers, *The physician as teacher* by Schwenk and Whitman (1987) or *Teaching techniques: A handbook for health professionals* by Foley and Smilansky (1980). It is when these books are not helpful, when problems arise which cannot be answered simply by drawing from accumulated wisdom that educational consultants are vital.

The consultant can function as diagnostician, coach, facilitator, negotiator, broker, mediator, conflict resolver, trainer, catalyst, and planner (Pilon & Bergquist, 1979). In these roles the consultant performs a number of functions — Ferguson (1968) has identified 17 of them — such as gathering information, analyzing the problems and issues, making recommendations for improvement, improving the interpersonal climate and encouraging the teacher. I will briefly describe some of these below so that you can get an idea of how a consultant functions.

## When should you engage the services of an educational consultant?

I have found that there are four levels of dysfunction which render teachers incapable of improving their own teaching:
1. Unawareness that there is a problem;
2. Awareness that there is a problem but ignorance of its cause;
3. Awareness of the cause of the problem but ignorance of the remedy;
4. Awareness of the problem and its remedy but lack of skill or will to implement it.

If you have problems but are not aware of them, if you are aware of problems but don't care, or have no teaching problems, you probably will not be reading this book.

The second level of dysfunction is a common one for people who will be reading this book. Teachers often receive critical feedback, usually through student questionnaires, that is too vague to provide a basis for improvement. Another common situation is the teacher who has a clear, but mistaken, idea of the problem, and therefore applies the wrong remedies. My memory of one of those situations is very clear, although it happened a long time ago, because it was an emergency call and teaching consultants get very few emergency calls. It provided me with some justification to tell my wife, who is an MD and often carries a beeper on her belt, that someday we educational consultants are going to be in such urgent demand that we will carry beepers too, and teachers will call us for advice during the break in their class.

The call was from an executive of the Faculty Association which, for those of you who do not work in universities, is the professor's genteel version of a union. It appeared that a professor was about to be fired for incompetence in teaching.

This is an extremely rare event in a university. The tasks that professors are called on to perform are, on the whole, so intangible that success is difficult to define; incompetence correspondingly difficult to prove. Clearly, I would be dealing with an unusual situation.

My initial conversation with the representative of the Association soon confirmed this. The teacher's students had unanimously excoriated his teaching and not a single voice had been raised in his defence. My job was either to contrive a defence, or effect enough rapid improvement in his teaching to avert his dismissal.

As he entered my office, he confined himself to a weak hello accompanied by a slight bow. He was a diminutive, bespectacled man whose fashionable clothes, embellished with a thin leather tie, seemed more appropriate to a mannequin than a professor.

"What do you think the problem is?" I ventured.

After a long pause, he answered in a whispered monosyllable: "Noise."

"Ah, I see. The students talk too much. That sort of thing."

"Yes," he said.

A scene assembled itself in my mind. I imagined a timid, introverted, and probably inaudible lecturer confronting two hundred robust and irreverent students ranged in tiers stretching to the ceiling, his hesitant reflections drowned by their noise.

"There are a few common remedies for noise. One of them is to let the students know that you hear them by, for example, asking them if they have a question."

The professor pulled a notebook out of his pocket and wrote down the advice. He said nothing. After I dispensed a few more tips and watched him jot them down I became suspicious, or perhaps I was struck by intuition. I asked: "How many students are there in your class?"

"Six," he said.

My image was shattered. Time for a house call. He was delighted when I offered to visit his class. His classroom was approximately three times as long as wide. At each end was a door. By one door was a round table at which the six students were huddled. Next to the other door, at the far end of the room, was a blackboard; it was through this door that the professor entered and it was on this blackboard that, without ever acknowledging the presence of the class, he immediately began to inscribe an unintelligible succession of notes. The note writing was occasionally punctuated by a mumbled comment which was presumably explanatory but, in any case, inaudible.

The students were completely at a loss. In a vain attempt to get his bearings, one student leaned over to another and whispered, "Are we on page seven?"

The professor, as though cued from off stage that his important role in the drama had arrived, raised his head and his voice sharply, fixed his glance at the little clot of students, and asked, "Do you have a question?" Well, he had certainly taken my advice. And if the problem had been one of noise, that advice might have been useful.

When we convened back in his office, I told him to forget everything I had told him about student noise and asked him if I could interview his students. He was delighted with my interest in his teaching and arranged for me to meet with them. The students spoke very freely and constructively. They obviously respected his expertise but they felt bad that, despite his obvious interest in their learning, he had been utterly incapable of engaging them in anything resembling human interaction. After the interview, I met with the professor again and asked him if he ever thought of joining the students at their table. I told him about some of the advantages of face-to-face contact in small groups. He said that he had considered it but rejected it, since there was no blackboard near the table. I suggested that he get a flip chart and place it right beside him at the table. I advised him to write his notes on the flip chart so that everyone in the group could see it, but to look at their faces, not at the flip chart, and to talk directly to them, and so on. According to his students whom I met subsequently, he did all those things and they made an enormous difference to his teaching — and to his ratings. I recently met him, smiling, at a Faculty Association meeting on tenure review.

Although the story had a happy ending, it was clear to me that this professor did not have a chance of solving his problem unaided. Although he had realized that his students were dissatisfied, he did not decipher the cause of their dissatisfaction. Having been made aware of the cause, he was not able to think of a remedy — an example of the third level of dysfunction. However, having been shown the cause and the remedy, he was able to carry the remedy out effectively. This is by no means always the case. Some professors, for instance, having placed the flip chart at the table, would have continued to address the chart rather than the students, an example of the fourth level of dysfunction.

## How do educational consultants function?

I have found that teachers have more confidence in, and find more profit in, the help that consultants give when they have some knowledge of the kind of assistance they can expect and of the techniques employed. Moreover, to succeed in such roles as diagnostician, coach, and facilitator, the consultant needs the teacher's understanding of and participation in the process. For these reasons I will attempt an account of how educational consultants go about their business. And I will be brief since I am aware that you may not intend to become a consultant.

What the educational consultant actually does, is, in a sense, to facilitate each step described in this book — gathering and analyzing information in order to diagnose problems and choose appropriate remedies, assisting teachers to implement those remedies, following-up to determine whether an improvement has taken place, endeavoring to enhance the interpersonal climate, and encouraging the teacher.

### Information gathering

Because students are afraid that they may offend the teacher who will later judge them, and teachers fear losing face, consultants have developed methods for students to communicate their views to the teacher indirectly. One way to do this is to ensure that the students' comments are anonymous. This is why the most popular student evaluation forms do not require students' signatures. Unfortunately, anonymity also liberates irresponsible and vicious students to write hurtful comments. I have suffered from such destructive comments and I don't know any teacher who has not. For this reason, some consultants prefer to report to the teacher only summaries of student questionnaires, from which such remarks have been expunged.

Even when the consultant gets information from students and teachers by talking to them rather than by getting them to fill out forms, she or he allays anxiety by seeing the students and teachers separately and, at least initially, reporting indirectly to each side what the other has said. This method is very popular, and its use in various consultation approaches may be found in *Face-to-face: A sourcebook of individual consultation techniques for faculty/instructional developers* (Lewis, 1988).

In addition, consultants gather information from several different sources so that the picture they assemble is more complete. Each student has a slightly different goal and a slightly different relationship with the teacher, and the perspective of the teacher is necessarily different from that of any student. The aim of the consultant must not be to eliminate these differences since it is precisely these kinds of biases that she or he needs to be aware of.

This multiplicity of biases was demonstrated dramatically in one of my teaching improvement workshops. An anesthetist gave a 15-minute lecture to a small group of colleagues on how to carve wooden ducks. Following my usual practice, I had asked some of them to take the role of students, and others to observe. The observers pulled their chairs back against the walls of the room and did not take part in the teaching-learning event. After the session, the teacher was asked to leave the room while the observers and I interviewed the "students" privately.

The teacher then rejoined us and we shared our impressions. It soon became clear that the perceptions of the teacher, the observers, and the "students" had been strikingly different. Since the teacher wanted to introduce the students to the joy of carving, his main concern was that he might have failed to achieve this. We observers had approached the exercise like theatre critics and were concerned with problems of presentation, for example, the fact that the teacher had omitted to put key words, such as the names of certain woods and ducks, on the board. The students, on the other hand, were concerned with neither of these issues. They were wondering where they could buy the carving tools and the wood.

Another reason consultants use a range of different sources of information is that each component of teaching is best evaluated by a different mix of sources of feedback. Professor Harry Murray (1980, 1987), of the University of Western Ontario, recommends that:

*Students* can provide reliable and valid information on classroom teaching and course management, but are not qualified to judge course content or extra-curricular teaching;

*Alumni* are in a good position to evaluate assessment practices and course management, and can provide neutral, long-term perspective on classroom teaching;

*Colleagues* are well qualified to evaluate all four categories of teaching, but given that students can do an effective job of assessing classroom presentation, colleagues probably should concentrate their efforts on the evaluation of course management, course content, and extra-curricular teaching, which students are not in a good position to observe;

The *department chair* can synthesize data from various sources and can contribute an institutional perspective to the evaluation;

*Self-evaluations*, such as descriptive reports of course objectives, extenuating circumstances, and extra-curricular teaching are valuable contributions to evaluation.

I will add one more source to Harry's list:

*Educational consultants* can provide valid judgments about innovative technique and whether the teacher has adhered to principles of good teaching and learning.

The consultant attempts to gather information, not only from a broad range of people, but also about the whole range of components of the teaching task. Typically, teachers receive only information that pertains solely to their presentations. They may be able to tell the consultant whether or not the students regard them as enthusiastic, clear, organized, or knowledgeable, but that is where it ends. There is usually no information about the other important components of teaching such as the currency and validity of the course content and the state of the emotional rapport between teacher and students.

The teacher's emotional impact on and relationship with the students is a very important component of teaching about which it is vital to gather information. Very knowledgeable teachers can be ineffective because of poor rapport with students. And poor rapport can be caused by negative feelings toward students. Particularly in the small group, negative emotions can destroy the class atmosphere. Any complex activity such as teaching requires more than mechanical skills. It requires a caring attitude and positive regard for students.

Although students can reveal their emotions on objective questionnaires, such instruments are rarely sensitive enough to be useful in gathering information about relationships, subtle aspects of the teacher-student interaction, and attitudes that underlie their emotions. My colleagues and I have found that free discussion methods are particularly effective in identifying student perceptions of the emotional climate in the classroom (Tiberius, Sackin, & Cappe, 1987; Tiberius, Sackin, Slingerland, Jubas, Bell, & Matlow, 1989). Interactive methods are superior because the rapid two-way conversation that they facilitate between students and the feedback facilitator tends to sharpen and clarify subtle issues. Interactive methods also enable the feedback facilitator to probe further information or gather concrete examples when the issue is subtle.

Finally, consultants use methods which overcome sources of inaccuracy. One cause of inaccurate feedback is simply forgetting. Questionnaires are typically administered at the end of the course when students can no longer remember the details. If students would give their feedback immediately, just as they think of it, it would be less eroded by the passage of time or distorted by competing thoughts than feedback that must be dredged up from the memory. Some consultants are currently experimenting with ratings filled out during classes. Although simulated teaching activities such as microteaching and laboratory teaching (Bergquist & Phillips, 1975) provide such "on-line" feedback to teachers, the setting is not the real classroom.

Another cause of inaccurate feedback is that students often

have great difficulty giving a complete and coherent account of their impressions. I remember one discussion process which began with a vaguely worded comment, "He's sort of weird." After 20 minutes of probing, this laconic comment blossomed into the following revealing account. "He throws people out of class if they come in late. This attitude may have been okay in the days when most students lived within walking distance of campus, but today's undergraduates have to fight heavy city traffic and depend on unreliable public transportation. Consequently, very conscientious students may be late for perfectly good reasons. But he doesn't give anyone the benefit of the doubt. He doesn't treat us like adults." The consultant's role, in this case, was to encourage students to be descriptive and concrete.

Inaccurate feedback can result also from poorly framed questions. Consultants can improve the accuracy of information gathering by choosing the right questions to ask. Since the questions on standard questionnaires are based on years of research into the characteristics of effective teaching, they cover the important characteristics of effective teaching, but the characteristics that are critical to the success or failure of your particular teaching situation may not be standard ones. In order to address such unique teaching issues, consultants sometimes write new questionnaire items or whole new questionnaires.

Interactive forms of feedback, such as unstructured interviews and discussion-based methods, are not so vulnerable to the problem of asking the wrong question as are methods which use prestructured questions. Interactive methods give students more control over the information they provide so that they can tell you what is important.

*Analysis and Recommendations*
Another central function of the consultant is analysis of the information and development of an improvement plan based on that analysis. In many cases, the nature of the remedy is made obvious by the information collected. Many problems are simple mechanical ones like increasing the size of the lettering on the overhead projection because it cannot be read from the back of the room. But other problems could be addressed by a number of remedies and the teacher's task becomes one of choosing the optimal one. For example, suppose that the feedback has revealed that the course requirements are insufficiently clear to the students. They need to be made clear, but there are many ways to do this. The teacher could simply explain to the class what the objectives are, could enter a carefully worded statement of requirements in the course syllabus and then reinforce that by reading them aloud in the class, or could go a step fur-

ther and provide examples of successful assignments from previous years. Consultants can sometimes help in such cases to broaden the spectrum of ideas and make recommendations based on what has worked in the past.

Of course, some problems are intractable. Disagreements over the objectives of the group or personality clashes among students are sometimes insurmountable for both consultant and teacher. When confronted with such cases, consultants can function in the role of negotiators, working out compromises or at least striving to reduce tension.

## Coaching

The educational consultant also helps teachers implement the appropriate strategies. Consultants can help by arranging conditions under which teachers can practice the new techniques. Not many people can perform a complex skill after simply reading about it in a book. There is a gap between thinking and action which Donald Schon (1987) calls the gap between technical rationality and practice. Teachers function well in our highly technical and rational world, but teaching is a practice not a thought game. When you first attempt to use a new suggestion, you may find that your facial expressions or actions are not communicating what you intended. Actors require years of training to learn how to translate their characters into physical and verbal motions. We teachers can't expect to do it over night. We may need coaching — including feedback on the spot — while we are acting.

One professor's students often told him they were reluctant to ask questions in his seminars because they felt that their questions were not welcome. He was dismayed by this and wanted to do something about it. One of the suggestions he learned at my workshop was to listen carefully and make eye contact with the questioner. He followed this advice but the same negative feedback persisted. Now here is the strange part. The professor had a habit of wrinkling his nose whenever he was asked a question, although he was unaware of it. When I asked him about it he said that he thought that he wrinkled his nose when he concentrated, for example when he listened carefully to a question. But students took his nose wrinkling as a sign of rejection of their questions. Here, then, was a case of a professor whose actions gave the impression that he rejected questions when he actually welcomed them.

Even if a teacher's implementation of an educational strategy is successful for some students, it may not be so for others. Undoubtedly, as a result of choosing between teaching strategies, some students will be disappointed. But their disappointment does not destroy the spirit of co-operation and good will if students realize that there is genuine disagreement among students and that the teacher has attempted to make a fair decision. A good coach can help the teacher explain conflicting interests in a way that communicates that although it's not possible to please everyone, he or she cares about the students.

### Follow-up

Most consultants follow up their teaching improvement efforts to gauge their effect. Teachers are sometimes impatient of this final step — they view it as an indulgence of the consultant who is trying to document her or his effectiveness. Actually, follow-up is an important part of the teaching improvement process for the teacher as well.

It is not sufficient simply to solve teaching problems or to improve your teaching. You must find out what you did to solve it or to improve. One of the best teachers in our faculty once told me that he would like to use the services of an educational consultant to evaluate his teaching so that he could find out what he was doing that was so popular with the students. He confessed that he was afraid that one day he would wake up to find that students no longer considered him a good teacher. And since he did not understand the basis of his teaching popularity, he would not know what to do in order to restore it.

## What if your university doesn't have a consultant?

Colleagues who have no training can help by observing your classes and by reporting their reactions to you if their observations are guided by special checklists or forms like the one presented in Weimer (1988). With the aid of one of these, a fellow teacher can be an invaluable source of feedback.

Teachers can be helpful to one another in the analysis and interpretation phase as well. But since this kind of task requires a rather large commitment of time, it might be useful for teachers to pair up so that each partner can benefit. Again, there are instruments available to aid peers to help one another to analyze their teaching (see Weimer, Parrett, & Kerns, 1988).

Teachers can also draw on their collective knowledge to increase their pool of ideas and suggestions for improvement. Collectively, teachers possess a vast store of ideas about causes and remedies; pooling these resources can be very helpful. One way to do this is team teaching, especially if the members of the team regularly attend one another's classes. Another method is a regular think tank in which teachers meet to brainstorm teaching problems.

The bottom line of all of these methods is that they encourage teachers by reminding them that they are not alone in their difficulties.

Any kind of consulting involves other people. But if you are simply unable to interest any other teachers to join you, there are still things you can do. The very first that I would recommend is to reduce the psychological barriers between yourselves and your students, to create a climate of trust and co-operation, so that you can benefit from student feedback and ideas. If teachers could reduce their power to that of their students, they could go a long way toward overcoming barriers to feedback. While they cannot do so in a hierarchical institution, they might be able to reduce the tendency for that power difference to block good communication between them and their students. Bill Alexander (1988), of the Ontario Institute for Studies in Education, reduces student fear by modeling acceptance of feedback. He says, "Write down three things you like about the course and one major concern or wish that you have, then sign it, and pass it in." He collects these comments and reads them out to the class, without the names. The language he uses in his request to describe criticism, "One major concern or wish," sets the tone for the class discussion to follow. The language is far removed from such confrontive language as "criticism" and "defense." Moreover, Bill opens the discussion with, "I've been in this business a long time. I've heard it all. So give me all the honest feedback you can." Having heard him say this, I must add that the relaxed, pleasant, expression on his face helps to convince the listener of his sincerity. He looks and sounds as if he will not fall apart, no matter what he hears.

Occasionally Bill goes even further in his efforts to demonstrate acceptance of feedback and conducts a training session in which he models accepting feedback. The centrepiece of the session is this diagram:

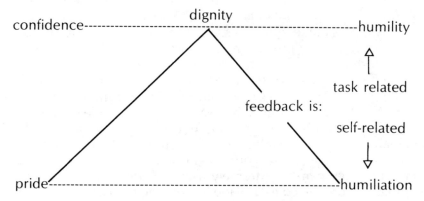

He discusses how fear can trigger us to become dependent on external sources of judgment. When this happens we drop to the bottom of the triangle. Feedback then defines our self-worth and is seen as a source of either pride or of humiliation. Understandably, students will be reluctant to provide feedback which is taken personally by the teacher. But if the teacher is confident and retains a sense of dignity, then neither pride nor humiliation is relevant. Feedback can be accepted without any sense of threat; it does not imperil our self-esteem.

Essentially what Bill is doing is giving students practice in providing personal feedback without embarrassment.

Another thing you can do is reduce your fear of listening to criticism by eliciting help from a special group of students, a group which is clearly sympathetic to you. Most of the feedback methods that include a process of direct interaction between teacher and students stipulate that the group which generated the feedback be different from the helping group that discusses the feedback with the teacher. Both the "Quality Circles" or advisory group method (Cross & Angelo, 1987) and face-to-face discussion methods (Lewis, 1988) identify a special group of class representatives or helpers whose role it is to funnel feedback from other students to the teacher or to help interpret the feedback from the class.

Finally, questionnaire design has evolved in recent years toward more flexible formats which allow teachers to choose questions to suit their specific situations. Such forms allow teachers to pinpoint relevant issues without having to rely on the diagnostic skills of a consultant. Most standard rating forms now include a few spaces in which teachers are encouraged to enter their own questions. Other feedback systems go much further toward offering flexibility by providing several hundred questions from which to draw. Finally, there are forms which enable teachers to devise the forms themselves (see Centra, 1982).

It is difficult to analyze information objectively and to make improvements without outside help. One of the best ways is the quality circles noted above, because the students in these groups not only provide information, they also help teachers interpret the information and decide what to do about it.

Joining a network of teachers outside your institution, such as the Professional and Organizational Development Network in Higher Education (POD), is a way to obtain outside help even if none exists within your institution. External networks are less valuable for gathering information because the information that you need is specific to your classroom, but for analysis and criticism they can be extremely useful. POD sessions, for example, are organized to provide lots of time to discuss teaching problems and to apply the concepts presented in the session to your own situations.

Practising is probably the most difficult component of a teaching improvement program to carry out without help. Again, quality circles are useful because these groups meet regularly with you so that they can give you feedback on something you try out.

Again, an external network can provide a rich array of opportunities, in action-oriented workshops, for practice of different teaching behaviors. Of course, practice in a simulated setting, among fellow teachers, may not entirely prepare you for the real world of your own class.

If you have the patience, and would like to know what is working and what is not in your actual classroom setting, then treat your classroom as a research laboratory. Make only one change at a time and ask students to provide feedback specifically on that change (see Cross & Angelo, 1987).

Whatever you decide to do, remember that talking with students is a most useful method of enhancing motivation for teachers at any level. For more information, see Tiberius, Sackin, and Cappe (1987) and Tiberius, Sackin, and Slingerland (1988).

## A final note

Obviously, I don't believe in the old adage that teachers are born not made. But people do have very different personalities, abilities, and styles. Sometimes the ideal suggestion cannot be carried out because it requires talents you have in short supply. For example, a science teacher received feedback from students that the organization of his lectures was poor. Despite his best efforts over a number of years he was unable to break the habit of digressing which destroyed the flow of his lectures. Finally, he provided students with a written syllabus. Although fewer students came to class, there was no criticism of his organization. The teacher didn't change his behavior, but he did improve his teaching because he improved his ability to facilitate learning. If we keep in mind that teaching is not a performance but a facilitation of learning, and that success in teaching is doing whatever helps the learner, we will not find this improvement process so unforgiving.

I like to think of this book as your book, and my role as scribe, noting the problems and situations that you have lived through and summarizing the suggestions that you have tried. I hope that, in future editions, it can become increasingly your book as I add your contributions. I would be very grateful for any problems, causes, remedies, and their outcomes that you could send me. I would like to attribute the contribution to you if you will permit me. Please write or call.

# References

Alexander, W. (1988, May). Personal communication.

Bergquist, W.H., & Phillips, S.R. (1975). *A handbook for faculty development.* Washington, DC: The Council for the Advancement of Small Colleges.

Boud, D., & McDonald, R. (1981). *Educational development through consultancy.* Guildford, Surrey: The Society for Research into Higher Education.

Cross, K.P., & Angelo, T.A. (1987). *Classroom assessment techniques: A handbook for faculty.* Michigan: The National Center for Research to Improve Postsecondary Teaching and Learning.

Eble, K.E. (1988). *The craft of teaching* (2nd ed.) San Francisco, Jossey-Bass.

Erickson, G. ((1986). Unpublished data from survey on faculty development services in colleges and universities. Kingston, RI: University of Rhode Island.

Ferguson, C.K. (1968). Concerning the nature of human systems and the consultant's role. *Journal of Applied Behavioral Science, 4*(2), 179–193.

Foley, R.P., & Smilansky, J. (1980). *Teaching techniques: A handbook for health professionals.* New York: McGraw-Hill.

Gulette, M.M. (Ed.). (1984). *The art and craft of teaching.* Cambridge, MA: Harvard University Press.

Lewis, K.G. (1988). *Face-to-face: A sourcebook of individual consultation techniques for faculty/instructional developers.* Stillwater, OK: New Forums Press.

Lowman, J. (1984). *Mastering the techniques of teaching.* San Francisco: Jossey-Bass.

McKeachie, W.J. (1986). *Teaching tips: A guidebook for the beginning college teacher* (8th ed.). Lexington, MA: D.C. Heath.

Murray, H.G. (1980). *A comprehensive plan for the evaluation of teaching at the University of Queensland.* Queensland, Australia: University of Queensland Tertiary Education Institute.

Murray, H.G. (1987). Acquiring student feedback that improves instruction. In M.G. Weimer (Ed.), *Teaching large classes well.* New Directions for Teaching and Learning, pp. 85–96, San Francisco: Jossey-Bass.

Pilon, D.H., & Bergquist, W.H. (1979). *Consultation in higher education: A handbook for practitioners and clients.* Washington, DC: The Council for the Advancement of Small Colleges.

Schon, D.A. (1987). *Educating the reflective practitioner.* San Francisco: Jossey-Bass.

Schwenk, T.L., & Whitman, N. (1987). *The physician as teacher.* Baltimore: Williams & Wilking.

Tiberius, R.G. (1986). Metaphors underlying the improvement of teaching and learning. *British Journal of Educational Technology, 17*(2), 144–156.

Tiberius, R.G., Sackin, H.D., & Cappe, L. (1987). A comparison of two methods of evaluating teaching. *Studies in Higher Education, 12*(3), 287–297.

Tiberius, R.G., Sackin, H.D., Slingerland, J.M., Jubas, K., Bell,M., & Matlow, A. (1989). The influence of student evaluative feedback on the improvement of clinical teaching. *Journal of Higher Education, 60*(6), 665–681.

Weimer, M., Parrett, J.L., & Kerns, M-M. (1988). *How am I teaching: Forms and activities for acquiring instructional input.* Madison, WI: Magna Publications.

# Index of Names

Abercrombie, M. L. J., 3
Ackermann, U., 81
American Educational Research Association (AERA), 166
Alexander, W., 207
Ames, C., 160
Ames, R., 160
Amidon, E. J., 101-102
Angelo, T. A., 162
Astin, A. E., 157
Barker, L. L., 28
Barnes, D., 29
Bayliss, C., 81
Bell, M., 162, 203
Bergquist, W. H., 18, 22, 65, 70, 101, 197, 198
Bligh, D. A., 110
Boud, D., 197
Brandenburg, D. C., 158
Brandt, R., 181
Braskamp, L. A., 158
Brinko, K. T., 70
British Columbia Teachers' Federation (BCTF), 67
Byrne, P. N., iv, 21, 48, 71, 73, 96, 149
Cappe, L., 24
Centra, J. A., 70, 158, 208
Clark, B. R., 158
Cohen, R., 186
Cohen S. A., 53
Cronback, L. J., 43
Cross, K. P., 162
Davidson, M. L., 44, 46
Doyle, P., iv
Eble, K. E., 197
Egan, G., 185
Elgin, S. H., 180
Erickson, G., 197
Ferguson, C. K., 198
Fisher, R., 178
Flanders, N. A., 101-102
Fleming, S., 24
Foley, R. P., 198

Froh, R. C., 158
Galbo, J. J., 2
Geis, G. L., 78, 158, 174
Gold, D., 148
Gold, R., iv
Grey, P. J., 158
Gronlund, N. E., 28
Gullette, M. M., 197
Hale Report, 3
Hobbes, C. R., 166
Hoffman, B., 24
Holmes, S., 137
Holubec, E. J., 181
Hunt, D. E., 42, 43, 99
Hunt Group, iv, 165
Jackson, P. W., 43
Johnson, D., 181
Johnson, R., 181
Jones, J. E., 26
Jubas, K., 162, 203
Kerns, M-M., 70-71, 162
Kibler, R. J., 28
Kindsvatter, R., 70
King, P., 41
Kitchener, K. S., 41
Knapper, C. K., 158
Kohn, A., 179
Kulik, J. A., 2
Lambert, L. M., 158
Lawson, J., 47
LeBaron, C., 148
Lewis, K., 197, 201
Lonsdale, M., iv
Lorraine, H., 88
Lowman, J., 197
Mager, R. F., 28
Maier, N. R. F., 34
Maslow, A., 147
Matheson, W., 18
Matlow, A. M. 162, 203
McDonald, R., 197
McKeachie, W. J., 3, 20, 73, 110, 197

McLeish, J., 18
Menges, R. J., 162
Miles, D. T., 28
Milne, P., 21
Miosi, T., iv
Murray, H., 158, 202
Oray, J. C., 158
Orme, J., iv, 111
Park, J. (1973), 18
Parrett, J. L., 70-71, 162
Pascal, C. E., 25, 158
Peikes, R., iv
Perry, W., 41, 42
Pfeiffer, J. W., 26
Phillips, S. R., 18, 22, 65, 70,
    101
Pilon, D. H., 197, 198
Pirsig, R. M., 74
Professional and Organizational
    Development Network in
    Higher Education (POD),
    165-166, 208
Porteous, J., 129
Powell, J. P., 106
Rasmussen, R., 34, 111
Rice, E., 157
Roberts, D., 126
Rooney, F., iv
Rudduck, J., 3, 66, 67, 83, 97,
    106
Sackin, H. D., 162, 203
Sanford, N., 46
Schmidt, J. A., 44, 46
Schon, D., 205
Schwenk, T. L., 198
Society for Higher Education
    (SHE), 166
Shore, B. M., 158
Silver, I., 24
Simpson, R. J., 2
Skolnik, M., iv
Slingerland, J. M., 162, 203
Small, P., 22
Smilansky, J., 198
Smith, R., 181

Strange, C., 47
Sullivan, E. V., 42
Taylor, I., 96, 149
Taylor-Way, D., 70
Tiberius, R. G., 24, 162, 203
Ury, W., 178
Weimer, M., 70-71, 162
Whitman, N., 198
Widick, C., 44
Wiener, N., 162
Wilen, W. W., 70
Wilson, J., iv

214